Enactments

EDITED BY RICHARD SCHECHNER

To perform is to imagine, represent, live and enact present
circumstances, past events and future possibilities. Performance takes place
across a very broad range of venues from city streets to the countryside,
in theatres and in offices, on battlefields and in hospital operating rooms.
The genres of performance are many, from the arts to the myriad
performances of everyday life, from courtrooms to legislative chambers,
from theatres to wars to circuses.

ENACTMENTS will encompass performance in as many of its aspects and
realities as there are authors able to write about them.

ENACTMENTS will include active scholarship, readable thought and
engaged analysis across the broad spectrum of performance studies.

Ron Vawter's Life in Performance

Theresa Smalec

LONDON NEW YORK CALCUTTA

Seagull Books, 2020

Text © Theresa Smalec
Photographs © Individual photographers

ISBN 978 0 8574 2 552 2

British Library Cataloguing-in-Publication Data
A catalogue record for this book is available from the British Library

Typeset by Seagull Books, Calcutta, India
Printed and bound by Chicago Distribution Center, Ill., USA

Contents

For those who knew Ron Vawter. And for those who wish they did.

Acknowledgements

Long before the chapters of *Ron Vawter's Life in Performance* began to cohere, Richard Schechner, my dissertation advisor in the Department of Performance Studies at New York University, saw the value of my project and encouraged me to persist. I am grateful for his unwavering faith and generosity. Others at NYU shaped my scholarly methods and interests: Barbara Browning, Barbara Kirshenblatt-Gimblett, André Lepecki, Peggy Phelan, Diana Taylor and the late José Esteban Muñoz. Committee members, editors and correspondents such as Philip Auslander, Gregory Mehrten, Ann Pellegrini, Martin Puchner, David Román, Mariellen Sandford and David Savran helped me to refine my ideas along the way.

My employment in the Department of Communication Arts and Sciences at Bronx Community College of the City University of New York has generated many new alliances and opportunities. I am particularly grateful to Dr Debra Gonsher, who has been an astoundingly supportive chairperson, trusted mentor and valued friend. Institutionally, I want to thank the Research Foundation of CUNY for a Professional Staff Congress-City University of New York Research Award. Additional thanks to Dr. Bridgett Davis and Dr. Shelly Eversley, Co-Directors of CUNY's Faculty Fellowship Publication Program.

Special thanks to Vawter's former collaborators, family members, friends, teachers, and lovers. I am grateful for my interviews with Joseph Cali, Linda Chapman, James Clayburgh, Meghan Coleman, Willem Dafoe, Kevin Daly, Father Vianney Devlin, O.F.M., Karen Finley, Norman Frisch, Jill Godmilow, Spalding Gray, James Griffiths, Gary Indiana, John Jesurun, Ken Kobland, Paul Lazar, Elizabeth

LeCompte, Joan MacIntosh, Gregory Mehrten, Father Daniel Nelson, O.F.M., Lola Pashalinski, Bruce Porter, Bruce Rayvid, Nancy Reilly, Leeny Sack, Father David Schlatter, O.F.M., Richard Schechner, Clay Shirky, Theodora Skipitares, Major General Michael Van Patten, Matilda Buttoni Vawter, Celeste Vawter Fonda and Marianne Weems.

Alongside the repertoire is the archive. Father Julian Davies, O.F.M. and PhD, assisted with my archival research about Vawter's years at Siena College. Patricia Markley gave me permission to use Little Theatre production photos published in the Siena College Yearbook. Charles E. Greene and Ben Primer, at Princeton University Library, assisted with permissions for the Richard Schechner Papers. Brian Keough, Head of Special Collections and Archives at the University of Albany, assisted with permissions for the Jarka M. Burian Papers. Jay Rosenberg, who photographed Burian's 1972 production of *Marat/Sade*, allowed me to publish his images here. I owe tremendous thanks to Clay Hapaz, Archivist for The Wooster Group, who helped with countless aspects of this project. Paula Court, a renowned photographer, allowed me to publish a medley of her rare and iconic images.

In the course of completing this book, I lost my dear parents, Franciszek Smalec and Kazimiera Matys-Smalec, as well as my beloved husband, Dale Kenneth Todd II. It could not have been written without them. My sister, Anna Schluff-Smalec, and her family, have been patient beyond measure. Finally, I am grateful for the support of my daughter, Zenona, who reminds me to be present, because time is short.

Introduction: What Remains?

While this book is not primarily theoretical in nature, my goal never-theless is to offer an expansive, well-researched—often revisionist—history of Ron Vawter the person/performer and his contributions to experimental theatre. Here, Vawter is positioned as an unsung hero of The Performance Group (TPG) and The Wooster Group (TWG) wherein I examine how he became the administrative and affective heart of both companies during his tenure with them. I also chart the means by which Vawter helped to develop and calibrate several of The Wooster Group's signature aesthetic practices. A short list includes the self-based performance personae; task-based scores as modes of developing character; acting as a form of 'standing in' for absent others—rather than trying to become those others psychologically; and the company's enduring attraction to media and its inherent mediations.

This book traces Vawter's career from his four years at Siena College, where he became a prominent actor and director in the cam-pus theatre club, to his move to New York City in 1972–73, where he encountered Richard Schechner's TPG, his first professional theatre company. I explore the tempestuous and protracted evolution of Schechner's TPG into Elizabeth LeCompte's The Wooster Group, and Vawter's key roles in navigating and assuaging that transition. I end with several independent projects that Vawter conceptualized and staged after his HIV-positive diagnosis, in the midst of the AIDS cri-sis and the urgency it engendered.

My methodology draws heavily upon what Diana Taylor has the-orized as the embodied 'repertoire'. The bulk of the knowledge inscribed in this book comes from oral interviews with Vawter's friends, colleagues, directors and lovers. Over the course of my research, diverse theatre artists agreed to discuss their interpersonal relationships and professional collaborations with Vawter. I also interviewed members of Vawter's family, his peers in the Little Theatre Club at Siena College, a former professor who mentored that club, and a retired Army General who completed Officer Candidate School with Vawter. Assembled here is a dense, intimate, multilayered and hitherto unwritten account of Vawter and the diverse communities to which he belonged.

In addition to the repertoire, my research engages with a combination of well-known and fairly obscure archives: enduring repositories of written or otherwise documented history. Examples of well-known archives include seminal books about TPG and TWG, such as Richard Schechner's *Environmental Theatre* (1973) and David Savran's *Breaking the Rules: The Wooster Group* (1988). Examples of the latter include several Albany-based newspapers that reviewed Vawter's performances in campus and amateur theatre, as well as New York publications that reported on his rise in the downtown avant-garde throughout the 1970s, 1980s and early 1990s. Other archival materials explored here include photographs, videos, scripts and press clippings pertaining to Vawter's performance career: records housed in the J. Spencer and Patricia Standish Library at Siena College; the Jarka M. Burian Papers in the M.E. Grenander Department of Special Collections and Archives at SUNYA; the Richard Schechner Papers in the Department of Rare Books and Special Collections at Princeton Library; the Ron Vawter Papers held at the New York Public Library for the Performing Arts; and The Wooster Group's archive, held at the Performing Garage.

Vawter is often eclipsed in histories of TPG and The Wooster Group by luminaries like Willem Dafoe, Spalding Gray, Elizabeth LeCompte and Richard Schechner. On the contrary, I claim that his influence on both companies was transforming. In subtle yet tangible ways, Vawter's self-presentation as himself (first as an Army recruiter, then as TPG's business manager and drummer, and later as LeCompte's tough right-hand man) led to changes in both TPG's and The Wooster Group's aesthetics—one being their increasing use of self-based performance personae. Vawter's college interest in Renaissance art and multimedia technologies also shaped his early work with The Wooster Group, particularly *Three Places in Rhode Island*. While various changes have affected The Wooster Group since its founding members began making theatre in 1975, the company's aesthetic is fundamentally rooted in two factors: media and mediation. Those familiar with the company's working methods emphasize its reliance on multimedia forms such as sound, music, video, and projected images—all of which function to disrupt, mediate and complicate the live action happening on stage. Before he joined TPG in 1973, Vawter had already recorded and projected a short, homemade film during a live performance at Siena College. His interests in projecting photographs onto performers' bodies, using audiotapes to 'stand in' for those whose voices had been recorded and the triptych visual form influenced various aspects of *Three Places in Rhode Island*. Vawter's preference for physical scores over psychological approaches to character also coincided with LeCompte's own interest in surfaces—although her surfaces tended to be more architectural, musical, and visual in nature.

While many people know the legend of Vawter's 'inadvertent' entry into theatre via the US Army, few realize that he began acting in high school, or that he was a rising star in campus and amateur theatre long before arriving in Manhattan in winter 1972. The details of Vawter's origins as a nonprofessional actor and director help to explain his later attraction to experimental ensembles like TPG and TWG. At the same time, his longstanding passion for bringing diverse people together sheds light on how and why he became a pivotal member of these collectives.

In one sense, this book is a traditional biography focused on an individual person and their accomplishments. However, it is also a social history—an ensemble biography, if you will—because it explores

3

the interpersonal and sociopolitical fabric of the theatre clubs and companies to which Vawter belonged. Through interviews with his peers, one is made aware of Vawter's propensity for community building. He was the quintessential member, collaborator, worker, friend and confidant. While he typically favoured margins over the spotlight and performed many of his most valued roles from behind the scenes, Vawter the ex-centric outsider also became paradoxically integral to every theatre group he joined.

CHAPTER 1

Stories of Origin

Ron Vawter's Early Stages

> The point of remembering is to reinvent ourselves.
>
> —Jean Carlomusto, 'Fever in the Archive' (2000)[1]

> I am a big liar, a pathological liar. When I was a kid, I invented things for no apparent reason. So it doesn't take much to bring that impulse back. You say to your audience: 'See how I'm lying.'
>
> —Ron Vawter (n.d.)[2]

Ron Vawter, a founding and core member of the Wooster Group, remained in relative obscurity for much of his career, but to those in the experimental-theatre world of Lower Manhattan, he was 'New York's Best Unknown Actor' (Wetzsteon 1989: 37). Vawter's brief career—he died of complications from AIDS in 1994, at age 45— engendered as much myth as admiration. Apart from the oft-cited

---

1 Jean Carlomusto made this comment at a panel discussion hosted by the Center for the Study of Gender and Sexuality at New York University on 6 December 2000. The panel was part of a week-long exhibition titled *Fever in the Archive: AIDS Activist Videotapes*.

2 'Ron Vawter (The Wooster Group) and Frank Vercruyssen (Stan): A Dialogue on Acting', undated transcript of a conversation, Box 1, Folder 3, Ron Vawter Papers, New York Public Library for the Performing Arts. All subsequent citations of source materials from the Vawter archive will simply list the box and folder numbers.

details that Vawter was a Green Beret and Franciscan seminarian, little else has been published about who he was or what he did before joining The Performance Group (TPG) in 1973. This opening chapter of the first book-length study focused on Vawter intends to change that by providing a detailed history, both oral and archival, of his accomplishments in campus theatre. In this vibrantly experimental context, Vawter first tried out some of the performance strategies and innovations that would shape his aesthetic for decades to come. In short, Vawter's onstage skills did not emerge in a vacuum or arise out of nowhere.

Many in the theatre community know the legend about the disaffected army recruiter who stumbled upon TPG's environmental production of Sam Shepard's *The Tooth of Crime* (1973) at their downtown theatre, the Performing Garage. However, scholars have a harder time explaining Vawter's remarkable rise in the experimental-theatre scene, first at TPG and then with the Wooster Group.[3] Even in the early 1970s, an era in which both nonperformers and the nonprofessional ensemble were valued,[4] it was not every day that someone with no prior exposure to theatre went on to become what Ross Wetzsteon described as 'the quintessential ensemble performer, the supreme downtown actor', going so far as to canonize Vawter as 'St. Ron' (1989: 38).

Contrary to the myth, Vawter's metamorphosis from army recruiter to avant-garde actor was not inadvertent. While a number of critics—perhaps recycling the same misinformation—posit Manhattan as the site of Vawter's 'accidental'[5] entry into theatre, he actually

---

3 The Performance Group is the Wooster Group's predecessor. Richard Schechner resigned from TPG in 1980 after giving Elizabeth LeCompte the lease on the Performing Garage. Under LeCompte's direction, the group renamed itself the Wooster Group.

4 Arthur Sainer historicizes the rise of the American nonprofessional ensemble in *Radical Theatre Notebook* (1975a: 22–4). See also Richard Schechner (1982: 21–3).

5 Julie Besonen, 'The Accidental Actor: Late Bloomer Ron Vawter', 1993 article, Box 1, Folder 9, Ron Vawter Papers.

started acting at Shaker High School in Latham, New York, while still a teenager. In 1967, Vawter entered Siena College, a liberal arts college located near Albany, in Loudenville, New York. There, he joined the student drama club, known as the Little Theatre. Over the next four years, Vawter built his reputation as one of the club's principal actors and directors. He performed in close to a dozen campus plays. As a student director, he oversaw several pioneering initiatives, including an intermedia version of the 1959 Broadway musical *Rashomon*. Vawter's 1970 rendition incorporated a silent film into the live stage performance. The following year, he directed a production of John Herbert's 1967 play *Fortune and Men's Eyes*, a controversial prison drama about a young offender's homosexual awakening.

By the time he graduated from Siena College in May 1971, Vawter had starred in several productions at the region's amateur theatres. He played Edmond in *Long Day's Journey into Night* with the Slingerland Community Players, and Tom in *The Glass Menagerie* at the Albany Civic Center (Kelly 1985: A5). In autumn 1971, Vawter went on to pursue graduate studies in drama at Stanford University. His time at Stanford was brief. He came home the following year and returned to the campus stage at the State University of New York at Albany, although he did not enrol in a degree programme there. At SUNYA, Vawter starred as Jean-Paul Marat in Professor Jarka Burian's production of Peter Weiss' *The Persecution and Assassination of Jean-Paul Marat, as Performed by the Inmates of Charenton, under the Direction of the Marquis de Sade* (1963), staged in October 1972.

Why has this formative period of Vawter's career been overlooked? Part of my task is to account for the gaps and omissions that hinder a fuller understanding of his body of work. As Vawter became increasingly well known in the 1990s for his work in the Wooster Group, and for his performances in *Roy Cohn/Jack Smith* (1992) and the film *Philadelphia* (1993), many reporters and scholars interviewed him about his origins. *BOMB*, *TDR*, *The New York Times*, *Vanity Fair*, *Variety* and the *Village Voice* are among the publications in which Vawter recounted how he became an actor. Not one published article mentions his extensive involvement in amateur theatre. And while Vawter did not author any of the texts that claim to recount his early life, he nevertheless played an integral role in the transmission of this incomplete narrative. Stephen Holden's interview with Vawter about *Roy Cohn/Jack Smith* is one incarnation of the well-known legend of Vawter's ostensibly happenstance entry into theatre:

> Mr. Vawter's background would seem to make him the most unlikely candidate for charter membership in New York's theatrical avant-garde. Born into a military family [. . .] he received his Army enlistment papers in 1966 as a 17th-birthday present and trained to become a Special Forces officer. Hoping to be a chaplain for the Green Berets, he was put on reserve status while he studied theology for four years in a Franciscan seminary and earned a B.A. in literature. On leaving the seminary he became an Army recruiter in Manhattan. One day, while walking to his office at 80 Center Street, he found himself attracted to the sounds coming from the Performing Garage. They turned out to be rehearsals by The Performance Group [. . .] of Sam Shepard's play, *The Tooth of Crime* (1992: 8).

Holden's account of Vawter's 'unlikely' entry into acting is one of many variations on a common theme. But why is Vawter's non-traditional background seen as especially noteworthy? After all, many theatre practitioners of the 1970s had no formal training. As Wetzsteon points out, the Wooster Group's early projects often involved such people: 'After the Wooster Group succeeded the Performance Group in the mid-'70s, the troupe's aesthetic came more and more to rely on non-performers' (1989: 40). In *Sakonnet Point* (1975), for example, the cast included Libby Howes, Ellen LeCompte (Elizabeth LeCompte's sister) and a young boy named Erik Moskowitz, none of whom were trained in theatre. The cast for *Nayatt School* (1978) included Joan Jonas, who began her career as a sculptor and later became a performance and video artist. Vawter had a relatively more extensive and conventional background in theatre than any of these people, yet his assumed inexperience becomes paradoxically central to how various prominent journalists of the arts have portrayed his rise.

The image of Vawter as an artless youth whose life changed by chance recurs in C. Carr's article, 'The Non-Conformist'. Carr stresses the belatedness of Vawter's interest in acting: 'Born into the military, a former Franciscan seminary student, Vawter was someone who had to search a while for his true calling' (1993: 38). Carr characterizes his 1972 encounter with TPG's *The Tooth of Crime* as a revelation of his undiscovered sense of purpose: 'He finally found it one day when, still a soldier, he walked past the Performing Garage and heard "incredible noises". [. . .] Vawter returned 30 or 40 times over the next couple months. He was home at last' (ibid.: 38).

Critics view the known facts of Vawter's upbringing as incompatible with the versatile performer he later became. Instead, they use the actor's personal charisma as an explanation of sorts for his elusive success. As Wetzsteon explains, Vawter 'is one of those performers whose work is characterized less by talent or technique than by persona or presence (which could be loosely defined as the penumbra of personality)' (1989: 38). Curiously, this definition sidesteps the very criteria (talent, technique) by which performers are usually judged.

Apart from its lack of precision, Wetzsteon's default to the nebulous notion of presence poses a more serious problem for theatre historians. How do we trace the emergence of skill in a man who ostensibly came from nowhere? How do we historicize the means by which Vawter developed his craft? The myth is widespread. The rest, they say, is history. But where might an effort to grasp this history's complexities begin? I began with his family.

Family Stories of Origin: Vawter's Early Life

I interviewed Vawter's mother in the cafeteria at Siena College on 22 November 2004.[6] We had spoken on the phone a couple of times but had never met. At the time, Matilda Buttoni Vawter was almost 80

---

6 All quotes attributed to Matilda Buttoni Vawter are from this interview.

years old. She worked on campus as a dining-service hostess for 31 years before retiring in 2006. Sadly, she passed away on 9 January 2010.

On the day we met, students and faculty greeted her warmly, 'Hey Mrs V!' as some of them passed us. Mrs Vawter wore an emerald skirt, suit jacket and blouse: she seemed almost regal. I later learnt from other campus employees that skirt suits were part of her daily attire, although her job did not require such formality.

I learnt retrospectively from Celeste Vawter Fonda (Ron's younger sister) that Mrs Vawter was in the early stages of Alzheimer's disease in 2004. Although she showed no signs of impairment during our conversation, her illness is an important detail, and perhaps throws some doubt on what she said. (In July 2008, Vawter Fonda explained via email that one effect of her mother's condition was her tendency to repeat almost anything anyone said to her; hence the need for constant care.)

Mrs Vawter seemed independent, composed and lucid when we spoke, although my hand-held voice recorder made her nervous and she requested that I not tape-record her testimony. Our interview covered some notable events of Vawter's youth, including his first onstage performance, his enlistment in the Army National Guard, his undergraduate years at Siena College and his brief involvement there with the campus Franciscan programme.

Matilda Buttoni was born to Italian immigrants in Whitehall, New York. Her parents were divorced, a rarity for Roman Catholics of that era. By age 20, the independent young woman worked for General Electric and earned good money, but she wanted more out of life: 'It was during the tail end of the war [World War II], and whenever you turned on the radio, you heard calls for women in service'. Mrs Vawter proudly recalled leaving Whitehall by joining the US Navy's female service, the WAVES (Women Accepted for Volunteer Emergency Service): 'I got up in the middle of the night. My mother knew what I was doing but my step-dad did not know. I tiptoed to the train station, boarded a train and went down to New York City for boot camp at Hunter College.'

Despite the popular belief that Ron Vawter came from a very conservative family, his mother's choice was hardly conventional. 'At that
time,' she explained, 'girls in the service were frowned upon. They were
called old bags.' Nevertheless, Mrs Vawter felt elated by her decision
to leave home: 'My only regret was that I didn't join sooner', she
chuckled, recalling the dorm inspections to which women were subject
at boot camp: 'We had to wax and polish the floors. Girls would put
Kotex on their feet and polish.'

After completing basic training, new WAVES could choose where
they would serve: California, Florida or New York City. Mrs Vawter's
first choice was California, where she became a teletype operator at a
naval air station in San Diego: 'It was like Western Union. You'd send
messages to ships at sea, and they'd send messages back. You had to
send out a lot of sad messages to parents.' However, her job was not
without its pleasures: 'Sometimes you'd teletype a message and some
sailor would type back "Hi!" and start flirting with you.'

Matilda Buttoni met Elton Lee Vawter at the Hotel del Coronado
in 1945, during a dance for US Navy personnel: 'He had beautiful blue
eyes, he was a good dancer *and* he had a good sense of humour! That's
the most important thing a man can possess. If you get some grouch,
then even if he's nice, forget it!' In addition to his charm, Elton Lee
Vawter was a member of the US Navy's Underwater Demolition
Team, which blew things up underwater. 'This was a very dangerous
job but he never got a scratch doing it. He never complained about
his job, either.' Mindful of Elton Lee Vawter's long military career—
he served nearly 30 years in the armed forces—I expected this account
of his professionalism. I was surprised, however, when Mrs Vawter
likened her husband to her son: 'He had a wonderful personality. He
was easy-going, like Ron.'

Matilda and Elton Lee married on Thanksgiving Day in 1946.
Their first child and only son, Ron, was born in Glens Falls, New York,
on 9 December 1948. Mrs Vawter fondly recounted the legend of how
Ron got his name: 'If a pilot takes off, he wires a flight plan. When he
gets back, he must send a return message to let the station know he's

back. But if he doesn't come back, he puts in an R.O.N., which means Remain Over Night.' She described her young son as 'quiet and soft-spoken', adding that he was 'good student' and a child who 'read all the time, anything he could lay his hands on'. Vawter also inherited his father's agility on the dance floor: 'He could make you feel like Ginger Rogers!' As a teenager, he loved music and played the drums in a high-school band called the Men of Note. 'Ron was a terrific drummer,' Mrs Vawter said. 'He could play paradiddles even the teacher didn't know.'

Yet the trait that stood out most in Mrs Vawter's mind was her son's ability to engage others: 'He was very curious and unassuming. He was comfortable in all walks of life, and could talk about any subject to anyone.' At times, her son made her think twice about her own demeanour: 'I'd be bitching about something, and he'd look at me kind of funny, "*Now, Mom . . .* ," he'd say.'

According to Mrs Vawter, her son began acting at Shaker High School during his senior year (1966–67). His first role was as Jerry in Edward Albee's *The Zoo Story* (1959), a play that forged Albee's reputation as an '*enfant terrible* of American theatre' (Kolin 2005: 16). Aesthetically, *The Zoo Story* fuses what Kolin describes as 'earthy naturalism and alienating, absurdist effects' (ibid.: 17). At the level of content, it is a long one-act play in which an erratic character named Jerry strikes up a conversation with a middle-aged executive named Peter. Jerry alludes to his teenaged homosexual experiences and discloses his inability to have long-term relationships with women. The play's homoerotic content is implicit in Jerry's speeches, but nothing happens by way of action until Jerry tricks Peter into holding a knife and then impales himself on it. The play ends when a horrified Peter realizes he has inadvertently assisted in Jerry's suicide.

With its slow-moving plot and its ghastly denouement, *The Zoo Story* is not a play one might expect high-school students to respond as strongly to as Vawter seems to have done. Nevertheless, something about this inaugural acting experience struck a chord with him. Perhaps it was Jerry's final, stunning transgression. Perhaps it was the underlying gay content. In any case, after starring in the high-school production, Vawter told his mother he would one day become an actor in New York. The earliest item found in the Ron Vawter Papers is a programme from the 1963 Broadway production of Albee's *Who's Afraid of Virginia Woolf?*[7] While it is not known if Vawter travelled to New York to see it, but he went on to demonstrate a lifelong interest in staging several of Albee's challenging plays, some of which are discussed in this chapter.

In 1965, with the Vietnam conflict looming, Vawter's parents already had other things on their minds than their son's theatre aspirations. Critics often cite the army enlistment papers Vawter received on his seventeenth birthday as proof that his father expected him to follow in his footsteps.[8] However, Mrs Vawter offered a more pragmatic motive during our 2004 interview: 'Ron joined the Special Forces, or he would have gone to Vietnam.'

Today, in the wake of America's global 'War on Terror' and its multiple fronts, National Guard units are routinely called up for combat,[9] which was not the case during the Vietnam era.[10] In an effort to protect his son from being drafted, Elton Lee Vawter used his rank as a Green Beret colonel and enlisted him in the New York Army

---

7 The programme is from a 20 May 1963 performance of *Who's Afraid of Virginia Woolf?* directed by Alan Schneider and staged at the Billy Rose Theatre (known today as the David T. Nederlander Theatre). See Box 8, Folder 3, Ron Vawter Papers.

8 See Helen Barlow (1995: 35), Stephen Holden (1992: 8), Erika Milvy (1992: 88), Amy Taubin (1990: 40), Ross Wetzsteon (1989: 39; 1994).

9 'One weekend a month, two weeks a year' was the National Guard's former slogan. It indicates the amount of time a guardsman must serve to be eligible for benefits. The National Guard dropped this slogan in 2004, as guardsmen began serving prolonged tours in Afghanistan and Iraq.

10 In the early days of the Southeast Asia build-up, the US Army tried to meet its manpower needs without drawing upon the reserves. However, in April 1968, 34 Army National Guard units and 45 Army Reserve units were called up to active duty. Of the 12,234 mobilized Army National Guardsmen, only one National Guard Special Forces unit was sent to Vietnam (see Mancini 1990: 68).

National Guard on 11 December 1965. After enlisting, Vawter became eligible to attend Officer Candidate School (OCS), where he could earn his commission as an officer. Non-commissioned soldiers of the Vietnam era received minimal preparation. Basic training programmes (also known as boot camp) typically lasted eight weeks. By contrast, OCS lasted 23 weeks. Since National Guardsmen only trained at the rate of one weekend per month, they completed OCS over two years. Mrs Vawter said her son's enlistment was meant to keep him out of harm's way for as long as possible. (Of course, Vawter could alternatively have got a college deferment, as millions of young men did.)

Major General Michael Van Patten (Retired) trained alongside Vawter during Officer Candidate School. Van Patten and Vawter began Phase I at Camp Smith (near Peeksill, New York) in summer 1966. Van Patten compared the 15-day training to a crime-deterrence programme for troubled youths: 'You know that programme Scared Straight, where they bring kids into prisons? That's basically what it was like.' Rugged topography, summer heat and acute stress soon convinced many candidates to drop out: 'Our OCS Class started out with 465 people in Phase I. But by the time we graduated, we only graduated with 168 people'.

Van Patten described Vawter as a model candidate: 'What I remember about Ron is that he was a real clean-cut kind of person, very strict in terms of military discipline. You know, he was a really good soldier.' Vawter also proved to be an excellent student throughout Phase II, which focused on military ethics and procedures. Training took the form of weekend seminars held once a month. There were written exams that candidates could only fail once. Those who passed returned to Camp Smith the following summer for Phase III, which was designed to test candidates on their leadership skills in combat situations.

Van Patten and Vawter graduated from OCS on 15 August 1968, earning their commissions as 2nd Lieutenants in the Army National Guard. Unlike a regular army commission, there was no particular type of service guardsmen had to perform to become officers. They could be called up for combat, but were more likely to fulfil their obligations through assignments such as recruiting, clerical duties or by serving in the Individual Ready Reserve.

Van Patten's graduation launched a 36-year career. He retired in 2001 as a two-star major general, the commanding general of the New York Army National Guard. For Vawter, however, the officer's commission opened onto a less straightforward path. While he immediately joined the Special Forces Group Airborne (a unit commanded by his father in Schenectady, New York), he also embraced the student anti-Vietnam War movement soon after entering Siena College.

Van Patten met Elton Lee Vawter on several occasions: 'Ron's dad was, if you want to use the term, a real 'man's man'. I mean he was a tough guy, an Airborne Ranger. He epitomized what you win medals for: a Green Beret-type guy'. Van Patten did not know how the elder Vawter reacted to his son's anti-war activism, but he admitted his own surprise when I told him about it: 'I knew nothing about that, actually'.

When Vawter entered Siena College in 1967, he still planned to follow in his father's path and join the Special Forces. However, it was in the Little Theatre club that a different kind of leader emerged. Even as he played it straight in his public demeanour, Lieutenant Vawter slowly introduced his fellow performers to the countertexts that compelled him: plays about social outsiders, iconoclasts and homosexuals.

The Little Theatre Club

During our 2004 interview, Mrs. Vawter recalled her son's first two years at Siena College, when he still commuted from home: 'We always had a ball whenever Ron came home for lunch. He explained everything he'd learnt to me, so it was like I was getting a college education, too'. In general, the young Vawter relished his new environment. However, his mother recalled one source of disappointment: Vawter had hoped to go away to college and live in a dorm.

15

One highlight of Siena College was her son's favourite professor, Dr John Murphy, an ordained Franciscan who had earned both his master's and doctoral degrees in medieval studies. Murphy taught art history, and Vawter was drawn to art of the early Italian Renaissance, an interest he would retain and share with The Wooster Group.[11]

Early in his freshman year, Vawter joined the Little Theatre, a student drama club. Father Vianney Devlin, an English professor assigned to moderate the club's activities, explained the student-centred structure of the Little Theatre:

> In the late 1960s and early 1970s, there was a transformation taking place. Previous to my arrival, the faculty moderator for the Little Theatre directed most of the plays, if not all of them. But the students whom I was moderating said *they* would like to do some directing of their own, and I said to myself, 'Why not? It's a club, not a professional company. It's a learning experience' (Devlin 2004).

When asked how the Little Theatre club decided what shows to stage, Devlin answered that members typically brought in ideas based on plays they had encountered in high school or on films and other popular culture genres. Devlin contributed to this medley of sources by encouraging more canonical plays. He recalled the Little Theatre as 'a very cooperative and imaginative group of students' who respected each other's initiatives.

Nevertheless, there were limits on what the club could stage. Siena College was a Roman Catholic institution, so plays with explicit language were sometimes modified. Devlin noted an even greater restriction—the literal size of the aptly named Little Theatre, which was located in the basement of the campus cafeteria: 'There were 99

---

11 In later chapters, I discuss the enthusiasm for Italian Renaissance art that Vawter shared with Elizabeth LeCompte. Their common interest in art of this period influenced the set designs used throughout the trilogy, *Three Places in Rhode Island*: *Sakonnet Point* (1975), *Rumstick Road* (1977) *and Nayatt School* (1978).

seats. [...] I had to be very careful about sticking to the fire laws because there were only two exits'.

Vawter and the other club's student members found clever ways to perform in this confined space. They also resolved other production challenges—when working on shows that called for female performers, they recruited young women from nearby Russell Sage or Skidmore College (at the time, Siena College was an all-male school). Students also designed costumes and sets, and handled the club's publicity. As a result, Vawter gained a lot of hands-on production experience at the Little Theatre.

David Schlatter, who joined the Little Theatre in 1968, emphasized the club's communal nature, and Vawter's key role in it: 'It was very much an acting troupe, a company. And it was pretty much everyone's opinion that Ron was one of the troupe's main players' (Schlatter 2004).[12] He also described Vawter as an outstanding actor, director and community builder. Students and faculty were the drama club's primary audience, but one professional writer also showed an ongoing interest. Martin P. Kelly, a drama critic for the *Albany Times-Union* (one of the region's two daily newspapers), reviewed several Little Theatre productions, and promoted many more in his column. While Father Devlin charged that Kelly 'always used to give us lukewarm if not negative reviews', on the whole, Kelly's reviews come across as balanced and detailed even as they often acknowledge the amateur quality of the club's endeavours.

At the level of actor training, the Little Theatre was a fertile testing ground for untrained theatre enthusiasts. According to Schlatter, there was 'no set philosophy in terms of how we went into theatre. We didn't have the Stanislavsky method or anything like that'. Father Devlin also had no formal training in theatre, so he encouraged students to develop their own approaches. Rehearsals were thus a space of experimentation where aspiring actors like Vawter could try out their ideas about acting and directing.

---

12 All quotations attributed to David Schlatter are from this 2004 interview.

The Zoo Story: 7–9 December 1967

Vawter introduced Edward Albee's *The Zoo Story* to the Little Theatre during the first semester of his freshman year, demonstrating his early leadership role in the club. It is unclear if Vawter had known by this time that Albee was gay. However, it is possible that he had grasped *Zoo Story's* gay content, since he had performed this drama in high school. *Zoo Story* is an intriguing choice of plays for someone as repressed about his homosexuality as Vawter later claimed to be.

The only extant documentation of Vawter's 1967 rendition of Albee's drama is a student review and two yearbook photos. Martin P. Kelly did not review the show and Father Devlin could not remember it. David Schlatter and the other former club members whom I interviewed did not attend Siena College until 1968. The review, titled 'Little Theatre Presents "Best" of Current Season', was published in *The Indian*, the campus newspaper of that era, and was written by an unnamed student reporting on a one-act play festival staged at the college that December. Unfortunately, this reviewer mainly summarized Albee's plot, and offered little in the way of description. Apparently, Vawter had portrayed Jerry as an empathetic anti-hero, as suggested by the critic's account of 'a desperate young man looking for a little human love' (*Indian* 1967: 6). However, the means by which he developed his character are unclear: 'The death scene was excellently portrayed, and Ron Vawter, who also directed the production, held the audience captivated during the most crucial moments of the performance' (6).

In effort to envision Vawter's production, I turned to the 1968 yearbook. Two photographs show a realistic-looking park bench, the only set piece used. These photographs also convey a highly unusual costume choice. In Albee's play, Jerry is a self-described 'permanent transient' (2004: 32). Scholars also stress his renegade position: 'Living on the margins of society, Jerry is the anti-establishment, counterculture hero. He is the dark stranger, the social outcast, the orphan, the Other' (Kolin 2005: 19). Friedrich Luft envisions Jerry as 'longing for death in blue jeans' (1986: 41).[13] Jerry (played by Vawter) should be easily distinguishable from the well-heeled Peter. And yet, the photos documenting Vawter's production generate uncertainty about who is who. In one of the images, a hefty young man sits on the bench, dressed in a suit and hat. A slighter young man approaches from behind; he wears a cardigan, button-down shirt, and loafers. With his brush cut and clean-shaven features, Vawter's Jerry resembles a stylish frat boy. Only his hard stare expresses what the dapper outfit conceals: a guarded and possibly menacing person. In the second photo, Vawter's Jerry stands behind the park bench, lecturing the other man. Here, Vawter resembles a haughty young schoolteacher.

If Jerry is, as Kolin argues, 'the precursor of the radical left, the Hippie, the Vietnam War protestors' (2005: 19), then Vawter clearly failed to look the part. One possible explanation for this incongruity is that *Zoo Story* directly preceded *The Happy Journey to Trenton and Camden*, a Thornton Wilder piece staged during the Little Theatre's evening of one-act plays.[14] in which Vawter played Pa Kirby, a middle-class American father. A photo of that performance shows Vawter wearing a suit-jacket and glasses, and looking very orderly. It is possible, the actor may have worn a similar outfit in *Zoo Story* simply because he did not have time to change between the two short plays.

However, Vawter's conservatively dressed Jerry may have also signalled his unique reinterpretation of Albee's character. Mindful of what Vawter's peers describe as his attention to detail, the young director may have wilfully portrayed Jerry as a closeted rebel: someone whose proper self-presentation did not set off bells. While his character wore an unadventurous costume, Vawter the actor displayed a profound magnetism onstage. Father Vianney Devlin noted: 'He was much more talented than in the ordinary sense. And he was much

---

13 Luft's review was originally published on 1 October 1959 in *Die Welt*, a German national daily newspaper.
14 The order of the four one-act plays presented by the Little Theatre was published in *The Indian* (1967: 9).

more *electrifying* than an average man at his age. He really knew how to use his body, hands and voice'.

Yet despite Vawter's skill for physically demanding roles, he tended to overact in plays that called for more subdued, pedestrian behaviour. To illustrate, Devlin mentioned Vawter's Pa Kirby in *The Happy Journey*. The set was again minimal: just four chairs representing an automobile. But Devlin recounted Vawter's great frustration with having to sit still and pretend to drive a car to a relative's house: 'He found that so restraining that he resorted to facial expressions. I said, "No, that's not appropriate for *this* particular type of play. This play relies on a different kind of kinetic than facial expressions"'. Despite Devlin's directions, Vawter could not seem to stop his face from performing: 'In fact, that was one of the big criticisms by whoever reviewed the show. Ron just did not know how to cope with that kind of a character'.

Exasperated, Devlin finally encouraged the young actor to look inward. But Vawter resisted using introspection to develop the quiet, unflappable role of Pa Kirby:

> He used to say, 'Well, what *can* I do'? And I said to him, 'This is something you're going to have to figure out yourself. My telling you how to react in this particular situation with the family would almost be like mugging, because [...] it wouldn't be you. You have to get down to a deeper level'. But no, he was not comfortable with it.

If a pattern starts to emerge from Vawter's years with the Little Theatre, it is that he preferred physicality to internalization, and surface to depth. As we will see throughout this chapter, Vawter often developed his early roles by observing and then replicating other peoples' outward actions and behaviours. Long before his years with The Wooster Group, he was a task-based performer who intuitively avoided psychological approaches.

Six Characters in Search of an Author:
14–16 November 1968

Vawter's sophomore year, (1968–69) introduced him to Joseph Cali, Daniel Nelson and David Schlatter. Cali was a regular student like Vawter, while Nelson and Schlatter entered Siena College as part of the Franciscan formation program, an initiative launched in 1968 to educate aspiring seminarians in a liberal arts context.

Father Daniel Nelson (who is now a psychology professor at Siena College) first met Vawter at an annual audition for the Little Theatre club. When we spoke, Nelson tried to put himself back in the mindset of young college student. His goal had been to impress the Little Theatre's senior members by presenting a scene with another new student from a play he knew well. However, Nelson quickly found out that these returning actors were equally familiar with his selection of plays:

> I noticed as soon as we said *Zoo Story*, everyone else was like, 'Oh no!', because Ron and Joe Cali had done it the year before. But [...] I found out later that Ron and some other people were really taken by it, because our interpretation was so very different from their interpretation. I was the stronger character as Peter the way we did it, whereas they'd done it the other way around. There was talk of Ron and I doing *Zoo Story* again, to produce a different interpretation and see how that would work (Nelson 2004).[15]

Although the Little Theatre never revisited *Zoo Story*, Nelson was invited to join the group. 'We went from there', he recalled, 'right into rehearsals for *Six Characters in Search of an Author*'.

A fourth-year student named Tom Mohler brought Luigi Pirandello's *Six Characters in Search of an Author* to the Little Theatre. Due to its theme of father–daughter incest, *Six Characters* caused a riot when first staged in Rome in 1921. The action revolves around a rehearsal disrupted by six mysterious people (The Characters) who demand to be cast in a play. The Characters beg the members of an

---

15 All quotations attributed to Daniel Nelson are from this 2004 interview.

acting company to let them stage the most traumatic moments of their lives: the scenes for which they were created. Meanwhile, the company's director (identified in Pirandello's play as the Manager) is soon distracted from rehearsing his own show, instead helping the Characters dramatize their lurid tale of adultery, incest, prostitution and suicide.

Nelson recalled the comic interactions between Vawter, who played the Manager in the drama, and Mohler, who directed the production: 'Ron always used to play with Tom, mimicking Tom's style of doing things'. Nelson explained that Vawter created his onstage persona in *Six Characters* by observing and then recreating Mohler's real-life habits and tics: 'Ron incorporated a lot of the director's mannerisms and ways of doing things into his role. [...] We would be hysterical! It took Tom a while to catch on'.

The 1969 Siena College yearbook includes a photo of Vawter in his role; the caption describes him as 'the pushy stage director'. The formerly clean-shaven Vawter now sported a thin goatee. The same page features Tom Mohler in a scene from another play, *The Public Eye*, with the same goatee, indicating that Vawter went so far as to incorporate his colleague's facial hair stylings into his role. Vawter's focus on the outward details of a role would recur in his early works with The Performance Group and evolve throughout his years with The Wooster Group; his one-man show, *Roy Cohn/Jack Smith*, was arguably the pinnacle of Vawter's passion for theatrical portraiture.

The Drunkard: 20–23 February 1969

The next production staged by the Little Theatre during their 1968–69 season was *The Drunkard; or, The Fallen Saved!*[16] That text had been adapted for the stage by William Henry Smith, and was performed under his direction at the Boston Museum in 1844, where it was shown more than 140 times. In revising *The Drunkard*, Smith

---

16 Scholars believe several people collaborated on the original manuscript (see IATH 1998–2012).

dispensed with the original manuscript's didactic dialogue, instead adopting the conventions of melodrama. The result is a slapstick portrait of a youth whose promising life unravels due to his compulsive drinking. Smith drew upon his personal struggles with alcoholism to give the title character surprising depth. Yet the play's larger purpose was not to browbeat audiences into sobriety. Instead, *The Drunkard's* unrivalled popularity stemmed from its ability to address a serious social problem through comedy. An announcement about *The Drunkard* suggests that this amusing approach persisted into the 1960s: 'The play, originally written as a temperance sermon, is now a leading example of this genre and is played for laughs' (Kelly 1969a: 26).

None of the Little Theatre members whom I interviewed recall whose idea it was to stage *The Drunkard*, although Nelson remembered that Vawter directed this show. Joseph Cali, who starred as Edward Middleton (The Drunkard), enthusiastically summarized the plot: '*The Drunkard* was a play about a young man who is in love with a girl. But the villain gets him drunk, and he goes down the path of destruction and ruin' (Cali 2004).[17]

Although the point of this play was no longer to raise awareness about the dangers of substance abuse, Vawter's peers admit that drinking and drugs were a ubiquitous part of that era's student life. Cali noted drug use when I asked what Little Theatre members did for fun: 'We'd get stoned a lot. We used to get stoned *a lot* because that's what you did back then, although not during the plays'. Schlatter agreed that drugs were part of the club's social activities: 'Things were in transition culturally, and we just went out and had a good time. There was some drug use, light drug use. Mostly pot is what I remember, but that's a whole other story'.

Nelson cited drug use as a subtle ground for division within the Little Theatre: 'I wouldn't call them cliques, because I never found them exclusive, but there were these natural groupings'. He identified Vawter as belonging to the Little Theatre's most experimental crowd: 'Sexuality was definitely a part of it. Drugs were another part of it.

---

17 All quotations attributed to Joseph Cali are from this 2004 interview.

And particularly then, more so than now, I was much more of a straight-laced kind of person'. Nelson recalled his mixed feelings about the club's thrill-seekers: 'For me, it was both an attraction, and wanting to keep a certain distance. [...] I was also concerned about a certain degree of self-destructiveness'.

Two 1969 articles offer clues about what may have motivated Vawter to direct *The Drunkard*. The first one, 'Little Theatre Presents Melodrama: *The Drunkard*', was written by an unnamed student who interviewed Vawter prior to the show. Vawter promised that his production would 'counterbalance the heavy drama contained in *Six Characters in Search of an Author*'. He 'fully expected active audience participation, from boos for the villain to cheers for the good guy' (*The Indian* 1969: 3).

Tom Whittemore's February 1969 review, 'Melodramatic Drunkard Entertains SRO Audiences', confirms that Vawter's cast succeeded in rousing a boisterous audience response: 'Most notable in this category is Tom Mohler's interpretation of the villainous Squire Cribbs. From his opening lines to the last scene of the play, Mohler is constantly swirling his cape, twirling his black moustache and sneering at the hissing audience. He trades insults with anyone within earshot in an air of mock defiance' (3).

Whittemore also applauded Vawter's interactive staging: '*The Drunkard* [...] depends as much upon the audience as the actors, and in this light its success seems quite evident' (3). Yet even as Vawter engaged the audience, the young director seemed to disengage from the darker, more taboo aspects of the drama. For example, the drunkard's struggle with alcohol addiction was treated comically, and the production raised no doubts that the character's problems would resolve themselves happily.

Making a Scene: St. Francis, 'The Seminary,' and the Anti-Vietnam War Movement

Vawter stunned his parents when he joined the Franciscan formation programme at Siena College during the fall of 1969, his junior year. Father Devlin recalled that Matilda Vawter telephoned him demanding answers. Neither she nor Vawter's father saw themselves as particularly religious, so their son's abrupt decision to become a priest came as a shock. However, when I spoke with her 35 years later, Mrs. Vawter seemed much less troubled by this period of Vawter's life. She matter-of-factly proposed that her son had joined the campus Franciscans to fulfil his dream of a residential college experience: a dorm room away from home.

The faculty members charged with leading Siena's Franciscan programme took its rituals seriously, and surely did not encourage new members to treat religion as a form of performance. For this reason, it is notable that Daniel Nelson's most vivid memory of Vawter performing is *not* with the Little Theatre, but in the context of a Franciscan mass. The Franciscans held a weekly mass in their residence hall, and took turns selecting readings for it. Shortly after Vawter joined the program, he chose to read a soliloquy from Edward Albee's *Who's Afraid of Virginia Woolf?* Nelson recalled how others reacted: 'Now I don't remember what it had to do with the mass. But I remember Ron's intensity and sense of drama. A pin could have dropped after it was over! And I remember people commenting on it. It was, at that time, a bit out of place.'

Nelson added that this liturgical performance was not an isolated example of how Vawter found opportunities to role-play: 'Many times, I felt like Ron drew upon roles to play, and I don't mean in the theatre. [...] Early on, it was hard for me to tell who Ron really was'. Nelson was not alone in his uncertainty. Other former classmates also noticed theatrical elements of Vawter's self-presentation. David Schlatter, for example, shared a rumour about Vawter's Army training: 'I believe he was trained to kill. Maybe it was said about him, or maybe it was he who told me—he had been trained in military martial arts. And of course when you hear that about a person, you never try anything, you never challenge the person'.

'It may have been his uniform that led to the rumours', Schlatter explained, 'It was different than what students in the ROTC programme wore'. Vawter, who was a commissioned 2nd Lieutenant, wore what Schlatter described as 'tall black combat boots with the pants tucked in, and the beret'. Partly because of his unusual manner of dress, Vawter was perceived as unique and mysteriously dangerous.

Others remember Vawter's impassioned role in the student protests against the Vietnam War, a position that gradually came into conflict with his role as a soldier. According to Father Devlin, Vawter and his friend Joseph Cali gradually came to be seen as controversial figures on campus because of their anti-war activities. The pair was popular in the Little Theatre club, but Devlin said their 'flamboyance' did not appeal to many students or faculty outside of that community: 'Siena was a very conservative college. As a result, they were viewed as rebels and outlaws'. Devlin's use of the word 'flamboyance' suggested a veiled reference to homosexuality, but when pressed, the priest laughed and clarified what he meant: 'They were passionate. They were good students, not part of what you might call the jock mentality. They were vociferous among a minority of students who had an opinion, or who were ready to stand up for it'.

While Vietnam helped to politicize Cali and Vawter, Cali also attributed their activism to the freedom of living alone: 'I moved off campus to a house on Route 7, near Crooked Lake. It was wild out there! We were doing acid. It was just that time in the culture'. Cali recalled losing old friends from high school because they did not approve of his new politics. However, his camaraderie with Vawter flourished, and their anti-war actions grew more radical.

For example, Cali and Vawter spearheaded a Vietnam War moratorium at Siena College from 13 to 15 November 1969. Cali elaborated: 'In 1969, we closed down the campus. We sat in front of the president's office. [...] We blocked Route 9—all of it! And that was very irksome to Ron's father, being in the military'. A front-page article authored by Cali appeared in *The Indian* a few days before the 15 November 1969 march on Washington, DC, that drew about 250,000 protestors from across the country. Cali urged Siena College students to oppose the war all year round, not just at special organized events:

> It has become clear to me that many moratorium workers in the area are beginning to ignore the November 13th and 14th dates and think only of the march in Washington. I am opposed to this kind of thinking. When I committed myself to the Vietnam Moratorium, I committed myself to the monthly activities until the war ended (1969: 4).

A photo of Cali accompanying the article identified him as 'Moratorium Committee Chairman at Siena' (1969: 5). Vawter was not mentioned, but Cali insisted that Vawter was his faithful partner in protest: 'Ron would do anything! He'd go anywhere, was smart enough to understand how he felt, and communicated it well. He was great'.

Vawter's anti-war activism complicated his hard-earned status as a commissioned officer. Cali recalled a general impression among Little Theatre members that Vawter had a difficult home life: 'I remember the vibe was that he had this strict and oppressive military dad'. Cali ultimately suggested that Vawter joined the Franciscans as a gesture of defiance: 'I'll bet becoming a priest would have just pissed his father off!' Additionally, Vawter's time with the Franciscans may have been an escape of sorts. When Vawter moved into Ryan Hall, a dormitory reserved for Franciscan students, the living arrangement released him from the watchful eyes of his parents. Even though he had a roommate, a curfew and certain religious ceremonies that he was supposed to attend, Vawter surely felt freer at school than he did at home.

Vawter later used the Franciscan programme as a form of narrative escape. In a 1992 interview with Jessica Hagedorn, he embellished and largely distorted that experience:

HAGEDORN. Let's start with the story of Ron Vawter. Legend has it that you were in the Marines.

VAWTER. The Special Forces. The Green Berets. I had just completed a year and a half of training and was all set to go to Vietnam but I didn't want to go. At the time, there were a couple of Green Beret Chaplains going to Vietnam and they were looking for people to replace them. Now, to be a Green Beret chaplain, you had to have trained as a Green Beret and then as a Chaplain. Very few people could get through both the theological and the military intensive training. I had already finished all of the military and as a kid I had always been religious . . . So they released me to reserve status and put me in a Franciscan Seminary Upstate. I spent the next four years training to be a Roman Catholic priest, and by the time I finished, I didn't want to be a priest or in the military (1992: 46).

Vawter's account of his theological training distorts the facts: he attended a liberal arts college where he received a secular education. Schlatter, who completed the Franciscan formation programme in 1972, stressed that Siena College was 'a regular college run by Franciscans. The so-called 'seminary' consisted of two floors in one of the dorms, but other than morning and evening prayers, we had regular lives as students'. Schlatter also disputed Vawter's claim that he spent four years with the Franciscans: 'Ron formally joined the programme in 1969, maybe for a year. All told, it could have been two years'.

Meanwhile, Dan Nelson speculated that Vawter's involvement was based on a desire for community, and fuelled by curiosity about a lifestyle that was foreign to him: 'The way I experienced Ron is that whenever something caught his attention, he wanted to go whole-hog into it. He didn't want to be on the sidelines. He met a lot of us seminarians through the Little Theatre, and I think he just wanted to experience this camaraderie—what the seminary experience was like.' Nelson's testimony suggests that Vawter's reasons for joining the formation programme were personal ones, and not part of a Chaplain training programme mandated by the Army.

Soon after moving into Ryan Hall, Vawter met Kevin Daly, a young Franciscan student who eventually became his secret boyfriend and lover. When I interviewed Daly in 2005, he explained how he first met Vawter:

> His room was next to mine, and we literally bumped into each other in the hall. I clearly remember him hustling out of the room in his Green Beret outfit so that he could get to practice, or wherever he was going. But he wasn't in the room all that much and was very involved in the theatre. He would still make frequent visits to his parents' home[18] (Daly 2005).

Daly said Vawter's roommate was a serious young man named Roberto González Nieves: 'They were certainly two very different people, thrown together in a college situation'. He added with a laugh, 'Ron didn't last in the dorms very long. I don't think the dorm life suited him'.

In 1999, González Nieves was appointed Archbishop of Puerto Rico by Pope John Paul II. I contacted González Nieves at his office in San Juan to ask about his memories of Vawter. To my surprise, the Archbishop responded personally via email. He shared a thoughtful reflection on his former peer:

> Indeed, Ron and I were roommates at Siena during the fall of 1969. We had long conversations that lasted well into the night and early dawn. I enjoyed his company. I remember him as a genuinely good human being, intense, compassionate and with a deep religious sentiment. He was filled with enthusiasm for beauty, truth, justice, joy, love, [and] good—in a word, for God—whose Infinite Mercy and Love have embraced him by now in the fullness of Eternal Life! I hope these few words are insightful. May the Lord bless you and keep you.
>
> Roberto, Archbishop of San Juan de Puerto Rico.
> (González Nieves 2008)

---

18 All quotations attributed to Kevin Daly, unless otherwise indicated, are from this interview.

As dissimilar as he may have seemed in relation to Vawter, González Nieves, at least retrospectively, seemed to like and respect his roommate.

Vawter's desires for community and social change were also fuelled by his fascination with St. Francis of Assisi. Daly mentioned a trip that Vawter took to Assisi, Italy, in the summer of 1969: 'I think it was a very cathartic experience for him. He talked about it frequently when I first met him that September'. Daly recalled Vawter's awe at being 'able to go to the same places in Italy where Francis had lived, and walked, and breathed'. Nelson also spoke of Vawter's identification with the famous saint. Vawter, he said, saw Francis 'as another person who experienced something very deeply, and who devoted himself wholeheartedly to it'.

Like the others, Schlatter recalled Vawter's sense of affinity with the historical Francis. Although he urged me not to construct a simple parallel, Schlatter noted that both Francis and Vawter gradually gave up their youthful ambitions as warriors in favour of pacifist approaches to life. Yet whereas Francis of Assisi ultimately rejected the worldly values of his merchant father, Vawter's relationship to his own father was far more conflicted.

Mrs Vawter said that 'Ron loved his father very much'. Daly identified Elton Lee Vawter as his former boyfriend's role model: 'He was a typical World War II veteran kind of father. And I think that had a lot to do with Ron's decision to be in the Green Berets. It was a matter of trying to win his father's approval'. Daly added that Elton Lee Vawter could be charming and affable: 'To us as outsiders, he was very gracious'. Nevertheless, he recalled Ron's reticence about the man: 'He didn't like to talk about him, and he felt that he had to be emotionally guarded around his father'.

To some extent, the college-aged Vawter seemed emotionally guarded around people in general. Vawter had a certain formality about him—so much so that Joseph Cali never saw his friend display anger in everyday life. However, Cali spoke with visible fascination about how Vawter often 'let that side of him come out as an actor in a role'. He described Vawter's stage anger as 'unbelievable', adding that 'an angry Ron Vawter was the most intense person you'd ever want to see'. Perhaps Vawter only allowed himself to express strong emotions in the permitted context of performance. Without claiming pejoratively that his religious and political commitments were merely theatrical opportunities, it is possible that both the Franciscan programme and the anti-war movement functioned for the young man as enabling sites of display. Unlike the army, which was the territory of his father, these were contexts in which, perhaps, Vawter's dissenting and volatile emotions could be authentically expressed.

Luther: 1–3 November 1969

John Osborne's *Luther* premiered in England in 1961, and was popular in the US throughout the socially turbulent 1960s. Although the play is set in sixteenth-century Europe, *Luther* offered modern-day relevance through its focus on an individual at odds with authority.

At Siena College, Father Devlin co-directed *Luther* with a student named Marion Drozd. Vawter played Hans, Martin Luther's father. In his stage directions, Osborne describes Hans Luther as 'a stocky man […] lower-middle class, on his way to becoming a small, primitive capitalist; bewildered, full of pride and resentment' (1961: 14). Hans only appears in Act 1, when he travels to Erfurt to witness his son's entry into the Order of the Eremites. Having made the 'rotten journey' (35) from his distant village, Hans donates 20 guilden to the Order. 'That's a lot of money to my father', an astonished Martin confides to a fellow monk, 'He's a miner, you know' (29). Yet despite his public generosity, Hans privately views his son's entry into the priesthood as wasteful and repugnant.

After watching a terrified Martin bungle his first Mass, Hans gets drunk while waiting for him in the convent refectory. When the young monk finally comes out after an agonizing bout with constipation (an ongoing problem for Martin), the father and son exchange their mutual bewilderment with one another:

31

MARTIN. Father, why do you hate me being here?

HANS. Eh? What do you mean? I don't hate you being here.

MARTIN. Try to give me a straight answer if you can, Father. And don't say I could have been a lawyer.

HANS. Well, so you could have. You could have been better than that. You could have been a burgomaster, you could have been a magistrate, you could have been a chancellor, you could have been anything! So what! I don't want to talk about it. What's the matter with you! Anyway, I certainly don't want to talk about it in front of complete strangers (38–9).

Osborne presents the stormy relationship between Martin and Hans in subtle and intricate ways. Hans frequently mocks his son's mental and physical anguish. Nevertheless, his fierce love for Martin is apparent despite his abuse. As he becomes drunker and less guarded, Hans finally reveals what bothers him about the monastery: its disavowal of the body, both its labours and its carnal joys. As much as he enjoys heckling Martin, Hans discerns a more private source of shame within his son, and warns that joining the Church will not resolve Martin's self-hatred:

HANS. That's fine talk, oh yes, fine, holy talk, but it won't wash, Martin. It won't wash because you can't ever, however you try, you can't ever get away from your body because that's what you live in, and it's all you've got to die in, and you can't get away from the body of your father and your mother! We're bodies, Martin, and so are you, and we're bound together for always (41).

As the others leave them alone, Martin abruptly reveals how much his father once meant to him: 'You disappointed me too, and not just a few times. [. . .] But I loved you the best. It was always *you* that I wanted. I wanted your love more than anyone's, and if anyone was to hold me, I wanted it to be you' (43).

Vawter sought to win his own father's love and approval by emulating his career path and public persona. However, there were also powerful reasons why the young man tried to distance himself from Elton Lee Vawter. Long after college, he reportedly shared a jarring memory with a former Wooster Group member (who asked to remain anonymous) while they were out drinking. The following anecdote offers important insight into the feelings of fear, shame and helplessness that may have shaped Vawter's early life:

> One of his earliest memories was sleeping in the room next to his parents' room and hearing his father smashing his mother's head against the wall. Through the wall, he heard his mother moaning or calling out his name, 'Ron! Ron! Ron!' And he was too scared to come to her defence. He was really traumatized by his father, and by his parents' relationship. And I think that [was] one of the reasons he was so protective of his mother in later life.

Mindful of Vawter's tendency to develop his onstage roles from the outside in (first observing and then repeating other peoples' behaviours) it is tempting to ask if Elton Lee Vawter was, in part, the model for his volatile portrait of Hans.

In contrast to his awkward portrait of Pa Kirby in Wilder's *The Happy Journey to Trenton and Camden*, Vawter's second attempt at playing a father figure was a striking success. Dan Campbell, a student who reviewed the Little Theatre's production of *Luther* in *The Indian*, praised Vawter for his physically convincing portrait of Hans:

> Two actors tie for the best supporting role honors, Ron Vawter who played Luther's miner father, and Joe Alaskey who portrayed Tetzel, the Augustinian Indulgence seller. Both men commanded their parts and put human feeling into the printed words of a fine script. Vawter, thin faced and clear-eyed, moved about the small stage and theatre area like a pro. He used his voice, his movements and the set stage lights to the best of his advantage (1969: 3).

Martin P. Kelly also commended Vawter's performance in his review of *Luther*. However, Kelly added that Cali's more reserved approach to the role of Martin Luther made the fiery exchange between father and son less than effective: 'In an early scene, Cali as Luther is confronted by a robust, earthy father, played vigorously by Ron Vawter, but the scene fails to catch fire. Cali seems to stand away from the tempest that swirls about him as the father mocks his decision to enter the priesthood' (1969b: 6).

Cali admitted he was sometimes taken aback by the anger Vawter displayed onstage. Other members of the Little Theatre also remarked on the explosive characters he created, and wondered where Vawter's impulses for those roles came from. David Schlatter saw acting as Vawter's form of release: 'He had this ability to just go into a character, and not worry about what other people would think'. Schlatter added that there was a pent-up dimension to Vawter's energy, which he was able to liberate onstage: 'It wasn't violent, and it wasn't intrusive. It was just what I call a coiled spring'.

Not long after the Little Theatre's 1969 production of *Luther*, Vawter quietly enacted his own form of rebellion against the religious organization he had worked so hard to join: he abruptly quit the Franciscan program. Vawter did not tell his peers why, but Schlatter speculated that the Franciscan dorm experience may have failed to meet his expectations: 'Many times, I've seen people get interested in the exciting person of St Francis. And then they come in and discover that life in a Franciscan order is part of the institutional Church, with rules and regulations'. Alternatively, Vawter may have succumbed to family pressure to quit. In any case, he did not return to Latham after leaving the campus Franciscans. Instead, he found an apartment in downtown Albany. There, Vawter finally seemed to discover the personal and sexual freedom that he had not been able to find at home or at school.

Rashomon: A Kabuki Myth: 29–31 October 1970

Vawter's final year at Siena College was transformative. On a personal level, he began a sexual relationship with Kevin Daly, his next-door neighbour in the campus Franciscan program. Their dormitory friendship slowly led to intimacy. 'Ron got his apartment off-campus', Daly explained during our interview, 'and it was probably in the spring of 1970 that we first became involved'.

Moreover, 1970–71 was also the year in which Vawter staged his most ambitious, experimental productions. The first of these was *Rashomon*, a play written in 1959 by Fay and Michael Kanin, based on the stories of Ryunosuke Akutagawa. The Japanese director Akira Kurosawa had already directed a film version of *Rashomon* in 1950. Akutagawa helped with the screenplay, and most of the film's action was based on two of his short stories: 'Rashomon' (1915) provided the setting, while 'In a Grove' (1922) provided the characters and plot. *Rashomon* reconstructs a rape and murder through the verbal accounts of four witnesses. Each account is self-serving and contradicts the others, ultimately leaving viewers uncertain of how the crime unfolded. *Rashomon* is inherently a play about perspective. The notion of multiple perspectives on a single event captivated Vawter at this particular time of his life.

Daly, who helped to design the set for *Rashomon*, identified Vawter as the play's director and auteur: 'It was all Ron's vision of what this was going to be'. Among the most striking changes Vawter made to the script was the addition of a movie section. 'This was before videotape', Daly explained, 'so I think we used either 8 mm or 16 mm film, or some kind of home movie camera'.

Gregory Mehrten, Vawter's later boyfriend and longtime partner, told me that Vawter had spent a lot of time watching movies in his youth. Kurosawa's *Rashomon* was a very famous film in its day, and Vawter may have seen it. Mehrten added that Vawter loved watching doubleheaders of the same show. For example, he took great pleasure in comparing Laurence Olivier's 1948 version of *Hamlet* with the adaptation that Sir John Gielgud directed in 1964. Perhaps his early fascination with competing versions of the same story led him to introduce a cinematic perspective of his own into a live stage play.

Vawter may also have heard about the practices of Robert Whitman, Allan Kaprow, Jim Dine and others. Allan Kaprow in 1959 and Robert Whitman in 1960 were the first American artists to use slides, film, and amplified sound in their work.[19] Of course, the surrealists and Dadaists had also used film in the 1920s and 1930s, but the 1960s marked a new burst of experimentation in film and theatre and crossovers between the two genres.

Regardless of how Vawter came upon it, his decision to combine film and live performance effectively doubled *Rashomon's* action. First, audiences heard the play's conflicted tales told onstage by four actors (Joe Cali, Joe Garren, Dan Nelson and Ann Maiella). Next, they saw the pivotal crime scene reenacted on film, but in an unfamiliar context. Daly explained that he, Vawter, and several others made a road trip out to Cape Cod. On a beach at the edge of the Atlantic Ocean, Vawter directed a pantomime featuring a second cast of actors who wore kabuki-style plaster masks. The central tale of *Rashomon*—the attack of the thieves, rape of the wife, and murder of the husband— was reenacted on the beach. Then, the four plaster masks worn by the actors were thrown into the sea. Vawter recorded the action on film.

To project Vawter's Cape Cod footage during the live performance at Siena College, the club's student technicians designed a special curtain. 'There was a stage we built', Daly explained, 'and as part of that stage, we designed a series of about four-inch wide vinyl strips that were attached top to bottom, so that it looked almost like a solid wall'. Daly estimated that this vinyl surface was roughly eight feet high, and six feet wide: 'The curtain was tacked, top and bottom, taut, so it would have a flat appearance when the movie wasn't playing on it. The movie would play up to a certain point, and then an actor would step *through* the slits'. The curtain looked like part of the set until it was time to project Vawter's film. At that point, it abruptly became an animate surface on which the silent seaside sequence played. Stage actors who stepped through the curtain's pliant panels revealed the

---

19 Michael Kirby chronicles Kaprow's use of projected slides in *18 Happenings in 6 Parts* in his book *Happenings* (1965: 67-83); Whitman also claims in his online 'Biography' that he was among the first artists to use film and slides in his work (2005).

literal threshold connecting their live performance to the recorded event. 'For that time', Daly said, 'this was a very progressive concept'.

Rashomon's intermedia innovations anticipate the early work of The Wooster Group. In David Savran's seminal book, *Breaking the Rules* (1988), Elizabeth LeCompte explains that it was Vawter who brought a slide projector to rehearsal during the making of *Rumstick Road* (1977). He also had the idea to project a slide of Spalding Gray's deceased mother, Bette Gray, onto the face of performer Libby Howes. LeCompte's testimony shows that Vawter remained interested in layering live performance and recorded media upon moving to New York. It also positions him as an intermedia innovator, even though he is best known as a performer.

Two years after *Rumstick Road*, in the summer of 1979, a filmmaker friend named Ken Kobland helped LeCompte and her performers shoot a silent film on Long Island Sound. 'By the Sea' was the final part of *Point Judith (An Epilog)* (1979). Stage action continued while the film was projected. Recalling Vawter's doubling, Libby Howes's actions onstage often corresponded to her actions in the film. Howes also held the smaller screen onto which a second film—a black & white Super 8 (also of the nuns)—was projected. The film commemorated Gray's decision to leave both TPG and LeCompte's emergent company to develop his solo monologues (Savran 1988: 134). Savran describes 'By the Sea' as 'underscoring the farewell, bringing together (although not synthesizing) a number of images from the Trilogy' (1988: 155). Vawter's earlier film at Cape Cod had similarly resisted the resolution of *Rashomon's* competing narratives. Daly described the film's ending as simple yet enigmatic: 'Ron basically just wanted the masks thrown into the ocean, and then washing back and forth in the waves, on the sand. That was the most important part of it for him'.

When I asked what it was like to work with Vawter on the film at Cape Cod, Daly replied that it was difficult:

DALY. 'Meticulous' and 'demanding' are two words that come to mind. [*Laughing*] It wasn't so much that he was hard to satisfy. It was that it was hard to understand what his vision *was*, because he wouldn't articulate it. It was only through repeated effort—on *your* part—that you would begin to understand, 'Oh, *now* I get what he's talking about'.

SMALEC. What do you think *Rashomon* was about for him? What did he want to dramatize?

DALY. I think he wanted to show the vagaries of truth, or the nuances and shades of meaning in truth.

When asked if he and Vawter ever discussed their sexual intimacy, Daly replied that this was another unspoken part of their relationship:

DALY. No, we didn't talk about it. But there was never any apprehensiveness between us—except for the first time, when we weren't sure that it was going to happen. [...] We must have been working late in the theatre one night, and he invited me back to his apartment. I was very excited to be invited over— that was the first time this had ever happened. We were very chaste; he went to bed in the bedroom, and I went to bed on the couch in the living room. And about five minutes later, I heard him calling my name. I went into the bedroom. I'd worked up the nerve to say, 'All right, I really do want this. I do know what is going on here'. And that was the only hesitation or anxiety I ever experienced in our relationship. We were always very at ease with one another. Even when Nancy [see below] came into the picture, I didn't really think anything about that. It just seemed like, 'Well, that's the—

SMALEC. Cover up?

DALY. Yes, that's the cover-up, and that's the path he's going on now'.

Nancy, the woman named above, was briefly Vawter's fiancée. Daly said Vawter dated Nancy for about six months: 'It was toward the end of his Siena College career'. Daly assessed Vawter's turn to heterosexual courtship as part of a social performance whose primary audience was Elton Lee Vawter: 'He was trying to appease his father by going with the girlfriend-engaged-married routine'. Meanwhile, Joseph Cali proposed that Vawter's engagement was not only sincere, but also deeply traumatic:

CALI. Ron had a girlfriend. She was really thin, really smart and really funny. And they were deeply in love, which is why I initially thought he was conflicted about becoming a priest.

SMALEC. Wow, what happened?

CALI. There was something crazy about the way they broke up, and maybe that was the beginnings of him discovering himself as being homosexual? There was a big sadness over that breakup. [. . .] It was kind of devastating for him. I don't know who broke up with whom. I think she broke up with him.

SMALEC. When did that happen, approximately?

CALI. I know it happened before I left Siena, so it would have been in 1970 or 1971 that they broke up.

Cali's testimony suggests that Vawter was still unsettled about his sexuality at the time. As it turned out, Vawter's choices of sexual partners remained fluid throughout much of his adult life.

Whereas Vawter's engagement to Nancy was known to his peers, Daly and Vawter, understandably for the time, tried to hide the nature of their own relationship. For instance, their dates took place away from the public eye, under the cover of nightfall:

DALY. Ron, for a long time, worked as the night clerk at the Northway Motor Hotel. He would pick me up around ten-thirty, and we'd go to the Northway Motel. We would sit around and talk all night, raid the kitchen, get a snack, and then at around three or four o'clock, I'd toddle off to a room to get some sleep. And when his shift was over, Ron would join me and nap before class. This went on several times a week, for months.

Surreptitious nights in motel rooms hardly suggest an ideal romance. Nevertheless, in a small town where people readily noticed deviations from the norm, the risks that Daly and Vawter took in order to be together are quite remarkable.

Daly fondly recalled several examples of Vawter's quiet affection. On one occasion, Vawter helped him build the set for *Rashomon*. On another occasion, Vawter sat with Daly while he studied for a final exam: 'My roommate was gone for the day, so we had the room to ourselves. As I sat at my desk studying French verbs, Ron entwined his hand in mine. For the next several hours, we played sweetly only with fingers and hands, without saying a word.'

In retrospect, Daly opts not to overanalyse his time with Vawter: 'I was young; he was young. I thought the world of him. So it's hard for me to take off those glasses and look at it in a more objective light now'. Even then, however, he accepted Vawter's limitations: 'He never told me he loved me, and it didn't matter. I loved him'.

While Vawter may have struggled to verbalize his emotions during this period, an article titled 'Little Theatre Production Nears Final Stages' offers a rare glimpse into how he expressed himself as a writer. Early in the piece, Vawter explains that what drew him to *Rashomon* is its apparent simplicity: '*Rashomon* is an ordinary story, one with grandeur, without risk' (1970: 6). Bypassing the play's heinous rape and murder, Vawter focuses instead on the smaller distortions inherent in the narratives people contrive. One of the play's storytellers is a woodcutter who witnessed the crime in the forest. His minor lie about how it unfolded eventually leads to his exposure as a thief who stole the murder victim's costly dagger. Despite the woodcutter's shameful admission, the priest who hears his tale absolves him, recognizing an honourable person who stole to feed his family. The priest restores the thief's self-worth by entrusting him with a baby they find abandoned at the decrepit Rashomon gate.

Vawter goes on to explain how he staged *Rashomon*'s abstract motif of humanity's endless flaws and rebirths:

To achieve the continuing and enduring quality of the imper-
fections of man as metaphorically given by the discovery of
the newborn infant, [...] I would have chosen a highly styl-
ized, symbolic form of theatre. It is for this reason I have sub-
titled the play, 'A Kabuki Myth'. Yet to employ a theatrical
style so exclusively preoccupied with form would require an
audience immensely knowledgeable in Eastern theatrical
notions, [...] so I decided to move the action to the West,
but in such a way as to transcend all periods of Western man
... The very essence of Kabuki (1970: 6).

One notable aspect of this passage is Vawter's apparent familiarity
with Kabuki. Where he learnt of Kabuki is unclear. Nevertheless, his
early interest in combining Asian and Western performance traditions
is another element that would recur in his later work with The
Wooster Group, particularly in *Brace Up!*

In 1970, Vawter assumed his college audience was not familiar
enough with kabuki to interpret its iconic movements and gestures.
Instead, he concluded his take on *Rashomon* with a more ambiguous
image: the four plaster kabuki masks tossed into the ocean. Significantly, he added that his silent film functioned as a kind of supplement
and reframing. It did not present a *different* version of the *Rashomon*
story than the ones narrated onstage. Instead, it defamiliarized the
action by placing it in a new context: 'The film shot to augment the
play is merely the enactment of the crime—but filmed in such an
obscure fashion that audiences themselves must decide and create their
own version of the story, their own truth, their own reality' (1970: 6).
By ending the live performance with his Cape Cod film, Vawter distanced viewers from the dramatic world they had come to recognize.
In a play about what it means to tell the truth, his silent film con-
cretized the idea that 'reality' is perspectival. In subtle ways, Vawter's
use of intermedia recalls Bertolt Brecht's *Verfremdungseffekt*.

After *Rashomon*, Vawter began working on *Fortune and Men's Eyes*,
his final production with the Little Theatre. In contrast to *Rashomon's*
timeless metaphors and narrative uncertainties, this latter play was

grounded in stark realism, and in homophobic realities of the early 1970s.

Fortune and Men's Eyes: 18–20 March 1971

Fortune and Men's Eyes, a prison drama written by John Herbert, premiered in New York at the Actors' Playhouse in 1967, but it took over a decade for Herbert's controversial play to be staged in his native Canada (see Wallace 2003). It is remarkable that Vawter staged Herbert's drama on Siena's conservative campus in 1971—just two years after Stonewall, and four years before the play's Canadian debut.

Fortune and Men's Eyes explores the violent interactions that transpire in a Canadian reformatory for juvenile offenders. The protagonist is a first-time offender named Smitty. Herbert describes him in the stage directions as 'a good-looking youth of clear intelligence and aged seventeen years. [. . .] He is of a type that everyone seems to like, almost on sight' (1967: 7). The plot revolves around Smitty's initiation into prison life, and his gradual degeneration into a sexual predator.

In an online article, 'John Herbert (1926–2001)', the scholar Robert Wallace argues that Smitty's education at the hand of other inmates and guards allowed Herbert to dramatize 'both the systemic corruption of Canada's penal system and the crippling effects of gender roles enforced by social norms' (2003). Wallace concludes with an ominous overview of Herbert's plot: 'Locked in a prison cell—the play's only setting—four male youths illustrate how sex functions as the currency of power in a homosocial milieu'. However, *Fortune and Men's Eyes* is also the story of Smitty's homoerotic awakening. Despite his initial homophobia, Smitty slowly struggles to accept his tender feelings for another man.

All of the Little Theatre members whom I interviewed said Vawter was responsible for bringing Herbert's text to the drama club. Father Devlin, in particular, recalled the anger of his fellow Franciscans when they realized he was serious about letting Vawter direct a play that dealt with homosexuality in prison:

DEVLIN. There was [. . .] an indignant response to the possibility of staging this play. I said to Ron, 'All right, you can do it, but let me guide you because there might be some language that you could—I won't say do away with—not use as frequently'. And there was cooperation on his part.

SMALEC. What kind of a director was Ron? How would you describe his approach to directing?

DEVLIN. It was intense. I think you have to keep in mind that putting on a play such as *Fortune and Men's Eyes* required a certain amount of daring [. . .] This was a kind of protest, although Ron and the students involved did not treat it in that kind of angry way.

SMALEC. It sounds like they were very brave.

DEVLIN. Oh yes. And needless to say, I got a lot of criticism.

Whereas Siena's faculty priests were offended, Kevin Daly told me that student members of the Little Theatre embraced Herbert's play as a provocation: 'By this time, we were coming off several huge successes with the company, so we were psyched to do something else—especially something that would be a slap in the face to all the bigots on campus'.

Daly added that Vawter 'pretty much had the play cast when he started it'. He selected 'a cute seminarian' named Joe Garren to play Mona. Joe Alaskey played Holy Face, the ruthless guard. John Konesky played the tough-talking bully, Rocky. Vawter took the lead role of Smitty. Daly noted of his boyfriend's decision to cast him as Queenie: 'That was the first acting role I ever had at Siena'.

Prior to *Fortune*, Daly's contributions to the Little Theatre had been backstage, but Vawter sensed the actor wanting to burst through his boyfriend's quiet demeanour:

SMALEC. What was your character like?

DALY. You mean with a name like Queenie? [*Laughing*] Queenie was very flamboyantly gay and did not try to hide it. She celebrated it! In the second act, she went into drag and sang a song.

SMALEC. How did this role relate to your own sexuality?

DALY. Oh, I was still totally closeted. And it was totally liberating to get up onstage and portray a character totally different from who I was offstage. I didn't lisp, didn't have overtly feminine gestures and I had never worn women's clothing before.

Daly's recollections make it clear that Vawter called the shots with respect to how *Fortune* was staged: 'I think it was very empowering for him, because he had almost total control over the production'. Curiously, however, published reviews, such as Mike Williams's 'Fortune: Gut Experience' identify Vawter's peers, James Hart and Traci Kachidurian, as the drama's director and assistant director: 'This is Mr. Hart's first attempt at directing and we cannot help but admire his courage in selecting this play' (1971: 19). Martin P. Kelly also named Hart as the drama's director.

Perhaps Vawter sought some critical distance from *Fortune*? Since he played the lead role of Smitty, he may have invited reliable friends to oversee this production. Another possibility is that Vawter asked Hart to take credit for directing Herbert's drama in an effort to mask his own leadership role. Vawter's sister, Celeste Vawter Fonda, told me that she and Vawter's mother attended all of his shows. Mindful of this audience, it was risky enough for him to star in *Fortune*, let alone acknowledge the show as his directorial vision.

Decades later, Vawter linked this turbulent time of his life to an image he had seen as a child, while watching his family's brand-new TV set. The image was of a young Roy Cohn whispering into Senator Joseph McCarthy's ear. Vawter recounted that primal scene in a 1992 interview published in *New York Quarterly*, simply titled 'Strange':

There was something about him that I recognized, even back then. I didn't know I was queer. I didn't know he was queer. But I recognized in Cohn something that was like me. I'm sure I saw in him a sexuality that was repressed and diverted and disguised, which was just what I was going through. I had homosexual impulses from the age of four, but I was told I shouldn't behave that way (1992: n. p).

Even as a child, Vawter recognized Cohn's whisper into McCarthy's ear as a kind of queer act: 'That actually made it a more powerful image for me' (1992: n. p). Only as an adult, however, did he grasp the furtive whisper's relevance to his life: 'I fully intended to have a career in the army, and had done a pretty good job of totally denying my homosexuality until about the age of 22' (1992: n. p). Vawter turned 22 on 9 December 1970, which makes *Fortune* the first production informed by his gay self-identification.

Fortune was also Vawter's final production at Siena College. Daly suggested that spearheading Herbert's play gave Vawter the freedom to take a progressive stance on homosexuality: 'I don't know for certain, but it could have been his first steps at coming out of the closet [...] without having to say, "I'm gay", or "I completely identify with the subject". You're at least making a public statement that you support the ideas being presented in this play'.

Vawter could not yet openly admit his same-sex desires, but performing as Smitty gave him a chance to rehearse them, and to find out what others would think. Decades later, Jessica Hagedorn asked him, 'Did you "discover" your sexual identity as you discovered yourself as an actor?' Vawter replied, 'It was a parallel process, yes' (1992: 49).

Those who reviewed *Fortune* were frank about the play's gay content, but troubled by Herbert's depiction of prison life. In his review, Williams depicted the drama as focusing on 'the brutality of prison life and the twisted kind of homosexual love it can produce' (1971: 19). However, this student reviewer seemed more alarmed by the coercion involved in the young men's sexual encounters (the play includes several scenes of forced sex, including an offstage gang-rape) than by the fact that these sex acts take place among men.

Kelly's titled his review in the *Albany Times-Union* 'Siena Play Lacks the Cohesive Fire'. Kelly wrote that Vawter played 'the leading role of the first-time offender far too casually in the initial act. The audience sees none of the fear or anxiety in the young man' (1971: 6). Kelly's criticism recalls Father Devlin's account of the 'deeper' emotions that Vawter could not comfortably access during his freshman year. Even in *Fortune*, four years later, the more experienced actor still had problems convincing his audience that he understood Smitty's vulnerability. Kelly's closing remark—'Vawter appears too controlled to be the victim of a seduction' (1971: 6)—confers an awkward rigidity upon the actor. His tendency toward formality seemed to interfere with his credibility in this role.

Vawter graduated from Siena College on 29 May 1971 with a B.A. in English literature, ending his involvement with the Little Theatre club. Vawter had already severed his ties to Kevin Daly when *Fortune and Men's Eyes* ended. Daly recalled volunteering that summer in Peekskill, NY, where he unexpectedly ran into his former boyfriend. Only then did Vawter share his plan to move to Palo Alto, CA, that fall. 'All I know was that he said he was going to Stanford, for acting', Daly told me.

In March 2015, I contacted Stanford's Office of the Registrar in effort to find out more about Vawter's programme and the dates of his enrolment. However, due to the Family Educational Rights and Privacy Act (FERPA), Stanford could not discuss this information with me. Additionally, the university's student records only became computerized in 1986, meaning that records from the 1970s are difficult to search, even if one has permission to access them.

Although I cannot confirm any official details of Vawter's time at Stanford, several people interacted with him in that context. In 2011, a Brooklyn-based writer named Bruce Pribram contacted me via social media to share his memories of Vawter. Pribram said he was an undergraduate at Stanford in 1971–72, the same year that Vawter performed with the graduate program. Pribram recalled that Vawter 'was a wonderful Mortimer in Edward II' (2011). Pribram did not remember much more, yet he added one curious detail: 'I don't think things ended happily for Ron at Stanford, but I really have no idea as to the whole story').

Like Kevin Daly, Joe Cali learnt by chance that Vawter was at Stanford. Cali had transferred to Berkeley in fall 1971 to complete his Bachelor's degree. Ironically, it was only in Palo Alto, after spending a night in Vawter's apartment, that he finally realized his friend was gay:

> At Siena, I wouldn't have suspected because he had his girl-friend. I really had no inkling at all. It probably became clearer to me after he broke up with her, and absolutely in Palo Alto, because he came on to me there. For the first time in our friendship, he crossed over the line. He wanted to have a rela-tionship with me. And I just said, 'It's not going to happen because I'm not gay. I love you. You're such a good friend of mine, but no'. I remember I stayed at his place that night, and it was cool; he was very cool. It didn't change our friendship in the least—once we got that stuff out of the way.

Not long after Vawter came out to Cali, both men headed back East. Cali married and moved to Manhattan in 1973. Vawter left Palo Alto in 1972, returning to Albany. And it was in Albany, under the direction of the late Jarka Burian, that he starred in the final and arguably most challenging performance of his campus theatre career.

Marat/Sade: 18–22 October 1972

Richard Schechner visited the State University of New York at Albany (SUNYA) in February 2006 to deliver the Burian Lecture, titled 'My Directing and Performance Studies'. Jarka Burian (1927–2005) joined the New York State College for Teachers (the predecessor of the State University of New York, Albany) in 1955, working as an assistant professor (1955 to 1959), associate professor (1959 to 1963), professor (1963 to 1993), and professor emeritus (1993 until his death). From 1971 to 1974, and again from 1977 to 1978, Burian served as the chair of the Department of Theatre at SUNYA. He also directed numerous productions at SUNYA and the Arena Summer Theatre in Albany from 1956 to 1991. After delivering his lecture, Schechner spoke with Grayce Burian, the widow of Jarka Burian. She recalled a production of Peter Weiss's play *Marat/Sade* (1963) that her husband had directed with Vawter in a leading role. Intrigued by this unlikely addition to what I had already told him about Vawter's amateur theatre career at Siena College, Schechner put me in contact with Grayce Burian.

The Jarka M. Burian Papers, held at the M. E. Grenader Department of Special Collections at SUNYA, include Burian's play files, which indicate that he began working on *Marat/Sade* in August 1972.[20] As for Vawter, it is unclear exactly when he returned to Albany after Stanford, or how he heard about the SUNYA production of *Marat/Sade*. Perhaps he knew someone attending college there. Perhaps he simply saw one of the posters found in Burian's play file:

Auditions. *Marat/Sade*
Directed by Jarka Burian
August 29-30-31, 7:30 p.m.
Main Stage Performing Arts Center
Open to All Students.

Although Vawter was not a SUNYA student, he turned up to audition with two of his former peers from the Little Theatre: Joe Alaskey and James (Jim) Hart. All three of their names appear on an audition schedule listing the names of 30 people invited for callbacks. Burian placed an asterisk beside Alaskey and Vawter's names, requesting to see them individually. The reason for these private meetings is not given. However, one possibility is that Alaskey and Vawter were not SUNYA students in 1972, as was required of everyone in the university's productions. When I met with her in 2006, Grayce Burian recalled that her husband got around that rule by having Vawter take a single course at SUNYA during the semester of the production.[21]

---

20 All documents pertaining to *Marat/Sade* cited in this chapter are from the Jarka M. Burian Papers (see Burian 1956–1991).
21 Neither Vawter nor Burian is alive to transmit their first-hand knowledge about the show, and I have been unable to locate either Hart or Alaskey. As a result, I have developed my account of *Marat/Sade* using Burian's papers, and using various published reviews of the production.

Professor Burian kept meticulous play files[22]. He documented every part of the process: auditions, rehearsals, expenses, publicity, critical reviews and his many correspondences about the shows. His 'Comments on Productions' folder contains Burian's reflections on each production, including a summary related to *Marat/Sade* that was written in 1998, decades after the 1972 production:

> The Vietnam conflict was still splitting the nation, campuses were still in agitation though the excesses had diminished, and revolution as an idealized concept was still in the air. [. . .] Notable in the cast were the actors of the two title characters: Ron Vawter as Marat, Joseph Alaskey as de Sade. Vawter (who had acted for Siena College and local community groups) went on to have a major career as an actor in the off-Broadway theatre, as well as work in TV and film. [. . .] *Marat* was also one of my major hits in terms of audience response, although the various critiques in the folder show clearly that not everyone was happy with the result.

Burian ended with a note about the visual documentation pertaining to *Marat/Sade*: 'As is evident in the folder, this was one of the most fully photographed of my productions'. Indeed, his play file contains numerous photos and slides. From warm-ups, to dress rehearsals, to performance, the contours and size of the stage, costumes and props, and performers themselves are all carefully preserved.

Yet it is also true that Burian's orderly play file is one man's selective arrangement of a much larger process. For even as he left behind a detailed record of a collective process, there are crucial personal experiences that Burian's papers fail to articulate.

On 14 September 1972, midway through the two-month rehearsal period for *Marat/Sade*, Elton Lee Vawter abruptly died of a heart attack at age 47. In the words of his wife, 'He was on military assignment in San Francisco, and they shipped him home in a box'. Matilda Vawter softly added: 'Ron never had a chance to say goodbye

---

22 'Marat Sade, Peter Weiss, November 1972', Series 1: Play Files, 1956–1991, Box 1, Jack M. Burian Papers, State University of New York, Albany.

to his dad'. Burian's play file does not mention Vawter's loss. However, there are subtle indications that Vawter may have shared the news of his father's death. Those clues reside in the play file, in the chronology of *Marat/Sade* rehearsal schedules. Rehearsals began on 5 September 1972, and Vawter was called to rehearse most days. On Thursday, 14 September 1972, the day that Elton Lee Vawter died, rehearsal began at 7:30 p.m. There is nothing in the play file to indicate that Vawter mentioned his loss that evening. Perhaps he did not know? During my interview with Willem Dafoe, the former Wooster Group member told me that Vawter's father had suffered a 'massive heart attack while celebrating with friends at the *Top of the Mark* [restaurant] in San Francisco'. Ron Vawter may not have learnt of his father's passing until later that night.

The schedule for Friday, 15 September 1972 states that rehearsal began at 7:15 p.m. with the entire cast. But then, abruptly, rehearsals come to a halt—or at least their documentation is interrupted. The next rehearsal schedule in the play file covers 9 October to opening night. What happened between 15 September and 9 October? Given Burian's meticulous record keeping, it's unlikely that the schedules are just missing, but there is no way to know for sure. It seems more likely that Burian took a formal break to give Vawter time to mourn, although it is curious that he did not continue to rehearse without him.

In the last days before the 18 October premiere, Burian took detailed notes on rehearsals and left copies for the cast to read. His 'Director's Notes' are often amusing, sometimes abrasive, but they always clearly convey what he wanted from the actors. Interestingly, it appears as though Burian gave Vawter more leeway than he did other actors. For example, on 16 October, Burian's note to Vawter stated:

> Very good overall; you've built this up to a fine performance. I especially liked the sequence with DeSade that culminates with the 'turn yourself inside out' lines. One slight reserva-tion—at times I'm not sure if you or the character has for-

gotten or stumbled on his lines—in other words, maybe cut back a little on this if you've been doing it deliberately.

Burian did not ponder whether the apparent mistakes of other student performers were, in fact, quirks they invented for their characters. In Vawter's case, however, he entertained the idea that the talented young actor had wilfully created a confused and faltering Marat.

The Ron Vawter Papers include an article by Stanisław Ignacy Witkewicz, a Polish avant-garde artist, titled 'On a New Type of Play'. Someone (presumably Vawter) underlined several passages in the essay. In one of them, Witkewicz compares two ways in which a theatre artist might affect his audience: 'In other words, an insane asylum? Or rather, a madman's brain on stage?' (99-100).[23] Vawter's apparent choice was to enact Marat's madness directly, without framing it as a deliberate performance of madness.

In his notes from the 17 October dress rehearsal, the director remarked again on Vawter's poor articulation, citing a particularly garbled speech: ' "Fill the rich man's *what*?" I couldn't understand it. Stare *past* Herald's staff as he lowers it in front of you. "Citizen Marquis" is now *too* spastic'. On opening night, 18 October, Burian noted Vawter's deficient makeup, 'Need whiter face', as well as his faulty diction, ' "They aren't trifles"—make the *negative* clearer; last night hard to know that you were rejecting Sade's point'. Finally, he asked why Vawter omitted a gesture normally performed by his character: 'What happened to the moment when you sweep stuff off the board?'

Vawter's lapses were hardly catastrophic in nature. Nevertheless, they suggest an uncharacteristic lack of attention to detail. Mindful of what Vawter's peers say about his discipline, it seems odd that he repeatedly failed to make the corrections requested by the director. Burian's final notes to the cast are from the closing matinee, on 22 October. His sole comment concerning Vawter's performance is scrawled starkly across the page: 'Marat over-spastic'. Elton Lee

---

23   For the copy of the S. I. Witkiewicz essay found in the Ron Vawter Papers, see Series I: Personal Papers.

Vawter's sudden death may have temporarily impaired his son's ability to focus.

Burian's stated concerns about the show were not the ones shared by critics. In his opening night notes, the director made a long list of 'things to work on, check, or control'. By contrast, the consensus among the reviews found in Burian's play file is that his directorial vision was far too sanitized: for a play about a mental asylum, there was hardly enough bedlam to go around.

Marjorie Feiner reviewed *Marat/Sade* in the *Knickerbocker News*. Her complaints about the show's costumes and lack of stage blood initially seem trivial:

> Marat, played by Ron Vawter, is clothed in a sheet draped almost Roman-fashion (I would have rather had something more revealing, to strip it down to the bare essentials). [...] He is supposed to scratch the sores on his body (these were non-existent) until the bath water is red with blood (1972: 7A).

However, Feiner's larger point was that the absence of chaos had a distancing effect: 'The rawness of insanity never touched the audience [...] arousing our deepest pity and aversion, thereby thrusting our madness back to us' (1972: 7A). Despite her early reservations, Feiner ultimately praised Vawter as a credible fanatic, especially during the second act, when he incited the other inmates to riot: 'In many places he handled his part with an appeal that was believable' (7A). Edward Hayes, who reviewed *Marat/Sade* in the *Albany Student Press*, likewise named Vawter as one of the play's outstanding talents (1972: 1A).

To my knowledge, Vawter never mentioned his work on *Marat/Sade* again, at least not in published interviews. Two months later, in December 1972, he moved to Manhattan, where he reportedly stumbled upon the Performing Garage while walking home from his job as an army recruiter.

CHAPTER 2

Scenes of Self-Recruitment

Ron Vawter's Entry into The Performance Group

In *Breaking the Rules: The Wooster Group*, David Savran succinctly repeats the oft-cited legend of Ron Vawter's inadvertent entry into theatre:

> Vawter came to the Wooster Group via the U.S. Army. He recalls working downtown in the winter of 1972 as a recruiting officer and passing the Performing Garage on his way home every evening. After hearing, night after night, strange 'experimental sounds' coming out of the place, he stopped in to see [Richard] Schechner's production of Sam Shepard's *The Tooth of Crime* which he was 'very taken with'. He gradually got to know the Group members and quit the Army in the summer of 1973 to become The Performance Group's administrator (1988: 4).

The Performance Group (TPG) began as a workshop led in November 1967 by Richard Schechner, a director and professor at New York University. Through the efforts of Schechner and others, the Polish theatre visionary Jerzy Grotowski came to New York in October 1967 to lead an actor-training workshop in which Schechner also participated. In convening his own workshop immediately thereafter, Schechner said one of his main objectives was to teach what he had learned from Grotowski in combination with the experimental work he had done in New Orleans at Tulane University.[1]

---

1 Richard Schechner, personal email, 9 March 2009.

By early 1968, Schechner's workshop consisted of about 12 young actors, dancers and designers, among them Joan MacIntosh, William Finley, William Shephard and Priscilla (Ciel) Smith. In March 1968, Shephard located a former metal stamping plant at 33 Wooster Street in what was to become SoHo. The building was (and still is) part of the Grand Street Artists' Co-Op. Schechner rented the space with an option to buy shares, which he did. He also formed a non-profit corporation called Wooster Group, Inc.[2] He named the company he had started The Performance Group, and called their theatre The Performing Garage.

In 2006, I reconstructed Vawter's route home to find out how he crossed paths with 33 Wooster Street. As a point of departure, I used Ross Wetzsteon's article, 'Saint Ron: New York's Best Unknown Actor', a text in which the *Village Voice* critic identified '80 Centre Street' (1989: 39) as the address where Vawter worked back in 1972.[3]

Upon arriving at 80 Centre Street, I found what is today called the Louis J. Lefkowitz State Office Building, or the District Attorney's Office. I spoke with the building's landlord, parking attendants, security guards and passersby. Most everyone remembered 80 Centre Street as the Department of Motor Vehicles—where people went to get their drivers' licenses during the Vietnam era. Confused, I searched both the Municipal Archives and New York Public Library for proof that an Army recruiting office had existed at 80 Centre Street. The documentation I found only deepened my uncertainty.[4]

---

2   Another New York corporation was already named 'The Performance Group,' so that name could not be used for this purpose. Schechner took 'Wooster' from the street where his theatre was located.

3   Stephen Holden also cites 80 Centre Street as the address of Vawter's army office in his interview with Vawter (Holden 1992).

4   Manhattan's 1973 Yellow Pages list five U.S. Army Recruiting stations: 43rd Street and Broadway, 215 West 125th Street, 1276 Lexington Avenue, 201 Varick Street, and 356 Broadway. This last address was just below Canal Street, but not where Vawter said he worked. The 1973 Yellow Pages confirm that 80 Centre Street (known by its cross street, 155 Worth) was the Department of Motor Vehicles. However, I eventually encountered one man who remembered an 'Army Induction office' at 80 Centre Street in the early 1970s. Known today as

Although I had already started to question the transmitted narrative of Vawter's rise as an actor, my inability to verify his workplace led to a more focused inquiry. What if Vawter's self-presentation as an Army recruiter had been a facade of sorts, an outward show that did not reveal the whole story? How did The Performance Group's early impressions of Vawter as a 'nonperformer' complicate his subsequent roles in TPG? Vawter's military demeanour—whether legitimate or, to some extent, artfully contrived—and his ensuing job as TPG's general manager became the foundations of his onstage persona in the Group's production of *Mother Courage and Her Children* (1975). With TPG, Vawter became a character by virtue of who he already seemed to be.

The implications of viewing Vawter's self-presentation as a kind of performance are threefold. First, except for Bonnie Marranca, who makes the (somewhat inaccurate) claim in 'The Wooster Group: A Dictionary of Ideas' that Vawter and Spalding Gray were 'both traditionally-trained theatre actors' (2003: 14), scholars have not questioned or investigated what Vawter did before joining TPG. Second, studying Vawter's entry into the Group offers a perspective on how his self-presentation converged with the emergent aesthetic interests of Spalding Gray and Elizabeth LeCompte who were romantically involved with each other. After several years of being directed by Schechner, they began collaborating in 1975 on theatre pieces that explored Gray's family history and his mother's suicide. Gray acted while LeCompte directed. Statements made by these artists as well as other former TPG members reveal that Vawter's self-presentation appealed to Gray and LeCompte. They liked him because he was an interesting person; they did not initially see him as an actor.

Finally, and perhaps most importantly, scholars today still police the borders 'between' theatre and performance. Michael Kirby famously partitioned these modes in his Introduction to *Happenings*,

---

Military Entrance Processing Stations, these are places where individuals are processed for enlistment into the armed services. Civilians, including National Guardsmen, could be employed at Army Induction centres.

when he aligned 'traditional theatre' (1965: 14) with the 'matrixed' performer, who 'functions in an imaginary time and place created primarily in his own mind', responding to 'often-imaginary stimuli in terms of an [...] artificial personality (17). By contrast, 'nonmatrixed' performers like the athlete or public speaker function 'as [themselves] in the same time-place as the spectators' (16). Significantly, Kirby also contrasted the physical labour of the nonmatrixed performers used in Happenings with the intellectual labour of those who assembled such events: 'The creation was done by the artist when he formulated the idea of the action. The performer merely embodies and makes concrete the idea' (17).

The dichotomies between matrixed and nonmatrixed performing are usually clear: artificial/everyday; role play / simple action; character/self, and so on. Yet the fact that Vawter's actual duties as TPG's general manager found their way into the Group's production of *Mother Courage* offers an intriguing opportunity to analyse the ways in which formalized performance—theatre, that is—can co-opt, adapt or complicate those everyday performances. Although critics tend to describe Vawter's work in *Mother Courage* as nonmatrixed performing—he simply did his job in front of an audience—his early self-presentation to the members of TPG was, in fact, a complex and formalized mask. Vawter acted, but as himself.

Enter Ron Vawter

In his *Village Voice* article, Wetzsteon cites Vawter's account of why he went from a promising career in the Special Forces to the unfamiliar terrain of Off-Off-Broadway: 'My father's death released me emotionally from that sense I'd had for years that I was destined for a military life' (1989: 39).

Mindful of this testimony, it seems conceivable that Vawter relocated from the Albany region to New York City shortly after Elton Lee Vawter's fatal heart attack, which took place during the rehearsal period for Jarka Burian's SUNYA production of *Marat/Sade*, on 14

September 1972. Finally, Vawter's releasable military service record indicates that if he was assigned to Manhattan, then it was only for a matter of weeks in December 1972.[5]

I contend that Vawter moved to New York with the goal of becoming a professional actor. Of course, since he died in 1994, no one can ask about his intentions. Yet we do have The Performance Group's memories of the eye-catching young man dressed in an army uniform who came to watch their show, *The Tooth of Crime*, and kept attending until they noticed him. Indeed, as TPG actor James Griffiths acknowledged during our interview, his earliest memory of Vawter retains an indelible air of bewilderment: 'He showed up in his Army captain's uniform [...] and we all said, "Who the fuck is this?" We had just finished this semi-political piece called *Commune* [1970], and we thought—not very seriously—that he was maybe with Army intelligence. This was obviously an enemy, right?' (2004)

Joan MacIntosh, a founding member of TPG who played lead roles in many of the company's productions, confirmed the unsettling impact of Vawter's appearance, adding an important detail about his habitual choice of seats: 'We were doing *Tooth of Crime*. Spalding played Hoss and I played Becky Lou. And we kept noticing, on the upper level of the Performing Garage [...] that there was this guy in a Green Beret uniform who kept sitting in the same place, up high.

---

5 I obtained Vawter's military record from the National Personnel Records Center. Due to the Privacy Act of 1974, his assignments were blacked out. Yet I could see that Vawter was assigned to a station other than his home unit (the Special Forces Airborne Group in Schenectady, New York) in December 1972. January 1973 was Vawter's last recorded assignment before his separation from the Special Forces on 11 July 1973. At that time, he was supposed to rejoin his home unit. Perhaps he returned to Schenectady in January 1973, fulfilled his duties there and then moved permanently to New York. This is not to suggest that Vawter's army recruiting job in Manhattan was a lie. Nevertheless, his explanation for his sudden abandonment of his military prospects feels incomplete. It is also unclear why a National Guardsman would have been detailed as a recruiter for the US Army, a totally separate entity.

[. . .] We finally said, "Look, this is getting really scary. There's this military guy who's been back here now 17 times "' (2004).[6]

Bruce Rayvid, TPG's technical director, likewise struggled to place Vawter's peculiar, repetitive habits. Unlike Griffiths and MacIntosh, who envisioned him as a likely antagonist, Rayvid characterized Vawter as someone overly obsessed by the show: 'I remember Ron kind of lurking—that's the best word for it—up in the balcony on several nights, in uniform. We did have some crazies' (2004).

While members of the group did recognize that Vawter's strange behaviour was not fully in line with the norms of everyday life, none of them considered the prospect that Vawter was neither a lone fanatic nor part of an organized response to TPG's politics, but a performer like them. Yet given the indisputable sense of drama engendered by his presence, what factors prevented the Group from perceiving it as an act of display staged for their benefit?

Perhaps the answer lies, at least in part, in what the sociologist Erving Goffman, in *The Presentation of Self in Everyday Life*, called a *front*: 'It will be convenient to label as "front" that part of an individual's performance which [. . .] functions in a fixed and general fashion to define the situation for those who observe the performance' (1959: 17). The implications of Goffman's definition are striking, if ironic. Even as Vawter's unusual front successfully captured TPG's attention, it also prevented the Group from discerning what should have otherwise been obvious: his interest in avant-garde theatre. Whether or not he projected it consciously, Vawter's Army uniform defined him, generally and inflexibly, as a nonperformer.

During my interviews with former TPG members, I noticed how often they switched military designations in describing Vawter's appearance. Sometimes they called him a Green Beret, sometimes an Army captain, and other times, a 'man in uniform'. In short, Vawter was generically 'military' to them. Jim Clayburgh, TPG's environmental designer, recalled the flagrant sense of transgression associated with

6 All quotations attributed to Joan MacIntosh in this chapter are from this interview.

military attire during 1972–73: 'It was during the end of the Vietnam War era, and it was such a courageous thing to be wearing a uniform at that point. It wasn't a neutral act!' (personal interview, 24 May 2004)

The incommensurability between Vawter's public image and the seemingly improbable role he secretly wanted to play becomes even clearer in Richard Schechner's 2002 lecture, delivered at a symposium titled 'Reflections on Ron Vawter':

> We'd had Performance Group groupies, but that had stopped at the end of *Dionysus in 69*. So it was strange when I saw this guy come two or three times a week, week after week. He was very . . . I would say 'straight-laced'. So I asked him what his name was and what he did. He said, 'My name is Ron Vawter and I'm a recruiting officer for the United States Army. I'm stationed down here, somewhere below Canal Street, but really I'm an actor'. And I said, 'Well, we are really in need of a business manager. Can you add'? He said, 'Sure'. So he became, for a while, the business manager of The Performance Group (2002).

In all respects save one, this testimony corresponds with TPG's general sense of Vawter as a mildly disquieting figure. Unique, however, is Schechner's memory that Vawter came out and told him: 'but really I'm an actor'.

Scholars define 'self-disclosure' as sharing with others what they would not normally discover or know. Self-disclosure involves risk and vulnerability on the part of the person sharing information, and Vawter likely confided in Schechner for a reason. Perhaps he assumed the older director held the power to decide if he could join TPG? Another possibility is that Vawter told other group members he was an actor, but his speech acts did not sink in. Even Schechner ultimately forgot or suppressed Vawter's pivotal admission. In a 2003 interview, Schechner would go on to contradict the anecdote cited above: 'The fact of the matter is that being roughly 30 years ago, I don't recall anything specific. I do know that I asked if he would work, doing our books and some of our business management. [. . .] *I didn't know he was an actor at the time*' (Schechner 2003; emphasis added). The hazards of oral history are one methodological insight to draw from this mutable testimony—even eyewitnesses cannot say for sure what happened decades ago. Another inference is Vawter's readiness to assume *any* role in order to join TPG—whether as actor, bookkeeper or volunteer.[7]

Finally, we might conclude that Vawter's front carried so much cultural baggage that his 'authentic' self was illegible: influenced by the army recruiter's clean-cut and orderly demeanour, Schechner failed to imagine Vawter as an actor, and typecast him instead as an administrator.

Spalding Gray was, in fact, the only TPG member to describe his first impressions of Vawter in overtly theatrical terms. During our 2004 interview, Gray surprised me by referring to Vawter as a *character*:

SMALEC. And so, as a performer in the show, did you think that this guy would join your company?

GRAY. No. No, I didn't think that. But yet, the show was environmentally lit, so you could see him as clearly as the other performers. You could see his face, and it was lit up just as much as—as all of us. So he became a character.

SMALEC. What kind of character?

GRAY. Well, the kind of character he was. I mean [long pause] dressed in a military outfit (2004).

Gray did not unequivocally mean that Vawter projected a matrixed character. On the contrary, he implied that Vawter's 'character' arose from his self-presentation in an environmental theatre context that made others notice him. Yet Vawter not only embraced the forms of activity and visibility available to all viewers, he also became the company's unlikely focal point: the very person whom they wanted to know more about.

---

7 Bruce Rayvid told me that Vawter joined TPG as a volunteer. Vawter volunteered for a year (if not longer), and eventually offered to do the company's books.

Despite TPG's early theories that Vawter was an army spy (and thus an outsider to their theatre), they soon began studying his presence more closely, describing it in ways that blur the lines between performers and audience. While Vawter did not assume a fictional role in *Tooth of Crime*, a certain kind of *life character* gradually emerged. In Wetzsteon's 'Saint Ron,' Spalding Gray recounted how that transition took place: 'It was totally weird, the way he stood out in the audience. [...] After a couple of performances, the actors became more aware of him than we were of each other. Finally, after a dozen times or so, we approached him and told him he could come free as our honorary guest' (1989: 39).

Gray's account of the free admission offered in exchange for Vawter's continued attendance suggests TPG was trying to appraise a social performance that, to them, signalled more than met the eye. Even as the Group was absorbed in staging a formal drama, Vawter's ongoing act of observing that process acquired a greater dramatic significance. When TPG failed to seriously recognize him as an actor, Vawter tactically amplified his front as a nonperformer.

MacIntosh, for example, recalled that Vawter subsequently presented himself as a general handyman: 'We're at a company meeting, and we get a letter from somebody named Ron Vawter, who says he wants to join the Group. He'll do anything to be part of it; he'll sweep floors, whatever. We're looking for a company manager at the time, so we hire him. And *then* we discover it's this guy who kept coming [to *The Tooth of Crime*] all those times' (2004).

Decades later, in a 1992 interview with Jessica Hagedorn, Vawter continued to foster that incomplete picture of his unplanned entry into theatre: 'I never thought I was going to be in the theatre. Nothing had ever propelled me to want a theatrical career. My parents were both military people; I was programmed to be in the military' (46).

Vawter's parents may have expected him to join the army, and perhaps he expected that of himself, but he had already starred in nearly a dozen productions by the time he met TPG in 1973. His 1971 move to Palo Alto to study graduate acting at Stanford further suggests that

Vawter had considered a stage career long before encountering TPG. Also there is the matter of Schecher's contradicting accounts of the army recruiter who recruited himself into theatre. Curiously, however, Vawter chose the less deliberate version to become part of his legend. By retrospectively presenting himself as having *no* prior actor training, Vawter forged what he clearly recognized as a valued niche: 'In the mid-1970s, there was this movement or trend that the purest actor was one who hadn't trained in a school. I sort of sneaked into theatre at a moment when being a non-performer was an approved and preferred way of performing' (1992: 49).

There are indications that experimental theatre during this period was moving toward including the 'untutored' artist among its ranks. One factor underlying the era's interest in amateurs was the evolution, since the 1950s, of avant-garde art forms that sought to distinguish themselves from conventional theatre, dance and visual arts. Happenings, Fluxus, early postmodern dance and the experimental theatre groups that preceded TPG all questioned virtuosity, who qualified as an artist and what behaviours and objects constituted art.

A second reason for recruiting amateurs and artists without specialized training was the counterculture's distrust of theatricality, based on the belief that the means of producing spectacle were already in the hands of those invested in maintaining the status quo. Arthur Sainer, a critic and a playwright, articulated the American avant-garde's resistance to both theatricality and specialized training in his *Radical Theatre Notebook*:

> We began to understand in the '60s that the words in plays, the physical beings in plays, [and] the events in plays were too often evasions [. . .] artifices that had to do not with truths but with semblances. [. . .] With the Bread & Puppets as a spearhead, the idea of the nontheatrical or nonprofessional ensemble began to take hold (1975: 15–23).

In some ways, of course, this ideology of the 'natural' was not specific to theatre of the 1970s (and not specific to that era, since it distantly echoes the Futurists' repudiation of artistic tradition and training while anticipating today's fixation with reality TV). Nevertheless, it was precisely through the young man's self-presentation as an artless army recruiter that his complex roles in *Mother Courage* began to take shape.

As a first step in tracing how Vawter's offstage comportment became part of the performance personae he fashioned in *Mother Courage*, I want to reconstruct the process by which TPG came to see him as a friend and possible colleague. In *Performative Circumstances*, Schechner describes *Tooth of Crime* as aimed at 'removing the "magic" from theatre' (1983: 83). To do so, he designed an 'experiment' whereby cast members dropped their roles and behaved as themselves during specific parts of the event:

> At intermission performers prepare and sell coffee, talk to spectators, socialize, and let everyone know when the second act is beginning. The difference between show time and intermission is clear, but there is no attempt made at hiding the non-performing life performers lead even in the midst of a night at the theatre. [...] Roles are seen as emerging from a full constellation of activities that include economics, logistics, hosting, and one-to-one relationships (83).

Although Schechner does not specify how performers' interactions with the audience enhanced their roles in *Tooth of Crime*, TPG members recall that their ongoing contact with Vawter expanded their perceptions of him. The mysterious Green Beret ceased to be seen as a stereotype. At the same time, certain people began to realize that his military 'front' could be used tactically in performance.

For instance, Rayvid recalled the compelling contradictions that Vawter exuded: 'He was totally the antithesis of his uniform. It was kind of a hoot, because it seemed like, "Oh man, you're working with the system! We're going to change the world, and you'll be the inside guy"'. Like Rayvid, Gray met Vawter at a pivotal juncture in his own career. Though he played a fictional rock star in *The Tooth of Crime*, Gray was increasingly drawn to presenting his real life onstage. During *Commune* (1970), Schechner asked TPG members to invent names as a basis for their roles in the piece. Stephen Borst chose 'David Angel'. Joan MacIntosh chose 'Clementine'. By contrast, Gray selected 'Spalding'.[8] The roles he ultimately played in *Commune* (a homicidal cult member; a murder victim's husband) had nothing to do with Gray's actual biography. Nevertheless, his self-referential act of naming marked the start of his fascination with the self-based persona.

When Vawter arrived on the scene in 1973, Gray quickly recognized him as a 'character', although it is unclear if he suspected that Vawter's weekly returns were part of a conscious routine. In any case, Gray grew to admire the newcomer's down-to-earth style: 'He was very aware of the people around him, and not solipsistic, not caught up in himself the way many actors are. He was easy to talk to because he was interested in a lot of things' (2004). Over time, Vawter's ability to engage with an audience while being himself led Gray to see the value of taking one's 'offstage' persona into the spotlight: 'Later, I made a piece with him at the Kitchen [in New York City] called *Interviewing the Audience*. He selected audience members, and then we both interviewed them. He was very good at that. [. . .] He was genuine in his curiosity and that in itself was an art'.

This recollection is complicated by the fact that today, Vawter is not recognized as co-originator of *Interviewing the Audience*—my conversation with Gray was the first time I heard of Vawter's involvement. That said, Gray's attention to Vawter's 'genuine art' of curiosity signals the paradox at the heart of his colleague's behaviour, and raises larger questions about Vawter's impact on Gray's formulation of the difference between *acting* and *performing*. In 'Performance as Therapy,' Philip Auslander argues that the path 'from being an actor pretending to be someone else to playing himself through other characters, led Gray to the autobiographical monologue form' (2005: 167). As stated previously, Gray himself suggests that, Vawter's self-presentation was an integral to the development of his own process. According to his

---

8 For Schechner's account of how his production pitted 'given' names against 'new or made' names, see Sainer (1975: 217).

testimony, both he and Vawter premiered *Interviewing the Audience* 'after The Wooster Group was formed.[9] It was in 1978.' (2004).

If this date is accurate, then their nonmatrixed interactions with an audience arguably would have laid a foundation for the self-based persona featured in Gray's monologues. While I have not found evidence that Gray and Vawter presented *Interviewing the Audience* at the Kitchen in 1978, I did locate a record of another performance, titled *What Happened on the Way Here*, which they did together at the Kitchen in February 1981.[10] Performing as himself, Vawter chatted with audience members as they waited for the show in the lobby, and identified people with interesting stories to tell. Once the show started, Vawter and Gray invited those people onstage and asked detailed questions about what had happened to them on the way to the theatre. Vawter had the gift of speaking easily and confidently, in a way that made people want to listen and believe him. During a 2005 interview, Elizabeth LeCompte described Vawter as an intriguing storyteller. At the same time, however, the details of her testimony suggest that Vawter constructed a social persona that did not quite align with the facts of his past: 'I didn't know anything about his acting background. [...] He talked much more about his Jesuit past, about his spiritual life. I knew him more as a Green Beret, and he wanted to be a chaplain for the Green Berets. [...] He'd gone to school mainly in Religious Studies, and he didn't mention that too much, except to joke around' (2005).

As discussed previously in the first chapter, although Vawter did join the Franciscan programme during his junior year, he withdrew after one semester and graduated with a bachelor's degree in English. Joking around about that part of his life to the other members may

---

9 Technically speaking, The Wooster Group did not exist until 1980, after Schechner resigned from TPG.

10 While reviewing microfiche at New York University's Bobst Library, I found an advertisement for a show starring Gray and Vawter, See *What Happened on the Way Here*, 1981 Village Voice, p. 90. In other words, it is possible that Gray misremembered the date (and title) of his early collaboration with Vawter.

have served to downplay Vawter's academic credentials, since portraying himself as what he actually was—a college graduate and luminary of his campus theatre scene—was likely the least hip thing he could have done. LeCompte made this point clear in our 2005 interview: 'I wasn't interested in good performers; I was always interested in interesting people'.

LeCompte's own aesthetic was never 'anti-theatrical' to the degree espoused by ensembles that wanted no part of traditional drama. For instance, she rejected Schechner's participatory environments and staged her pieces with the traditional stage and audience separation. Nevertheless, LeCompte identified with what she perceived as Vawter's position on the margins, having come to TPG with a graphic arts background: 'He was an outsider, like I was. We came to performing from a different place: not from the traditional theatre background' (2005). Vawter appealed to LeCompte not because he lacked training, but because his training *beyond* the theatre spoke to her experiences.

Like other TPG members, Schechner accepted Vawter's self-presentation at face value. The Performance Group's former director recalled that Vawter neither raised flags nor invited curiosity about his life outside the workplace: 'I had no notion at that point whether he was straight or gay. It never entered my mind one way or the other. He was correct; he seemed to me to be a much more ordinary, conventional, strict person that the rest of us, who were sort of like hippies' (2006). Vawter's early relationship with Schechner established a clear-cut hierarchy. Bruce Porter, who joined TPG as a stagehand in 1975, explained: 'Ron certainly knew how to take orders, which worked well with Richard, in that Ron saw himself as "the doer" based on what the inner circle wanted' (2004).

Vawter's everyday performances within The Performance Group come across, from the start, as strategic. He seemed to vary his self-presentation depending on his audience, and what he thought they wanted from him. That said, however, I do not doubt that Vawter was sincere in carrying out the duties assigned to him. The question is what happened when he transitioned from doing his everyday jobs as

TPG's general manager, to performing those tasks *onstage* in a formalized way?

In a letter to Bertolt Brecht's son dated 11 April 1974, Schechner requested Stefan Brecht for permission to stage *Mother Courage and Her Children* (1939) and outlined his plan to combine the play's dramatic motifs with the prosaic labour that normally happened offstage: 'Also Clayburgh and Vawter will perform, and the technical aspects of the production will be fully integrated into the scenography, and even the narrative. The actual business of the theatre will be a metaphor for the business transacted in the play'.[11]

Schechner's use of the word 'metaphor' is striking. The director suggests that even the most literal tasks (changing sets, running the box office, and so on) take on symbolic values when performed in the context of a formal score. Rayvid extended this idea during our interview by citing Schechner's precept: 'The show starts when the first audience member walks in, and it ends when the last audience member exits'.[12] He added a remark about *Mother Courage*: 'So yeah—the show started when Ronnie got in, and he was into his role' (2004). Here, Rayvid not only implied that Vawter created a subtle matrix of character by getting into his role as company manager, but also that Vawter functioned as the initial audience to Rayvid's act of opening the theatre. That solitary task performed by Rayvid as company technical director became part of the larger drama when Vawter became a more formalized spectator to his own routine-as-performance.

As noted at the beginning of this chapter, Vawter's self-based roles in *Mother Courage* present a chance to examine the ways in which theatre co-opts and sometimes modifies Goffmanian 'daily performances'. Vawter's job as TPG's general manager involved tasks that exemplify what Kirby defines in *Happenings* as nonmatrixed performing: 'the execution of a generally simple and undemanding act' (1965: 17). When I asked Jim Clayburgh what Vawter did in *Mother Courage*, the

---

11 'Letter to Stefan Brecht', Richard Schechner Papers, box 167, folder 3.
12 Schechner offered a similar definition of when a performance begins and ends in Environmental Theatre ([1973] 1994: xxix).

environmental designer replied that his colleague managed 'the day-to-day, in-and-out cash flow, which wasn't very much, but [. . .] he started to get his signature on the checks at that point' (2004). The Richard Schechner Papers confirm this was the case. A folder titled 'Mother Courage: Box Office'[13] includes accounting statements that Vawter signed as early as January 1975. After each show, Vawter tallied the number of tickets sold. As part of their commitment to the politics of *Mother Courage*, TPG also sold full and partial dinners to audience members who wanted a hearty yet inexpensive meal before the show. Vawter added the number of dinners purchased, subtracting the cost of food to determine TPG's revenue.

Vawter's performance persona in *Mother Courage* required him to complicate—and arguably even to *fake*—that straightforward activity. In *Performative Circumstances*, Schechner writes that Vawter 'counted the night's receipts at his desk near the drum set', adding that 'real cash [was] used as props,' with 'about $50 in circulation' (1983: 35). This detail implies that Vawter normally did the job without fanfare; yet during the show, he flaunted TPG's real-yet-theatrical capital for all to see. In his symposium lecture entitled 'Reflections on Ron Vawter', Schechner elaborated on some of Vawter's other activities in *Mother Courage*:

> Every time money was mentioned in the play, Vawter would ring the cash register. At a certain point, he'd come out [from behind his desk]. There are lots of signs in a Brechtian production, and he'd hang up—just like in a church—the number of people in attendance and what the total box office was. [. . .] He didn't have a speaking role yet because I didn't know him as an actor, and just never cast him (2002).

On the surface, Vawter seemed to function as himself: photographs of the production indicate he wore a range of street clothes, presumably whatever he had on before arriving at the theatre. Yet his nightly performance *Mother Courage* as TPG's general manager was

---

13 'Mother Courage: Box Office', Richard Schechner Papers, box 167, folder 2.

now codified and even fictionalized to some extent—no longer *simply* what he did in everyday life.

As the show's percussionist, Vawter again used actual skills (he was a talented drummer) to convey *Mother Courage's* manufactured reality of constant war. A marked script held in the Schechner Papers reveals constant cues for 'Drums'.[14] Vawter's ostensibly task-based work on the snare drum became the symbolic (ominous, militaristic, relentless) beat to which Brecht's action advanced. In retrospect, his technical performances raise provocative questions about his relationship to the play. Did Vawter simply see himself as TPG's employee, or did he think of himself as a character in the play?

Legacies of a Stealth Performer

In 1980, Schechner left TPG while LeCompte, Gray, Vawter, Clayburgh and several new people officially incorporated as The Wooster Group—a transition explored in Chapters 4 and 5. For now, it is worth noting that colleagues who met Vawter through TPG only began to recognize his self-presentation in theatrical terms after working with him on several Wooster Group pieces. For example, in an essay by Philip Auslander based on an interview with performer Willem Dafoe, the latter pointedly blurred the discourses of theatre and life to explain Vawter's core personality as The Wooster Group's no-nonsense bureaucrat: 'If you want to get real blocky about it, Ron is tense, kind of officious; he's the guy who's the link to the structure, he stage-manages the thing, he pushes it along, he's got a hard edge' (Auslander 1997: 40). Here, Dafoe's description refers not only to Vawter's administrative role in the company, but also to several of his performance personae in shows like *Route 1 & 9* (1981) and *L.S.D. (. . . Just the High Points . . .)* (1984). By contrast, Vawter's task-based activities in *Mother Courage* are still inchoate as theatrical roles.

The journalist Helen Barlow illustrates a general tendency to ignore Vawter's early, self-based yet formalized performances with

---

14 'Mother Courage: Notes', Richard Schechner Papers, Box 167, Folder 6.

TPG, such as his roles in *Mother Courage* as an Army recruiter and a business manager: 'When LeCompte began directing in 1975, she asked Vawter if he wanted to try acting. [. . .] Finally, he had discovered his life's calling—and he found it easy. "I don't know what all the fuss is about. Acting is just playing around, being able to relax and be sensitive to what's happening in the room"' (35).[15]

Wetzsteon also disregards Vawter's contributions to theatre before The Wooster Group: 'Vawter told new director LeCompte he'd be interested in working onstage as well as off, his lack of performance skills now an asset rather than a liability' (1989: 40). Yet even though critics rarely acknowledge *Mother Courage* as part of Vawter's professional body of work, I contend that his roles in Brecht's drama helped shape and set in motion what scholars identify as The Wooster Group's signature methods.

In *Breaking the Rules*, David Savran first voiced his position that The Wooster Group redefines *acting*—a practice that traditionally requires a performer to 'surrender his identity' to the character whom he plays: 'In all its work, The Wooster Group breaks with this pattern by asking the performer [. . .] to [. . .] simply stand in for someone else. The performer will make no effort to impersonate, to portray a character with any fullness of psychological depth. He just goes through the motions' (1988: 114).

A few years later, Euridice Arratia unsettled Savran's claims about the company's lack of impersonation when she published her observations of the rehearsal process for *Brace Up!*, claiming that 'two kinds of performances are thoroughly explored' by The Wooster Group: 'One imitates soap opera acting (images of 'real' soap operas such as *All My Children* are shown on the monitors). The other is a presentational style, less emotionally invested than the first. These two styles

---

15 There is a factual error in Barlow's account. LeCompte directed her first TPG project (*Sakonnet Point*) in 1975; however, she did not invite Vawter to try acting until autumn 1976, when she and Gray began to develop *Rumstick Road*.

constitute two ends of a continuum, with many other styles in between.' (1992: 134)

Despite Arratia's attention to The Wooster Group's range, she ultimately names Vawter as an exemplar of the 'presentational style', which she calls 'a Wooster Group signature', and which she characterizes as 'related to reporting rather than reenacting' (134). Meanwhile, Philip Auslander has supported both Savran's and Arratia's positions, arguing in 1997 that Wooster Group performances are 'less representations of an exterior reality than of the relationship of the performers to the circumstances of their performance' (1997: 41).

The assessment among these scholars is that Wooster Group members 'stand in' for, 'present', or otherwise mediate their onstage personae—as opposed to *acting* a character in the usual sense. Vawter's early self-presentation converged with LeCompte's formulation of a distinct aesthetic and the Group's performance style as it was developing. From the start of her tenure as The Wooster Group's director, LeCompte expressed an interest in the very type of person that Vawter seemed to be: someone with a life *outside* of the theatre. In 'Always Starting New: Elizabeth LeCompte', an interview by Lenora Champagne, LeCompte stated that she 'doesn't look for actors, but for people who have clear ideas of who they are, where they're going' (1981: 25). Meanwhile, Champagne corroborated the legend that most critics and historians transmit, again conferring on Vawter 'non-actor' status, stating that he became a member of TPG 'after a stint as a Special Forces recruiting officer and paratrooper chaplain' (1981: 25).

LeCompte (like Kirby, Schechner and others working in the burgeoning field of performance studies) split hairs over specific *types* of self-presentation during this inaugural period: 'The work performers do has different requirements than acting. Performers have other qualities. They must be full-bodied people' (in Champagne 1981: 25). LeCompte insisted that performers bring one thing (namely, 'action') to the stage, whereas actors bring quite another ('affect'). As Arratia observed first-hand when allowed to sit in on rehearsals during the making of *Brace Up!* roughly a decade later, 'the opposition [of]

71

action/emotion [was] a recurrent theme' (1992: 133). She quoted LeCompte, who said, 'Everybody has to be aware [that] I don't want anyone to fill any section with emotion. I want to fill it with your presence in the space. I want you to be who you are. I want physical actions, not emotions' (1992: 133).

Not unlike those scholars who built their reputations on drawing distinctions between conventional theatre and the avant-garde and exploring the implications of the dichotomies they found there, LeCompte patrolled the borders between task-based performing and acting. Yet even as the director discouraged her cast from conveying emotions and/or personae, not their own (forbidding 'character' in the traditional sense), she ultimately advanced a vision of theatre that recalls the complex nature of Vawter's self-presentation in *Mother Courage*.

Vawter's 'hybrid' performance persona in that production emerged from the convergence of three different modes of performance. The first was Brechtian *Verfremdungseffekt* à la Schechner.[16] For instance, in TPG's *Mother Courage*, Vawter played the minor role of an Ordnance Officer. He acted out scenes based on the Ordnance Officer's lines in the play. In Act 3, for example, he briefly haggled with Mother Courage over the price of a gun. As early as this 1973 show with TPG, Brecht's gestural acting already informed Vawter's hybrid performance persona: he was an actor playing an actor playing a part.

A second layer of Vawter's performance persona in *Mother Courage* arose from his actual roles in the group. As noted above, he functioned during the show as TPG's general manager and as a drummer. Yet unlike those TPG actors who broke character during *The Tooth of Crime* (by making coffee and socializing with the audience at intermission), Vawter consistently maintained his task-based performing throughout Brecht's drama, thus infusing his labour with a radical uncertainty. In 'The Brilliant Kids Show Us How', the critic Arthur

---

16 Brecht argued that a 'representation that alienates is one which allows us to recognize its subject, but at the same time makes it seem unfamiliar' ([1964] 1977: 92).

Sainer used ellipses to convey the ubiquitous, almost metaphorical nature of Vawter's presentation as drummer: ' . . . and always there are the drums announcing the next moment—is there never going to be an end to these next moments? . . .' (1975: 137).

Third, and most importantly, Vawter's hybrid performance persona arose from the peculiar circumstances under which he joined TPG. Since he was not initially recognized as an actor, Vawter did not develop his roles in the same ways that other members did. Most notably, he did not partake in the three-step actor training method that Schechner described in *Environmental Theatre* as 'a synthesis of physical, vocal, and association exercises' ([1973] 1994: 129). Schechner explained the association exercises as 'something private', a method by which 'the body will break open and all kinds of horrid things will spill out [. . .] all the dark secrets of the inside' (137). By contrast, Vawter's entry into *Mother Courage* was literally through the surface. He entered the world of that drama just as he had entered *The Tooth of Crime*: from the vantage of a spectator. MacIntosh recalled how Vawter 'watched rehearsal after rehearsal when he was first our general manager' (2004). Vawter later encouraged MacIntosh to believe he had acquired his onstage skills by observing her performances: 'He used to tell me—it could have been true, but I also know Ron enjoyed saying the right things at the right time—he'd learned everything he knew about acting from watching me' (2004).

Through his ongoing interactions with The Performance Group, Vawter acquired a spectrum of new identities: suspect outsider, trusted onlooker and the tough guy who got things done. Yet the one trait that the company held on to regardless of anything conscious Vawter did or did not do was his genuineness. Ironically, the role in which TPG members came to believe most fervently was not the army recruiter or ex-seminarian, but the heartfelt young man who had stepped into theatre wholly by chance. In this respect, Vawter's peers had no doubts about the 'realness' of what he presented.

CHAPTER 3

From Stealth Performer
to Shadow Governor

Vawter's Rise in The Performance Group, 1974–1976

Although Ron Vawter was known for letting others take the spotlight, he played increasingly powerful roles behind the scenes. The Performance Group's first impressions of Vawter as reserved and straight-laced changed dramatically over time. But how did he effect the transition from business manager to actor, from guy off the street to rising star? How did his self-presentation as a nonperformer continue to inform the roles he played onstage? And how did he generate a growing influence on the group, both as an actor and as an administrator?

Let us begin with Vawter's performance in *The Marilyn Project* (1975), a play written by David Gaard.[1], which follows a day in the life of Marilyn Monroe. As developed by TPG, the play featured a doubled cast that performed the play simultaneously. This doubling was first conceived out of necessity during TPG's summer 1975 residency at American University in Washington, DC. Schechner wanted to work on Gaard's play, but there were more students in the workshop than roles in the play. He solved this problem by casting

---

1 For a detailed history of Gaard's work on this play, see '*The Marilyn Project* 1974-1975, 2004', Box 9, Folder 4, Gaard (David) Theatrical Works and Short Stories, Online Archive of California, California Digital Library.

two performers in each role, thus accommodating academic needs while also finding a way to stage the play.

When Schechner restaged *The Marilyn Project* in New York that winter, he retained the doubling of roles.[2] The Performance Group's December 1975 *Marilyn Project* was mounted on the upper floor of the Performing Garage (a space later used for *Rumstick Road*). A few members of the cast were American University students, but most were TPG regulars. In her review for *Soho Weekly News*, 'Mirroring the Marilyn Mystique', Bonnie Marranca described the show's unusual methodology:

> [T]his production [...] is carried out in double images: action is shown simultaneously on the east and west sides of the performing space. There are two actors for each role, two stage sets. The mirroring effect is further duplicated in mirrors on either side of the stage, in the instantaneous pictorialization of the set on video monitors, and in the multiple sound images produced by the use of microphones. (1975)

Marranca added that *The Marilyn Project* 'takes place on a Hollywood sound set', and 'adopts a cinematic metaphor in performance'. This trope of filmmaking informed TPG's production in many ways, including the casting.

Bruce Porter, who joined TPG as a stagehand in 1975 and went on to become an instrumental sound technician, finally noticed Vawter as an actor during *The Marilyn Project*, even though Vawter had performed in *Mother Courage*, Porter's first tech job with TPG. 'Ron played the Director', Porter recalled, 'He played one of the directors. And *that's* when everyone realized that this guy was really a talent' (2004). Porter described what stood out about Vawter's performance

---

2 The lead role of Marilyn was played by Joan MacIntosh and Elizabeth LeCompte. Previously, LeCompte had played one of the Keepers in *The Tooth of Crime* and several roles, including Yvette, in *Mother Courage*. MacIntosh began her work with TPG when she performed Agave in *Dionysus in 69* (1968), a role that Schechner also doubled. Priscilla (Ciel) Smith played Agave at the same time as MacIntosh.

in the part, which was, along with Marilyn, a principal role in the play: 'Ron was the stealth performer! [. . .] He had this presence that was unmistakable. [. . .] It wasn't like he was trying to *be* anything, from what I could tell. He was just himself, and he just had a very interesting persona' (2004).

The *Oxford Dictionary of English* defines *stealth* as 'cautious and surreptitious action or movement: the silence and stealth of a hungry cat'. Yet despite Vawter's apparent care not to reveal much about his prior acting experiences to TPG, Porter's moniker, 'the stealth performer', signals his recognition of Vawter's craft. Moreover, Porter's claim that Vawter 'was just himself' initially seems at odds with his attention to Vawter's 'interesting persona'.

These apparent contradictions inform my thesis that Vawter's entry into TPG at once coincided with and intensified the company's interest in life characters: onstage personae derived, to some extent, from members' offstage roles. TPG's *Commune* (1972) featured what the critic Arthur Sainer described in *Radical Theatre Notebook* as 'alterations of performers as characters and as their biographical selves' (1975: 172). By contrast, Vawter's early act of attending the theatre in his military uniform and his subsequent performance as TPG's business manager in *Mother Courage* demonstrated that self-presentation could *simultaneously* function as an ambiguous kind of persona.

So how did Vawter go from carrying out his everyday tasks to being recognized as a performer? Technical director Bruce Rayvid said it took him a while to realize that Vawter wanted to act: 'I just remember him helping with everything and thinking, "Oh, this guy is great!" It wasn't till he kind of brought it up that people became receptive, because he was just an interesting guy' (2004).

Performer James Griffiths agreed that Vawter took the initiative in his slow transformation from backstage to onstage. In our interview, he recounted how Vawter stepped up and volunteered to play a role that he himself had declined: 'In some ways, I gave Ron his start in the spring [of 1975]. Elizabeth LeCompte's sister, Ellen, had written a piece, and she asked if I would be in it. I said, 'No, I want to do my own play', which turned out to be just god-awful. So Ron took the part that I was going to play for Ellen' (2004).

In June 1975, Ellen LeCompte staged *A Wing and a Prayer* in the upstairs space at the same time that Spalding Gray and Elizabeth LeCompte's *Sakonnet Point* premiered downstairs, in the *Mother Courage* environment. (During the 1970s, the Performing Garage was organized very differently than it is today. There was a large perform-ance space downstairs, and a smaller one upstairs, where The Wooster Group's archives and administrative offices now exist.) Griffiths never saw *A Wing and a Prayer*, but heard that Vawter was 'a natural per-former' in his adopted role. 'It was the first piece Ron ever did at the Garage', Griffiths added, indicating that he, like Porter, did not rec-ognize Vawter's earlier performances in *Mother Courage* as acting per se.

At its core, *A Wing and a Prayer* explored a 1970s relationship. Elizabeth LeCompte played Rose, a character whom Arthur Sainer described in his *Village Voice* review, 'Walking Souls, Traveling Whites', as a 'determinedly modern young woman' (1975: 86). Vawter played Joe, her lover. In our interview, Elizabeth LeCompte recalled little about performing in *A Wing and a Prayer*, except that it 'was imitative of Richard Foreman, so it was very abstract. I remember we played badminton or something like that. We danced' (2005). Sainer's review of *A Wing and a Prayer* offers more clues about the play's experimental strategies:

> Rose has a man named Joe. [. . .] They're both elegant. Smart. They tango and lindy. They beat each other up. [. . .] The piece keeps shifting styles, moving from one smart-assed avant-guardism to another. [. . .] It's tough and interesting and perhaps a little too determinedly urbane. [. . .] In addi-tion to the fine work of Liz LeCompte there is nice energy from Ron Vawter. (1975: 86)

Such fleeting sketches and memories are not much to go on, but it's notable that both LeCompte and Sainer mention the dancing. Photo contact sheets from *A Wing and a Prayer* (held in The Wooster

Group archive) show Vawter and Elizabeth LeCompte posed in classic ballroom dance moves. Vawter wears a button-down shirt and slacks; she wears a shapely dress. Although they look like a couple from the 1950s, their affection for one another is fresh and palpable. LeCompte not only recalled dancing with Vawter in her sister's play, she also mentioned this as one of his favourite social activities outside of the theatre:

SMALEC. What about Ron was interesting to you?

LECOMPTE. That he had been a Green Beret. He was very high-living: lots of drugs, lots of dancing, lots of sex. And he was religious, too.

SMALEC. Do you know what sorts of drugs he did?

LECOMPTE. He was doing a lot of LSD. Then later, he was doing poppers [. . .] a lot of things to keep him up all night because he liked to stay up dancing. [. . .] We went out with him sometimes. He would pick up people, and get picked up and dance all night, dance wildly all night. It was the disco era.

Vawter's nocturnal disco dancing may seem worlds apart from his tango and lindy in *A Wing and a Prayer*. Yet the dancing in *A Wing and a Prayer* was an important opportunity for Vawter to bring to the stage one of his offstage interests. Vawter's counting of receipts in *Mother Courage* referenced the commerce at the heart of Brecht's drama, as well as his actual role as the company's business manager. By contrast, dancing let Vawter showcase a personal pastime that he loved and did especially well.

Whereas Vawter's friendship with LeCompte included all-night trips to disco clubs, his early interactions with Schechner (who was 15 years older) were more businesslike. Precisely because Vawter seemed so unremarkable, Schechner initially took little interest in his personal life. Only decades later did the director acknowledge Vawter's agency in creating a highly normative persona that would deflect attention away from the parts of himself that were still closeted, including his homosexuality (personal interview, 7 November 2006).

The Marilyn Project uncovered even more of Vawter's private side, beyond his passion for dancing and his sexuality—namely, his skills as a performer. The Richard Schechner Papers reveal that Schechner originally cast Vawter as a musician in the piece, a nonspeaking role.[3] Stephen Borst, a veteran TPG member, was supposed to play the director to one of the two Marilyn's, but when TPG began rehearsing its New York production of *The Marilyn Project* at the Performing Garage, Schechner asked Vawter to stay on as the director of the Marilyn played by Joan MacIntosh. Robert Fuhrman, a graduate student at American University, directed Elizabeth LeCompte's Marilyn on the opposite side of the stage. It is not clear how Vawter went from having no lines to playing one of the leads. Nevertheless, his performance made a big impression on the group. Rayvid agreed with Porter that Vawter's instinctive knack for the stage seemed almost too good to be true:

> I got that sense, too: the world was just exploding for him, and he was finding parts of himself he hadn't known existed. And *we* were amazingly surprised, too, because it was such a hidden talent that came out so confidently. He wasn't shy at all about his performing. So it seemed like, 'Oh my god, you've never trained!'

While Vawter's assertive performance as Marilyn's director astonished his colleagues, the set design for The *Marilyn Project* was also remarkable. It included functioning video cameras that recorded the action onstage, simultaneously projecting it on video monitors positioned above the stage, in all four corners of the playing area. Jim Clayburgh, who had designed *Mother Courage*, again created this media-rich environment, which LeCompte would later revive and modify in many of her own productions involving Vawter and other performers. Today, many scholars assume the LeCompte began working with video on her own. Yet it was actually Schechner who wrote to the Media Equipment Resource Center (MERC) in October

---

3   See 'Marilyn Project: Notes', Box 166, Folder 17, Richard Schechner Papers.

1975,[4] applying for permission to use MERC video equipment in *The Marilyn Project*. In that letter, Schecher mentioned his prior experiences of combining visual technologies and theatre, and explained why video was crucial to *The Marilyn Project*:

> It is important in this play about media [...] that decisive images be seen not only 'in person' but on monitors; that the audience can compare the live and the mediated image; it is also important that the work of 'making a film' be replicated accurately and the presence of video will help us do that'.

In addition to Schechner's provocative use of video to record and reframe a live performance, this was the first time TPG used microphones to amplify and relocate sound. Clayburgh explained: 'The voice of Liz would go to Joan's side of the stage through the microphone, and the voice of Joan went to Liz's side'. Both techniques (using video to transpose and transform various visual texts, and the amplification and distortion of performers' voices by means of microphones) would later become instrumental to The Wooster Group's own working methods, and particularly instrumental to Vawter's techniques as a performer within that new company.

During our interview, LeCompte took no credit for *The Marilyn Project*'s experiments with audiovisual media or its divided stage, although she listed these as reasons why she agreed to do the show. Unlike other TPG members, however, LeCompte already knew Vawter as a gifted performer because she had seen his prior collaborations with Stephen Borst, a veteran of TPG who was openly gay:

> They had their own company upstairs, and they worked together for over six months to a year. [...] I can't remember the name of the company, but Ron and Steve were very much at the heart of it. They did a play that we came to see, and Ron was just spectacular. This was before *A Wing and a Prayer*.

---

4 See 'Marilyn Project: Notes', Box 166, Folder 17, Schechner Papers.

Borst was the first to stage his own projects under TPG's administrative umbrella when he directed James Griffiths, Joan MacIntosh and Timothy Shelton in a 1973 production of Michael McClure's *The Beard* as Schechner supported projects initiated by TPG members throughout the company's lifetime.

Vawter never performed in *The Beard*, but there is published evidence confirming LeCompte's memory of the company he formed with Borst, Shaman Company. *Village Voice* advertisements from 1975 promote a show called *Sly Mourning* by the group, billed as an affiliate of TPG. *Sly Mourning* was described in those ads as 'A sequence of events from a lesbian and gay men's theatre company'.[5] Previews began on 10 October 1975 and the show ran until 23 November 1975.

A review of *Sly Mourning*, titled 'Love and Death and Sick Psychiatry' appeared in *Soho Weekly News*. The reviewer, Rosalyn Regelson, said Shaman Company consisted of 'three men and four women' who performed 18 short scenes 'drawn from their lives or fantasies about their deaths'. She added that this 'flow' of experiences and imaginings revolved around 'love, madness, criminal arrest, physical disease, and psychiatric persecution' (1975). Moreover, she identified the Company's use of a discourse of pathology to stage performers' struggles with homosexuality and death: 'The device they use to handle both subjects is the reading aloud of medical texts describing physical or mental diseases, while the flesh and blood victims stand before us suffering the liquidation of their identities as individual human beings' (1975). Regelson's account of these specific performance practices she observed in *Sly Mourning* included an approach that would recur decades later, in Vawter's solo project, *Roy Cohn/Jack Smith* (1992). When he began creating his portrait of Roy Cohn, Vawter asked playwright Gary Indiana to write a script using cultural texts that defined homosexuality as a mental illness. In an interview with Schechner titled 'Ron Vawter: For the Record', the actor explained his

---

5 *Sly Mourning* by Shaman Company, advertisement, *Village Voice* 13 October (1975: 12).

dramatic and personal interests in staging arguments that refused to normalize same-sex desire:

> [W]e decided we were going to try to write the most intelligent persuasive denunciation of homosexuality that we could possibly muster. We went through all the psychiatric writings pre-'73 [. . . W]e were looking for good arguments, for intelligent, sensible arguments. If people believed that being gay was a disease, why did they? (1993: 20)

Vawter's Cohn functioned as a mouthpiece for the homophobic theories and attitudes of the famous lawyer's era. However, Vawter's portrait also suggested how Cohn's public advocacy for gay men to exercise self-restraint was part and parcel of the social repression that privately destroyed him. *Sly Mourning* seemed to operate in a similar vein. Once the play's 'psychiatric gobbledygook is brought into question', Regelson wrote, 'we begin to wonder about the medical descriptions of cancer and heart disease' (1975). In effect, *Sly Mourning* invited viewers to deconstruct the certainty espoused by our culture's most authoritative discourses. Regelson did not discuss individual scenes, but she did name the cast (David Barr, Jack Jason-Deneault, Marilyn Gelfin, Mickey McQuaid, Michele Schwartz and Ron Vawter), concluding that all of them 'project a rare quality of live, struggling being, not faking it' (1975).

In addition to Vawter's work on *Sly Mourning*, another document attesting to his early commitment to gay and lesbian drama is an undated photograph found in the Ron Vawter Papers. Taken in San Francisco by Ron Blanchette, the photo features Vawter and Borst. A handwritten caption identifies both men as 'co-directors of the National Gay Theatre.'[6] Mindful of these records of Vawter's involvement in gay and lesbian theatre, it is curious that only LeCompte recalled his work with Shaman Company. No one else from TPG mentioned it.

---

6 See 'Ron Vawter and Steve Borst', photograph, Box 8, Folder 16, Ron Vawter Papers.

Perhaps one reason for the tendency to overlook this part of his career is that prior to *The Marilyn Project*, Vawter basically presented himself as TPG's 'straight man': the serious, asexual workman who got things done. Schechner described the discretion and quiet professionalism that underpinned Vawter's approach to playing Marilyn's director: 'He always took everything very seriously [. . .] and he was extremely intelligent as an actor. By that, I mean he knew what emotions to access, and what emotions not to express' (personal interview, 23 June 2003). MacIntosh noted that Vawter applied his workplace demeanour to Gaard's play: 'In *The Marilyn Project*, the kind of precision, detail, and discipline he put into being the company manager translated into his acting'. Only Rayvid suggested that this transposition of Vawter's workplace behaviour to the stage was ultimately limiting: 'In *The Marilyn Project*, Ron was efficient and played one character. He got it; and that's what he was. He didn't have the range'.

Yet even as Vawter's character in *The Marilyn Project* showed little emotional range, it also gave rise to a specific performance persona. Arthur Sainer pinpointed what would become a staple of Vawter's public image in a review titled 'Marilyn's Back and Wooster Street's Got Her': 'The straight toughness of the director who is certain that his chopping of film frames is what creates Marilyn is finely conveyed by Ron Vawter' (1976: 73). In other words, *The Marilyn Project* crystallized a persona that would often recur in Vawter's life/work: the rigid, overtly masculine, straight-acting administrator. He was, once again, the nonperformer.

And yet, the drama also allowed Vawter an opportunity to present another self, one that was incongruous with his 'straight toughness'. A photo caption found in Schechner's *Environmental Theatre* describes the play's final scene: 'Two men take the famous "calendar girl" pose of Marilyn Monroe as Marilyn photographs them with a Polaroid camera'. In that image, Vawter and Fuhrman lie symmetrically beside each other on a tarp. Their buttocks almost touch; their genitals are exposed to Marilyn's cameras. Without clothes on, they are no longer identifiable as the play's authoritative directors; they are simply two men, and the homoerotic potential of their proximity to one another is obvious.

When I asked who instigated *The Marilyn Project's* naked finale, Porter replied, 'I'm sure it was Richard's idea. But Ron certainly had no reservations about vamping on the Marilyn pose himself'. Vawter's acceptance of Schechner's invitation to strip is pivotal. Decades after that show, in an article titled 'Curtain Call' by Helen Barlow, Elizabeth LeCompte reflected on Vawter's literal sense of performance as a mode of self-revelation:

> I think what kept Ron going was showing himself. He was an incredible narcissist, so to get up and show himself and to have some people look at him, no matter what they were looking at, was life-giving for him. [. . .] And when he was unable to stand on the stage and have enough strength to take his clothes off, then he had to die (1995: 36).

I asked LeCompte to elaborate on her remarks during our interview. Her response led me to see that Vawter's early onstage nakedness had a far-reaching influence on his approach to theatre:

LECOMPTE. The first thing Ron always did whenever he rehearsed a play—and whenever we rehearsed *any* play—was take his clothes off, all of them.

SMALEC. Did he ever tell you why he did that?

LECOMPTE. No, and I never asked. It was just something I accepted, and that was part of whatever performance he did (2005).

Disrobing not only became an essential part of Vawter's warm-up, but a recurring aspect of his performances. In *Rumstick Road* (1977), he crossed the stage naked carrying a flashlight before entering the small red tent (see Bierman 1979: 21). At the end of *Nayatt School* (1978), Vawter and a female performer named Libby Howes exited the stage naked, scurrying across a narrow ledge, roughly 14 feet in the air. In *The Balcony*, directed by Schechner in 1979, Vawter entered the stage wearing his street clothes. He then stripped naked in front of the audience, and slowly (over the course of several scenes) dressed up in drag to create his role as Irma, the brothel madam, and her transformation into the Queen. In *Hula*, staged by The Wooster Group in 1981, Vawter and his fellow performers danced naked except for Hawaiian leis and grass skirts. At the end of the 1984 production *L.S.D. (Just the High Points)*, Vawter and Willem Dafoe bared their chests while assisting Kate Valk with the Shoe Dance. This is but a short list of the early occasions on which Vawter performed in varying states of undress.[7]

None of Vawter's Siena College peers mention nakedness as something he explored with the Little Theatre. Nor does the late Jarka Burian note this tendency in his play file for *Marat/Sade*, although Vawter wore just a bed sheet in that production (see Burian 1956–1991). This suggests that Vawter began disrobing onstage during *The Marilyn Project*. This was not incongruous, as nudity featured heavily in the works of Schechner and TPG—From *Dionysus in 69* onwards, almost every show had some degree of nakedness (*Makbeth* and later *Cops* were the exceptions). Even *Mother Courage* had performers change costumes in the fully visible Green Room. Without trying to offer an explanation for Vawter's inclination to undress, it seems notable that he first came to the Performing Garage dressed in an army uniform, concealing not only his sexuality, but also his desire and ability to act.

Over time, Vawter revealed his sexual orientation to trusted allies through activities such as dancing in gay clubs. Rayvid says it took over a year before Vawter invited him to go clubbing after work. *The Marilyn Project* gave Vawter the opportunity to 'out' another precarious part of his background: his prior training as an actor. If he revealed that he was not exactly a 'natural', but someone whose stunning virtuosity came from years of practice on various college stages, Vawter risked forever altering TPG's favourable perceptions of him.

---

7 For detailed descriptions of *Nayatt School*, *Hula*, and *L.S.D.*, see Savran, *Breaking the Rules* (1988).

As luck would have it, Vawter did not need to disclose this aspect of his repertoire after all. By December 1975, the general manager's promise onstage was patently clear to the rest of the company. He could safely stay under wraps as 'the stealth performer' whose talent and timing seemed to materialize from out of nowhere.

Mother Courage in India: February–April 1976

The Marilyn Project closed in January 1976, followed by TPG's tour of *Mother Courage* in India. Performer Leeny Sack noted during that this tour coincided with India's Emergency: 'Had we been an Indian company, we probably would not have been allowed to perform that piece because of its political content and staging' (2004). 'The Emergency' in India refers to the imposition of authoritarian rule for a 21-month period lasting from June 1975 until March 1977. During that time, President Fakhruddin Ali Ahmed acted upon the counsel of Prime Minister Indira Gandhi and declared a State of Emergency under Article 352 of India's Constitution. Elections and civil liberties were suspended. Freedom of the press and the powers of the judiciary were curtailed. Schechner explained via email that there were many posters at the time of a severe-looking Indira Gandhi staring out at the Indian public with the accompanying caption: 'She saved the Republic'.[8] He added that Vawter was 'very enamoured of this stern Mother India look, partly because Gandhi looked like a guy in drag' (22 October 2008).

Rayvid outlined the ideals of intercultural exchange on which TPG's tour was founded: 'We were going not only to bring radicalism to India—the radicalism of Brecht and of *Mother Courage*—but also to learn from the greats. There was an amazing amount of teaching that we were interested in: Indian theatre, Indian dance' (2004). Despite these laudable goals, however, tensions soon arose within the company (Schechner 1983: 37–56).

8 In a personal email sent on 22 October 2008, Schechner acknowledged that his memory of the caption on the Gandhi posters was imprecise. Nevertheless, it was something along these heroic lines.

Less well known are the problems of audience reception. As suggested by numerous performance reviews held in the Richard Schechner Papers, Indian critics who reviewed TPG's *Mother Courage* in major cities generally had favourable responses.[9] In Bombay, a reviewer writing under a generic name, 'Our Drama Critic', praised TPG in a review titled '*Mother Courage*: Never Before Such a Play':

> Fantastic! Never before has a Bombay audience been exposed
> to such an enriching theatrical experience [...] It has every-
> thing. Action, activity (often frenetic and bewildering, often
> physically stunning), laughter, pathos, tension, ribaldry,
> humour, music, biting remarks against war and injustice. A
> summative statement on drama; an unforgettable event.

Yet even this glowing assessment suggests that part of TPG's appeal was that Indian audiences did not necessarily have to grasp the play's content: 'Thrice tears welled up in my eyes. It doesn't matter when. All I need to remember is that the tears came'.

In Delhi, the writer who reviewed *Mother Courage* was also called 'our drama critic.' (Perhaps this *nom de plume* was simply an Indian convention, or a way to avoid trouble during the Emergency.) In 'Environmental Group Comes to Capital', this critic as well downplayed Brecht's plot and instead emphasized performers' interactions with their environment: 'What makes this performance memorable is the way the actors explore or live through spaces. The level of their performance is dependent upon the degree of relationship or intimacy they are able to build with spaces around them or the space in which they perform'.[10]

India's cosmopolitan critics approached TPG's work with theoretically informed insights and vocabularies and seemed well aware of the multiple levels on which *Mother Courage* communicated. Even so, several TPG members experienced a deep sense of disconnection from

---

9 For further information about the Indian performance reviews cited in this chapter, see 'Mother Courage: India', Box 167, Folder 4, Richard Schechner Papers.

10 See 'Mother Courage: India', Box 167, Folder 4, Richard Schechner Papers.

their Indian audiences, especially outside of India's urban hubs. Rayvid recalled why some TPG performers began breaking character onstage during rural stops along the tour:

> What I remember most about going to the smaller villages was the invisibility. Even if they understood every single word, these people didn't have a *clue* about what we were saying! [...] Stephen [Borst] and Ron [Vawter] started to joke about it. Leeny [Sack] really got into it, too. Everybody else was seriously trying to do their roles, and then Steve and Leeny would change words, saying nonsense to see if anyone picked up on it. Not a clue! (2004)

For an ensemble intent on conveying Brecht's political ideas, it was jarring to discover that many Indians came just for the spectacle. 'Some of these people had never seen Americans before', Rayvid said. 'We felt almost like Martians on their planet!' He added that feeling foreign in relation to their audiences caused many TPG members to 'start spending a lot of time together'. On the other hand, Schechner and MacIntosh had been to India before, so they didn't feel the same degree of culture shock. Schechner stressed that most city audiences spoke excellent English. Moreover, he noted that by the 1970s, there was a decades-long history of staging Brecht in India, both in English and in various Indian languages.

Sack acknowledged Rayvid's account that TPG members spent ample time together in India, but saw this largely as a function of the company's hectic itinerary. In short, there was always the work of packing, setting up, and rehearsing. And although Vawter was usually one of the reliable people who packed sets and built them again, India gave him many opportunities to venture into far less familiar terrain.

Vawter never actually joined Borst and Sack in reportedly changing lines like 'Get a musket' to 'Get a muskrat' during the show.[11]

---

11 Gray offered this example of TPG members' tour-induced antics in his monologue, *India and After* (1979). Meanwhile, Schechner countered that if such line changes took place at all, they only happened in Sinjole, West Bengal, and not in any of the cities where *Mother Courage* played.

However, he gradually enacted other forms of deviation offstage. Jim Griffiths recalled an adventure that he, Vawter and Stephen Borst shared in Lucknow, the second stop on the tour. Since they were not scheduled to perform the night they arrived, the three men went for a walk, in search of something to do. They soon noticed some hijras[12] walking down a main street. Griffiths recalled: '[the hijras] took off down an alley. So we followed them. Ron and Steve were shouting, "Oh yeah! Let's go!" And we walked into this interior courtyard, where there was a pre-wedding party going on'. In the courtyard, the hijras unexpectedly drew the foreigners who had chased them into an erotic ritual:

> They would dance, and you were supposed to take rupee notes and shove them down their bras [...] so that's what we did. Throughout this time, the whole village was there. We were standing around in a circle, and they brought out chairs for us. We said, 'No—we're not even supposed to be here'. But they were completely welcoming. In fact, their babies were passed from person to person around the circle [...] It was a really inclusive, lovely moment (2004).

While Brecht's renowned play failed to achieve TPG's goal of intercultural exchange, something more bawdy and nonverbal worked. One might argue that Vawter and Borst initiated this unexpected scene of inclusion by chasing the hijras into the courtyard. In any case, the migration of gay desire from an alley into a more public space would normally be viewed as scandalous. While it is unclear if the Indian partygoers were aware of the intruders' intentions, they nevertheless responded by temporarily embracing all that was foreign and disruptive.

---

12 The hijra community counts among its members transgenders, transsexuals and transvestites, including intersexed individuals, eunuchs and other various gender-nonconforming identities. While they often are shunned in daily contact, their presence at births and marriages is considered auspicious, where their function is to bless newborns and newlyweds.

Unfortunately, however, such convivial moments were few and far between. When asked what she remembered about touring India with Vawter, LeCompte emphasized his general unhappiness: 'It was an extremely anti-gay scene. There were no gay clubs, no gay anything, and he couldn't have sex with anyone. And so, my most vivid memory of Ron is that he would get people to give him hand-jobs in his hotel room'. She clarified that Vawter bought sex from locals: 'Yeah, he'd get the guys who helped out with cleaning. They'd come up and give him blow-jobs and stuff. That's how he made it through' (2005).

For Vawter, India seemed to bring back the shame of the closet, the furtiveness he associated with being gay before moving to New York. Although he did not break wholly from his role as TPG's orderly caretaker, Vawter displayed more dissident forms of behaviour than others had noticed at home. Rayvid said that Vawter often accompanied Gray in the latter's quest to find 'the dark side' of each town they visited: 'Spalding could find it in any city. And Ronnie was gung-ho for adventures. They were older, but also wilder. I remember feeling liberated by being around them.' Vawter and Gray dealt with the strangeness they experienced in India by searching for even more deviance. They went out at night in pursuit of what Rayvid remembered Gray calling 'the shadow of town' (2004). Mindful of their quest to experience life on the underside of power, it seems appropriate that Vawter slowly emerged as the company's 'shadow governor': the person who kept TPG together and running from behind the scenes.

After India: Vawter's Increasingly Central Roles in TPG

Despite the restlessness that Vawter displayed in India, a TPG meeting in Calcutta prompted a poignant admission on his part. Schechner documented it in a journal entry dated 14 March 1976: 'Ron said he was really upset by the possibility of fragmentation—he loves producing plays for people he loves—and he didn't want to stop doing that. If the Group fragmented he'd try to find some way to hold on to the pieces'.[13] Here, Vawter's heartfelt devotion to TPG is clear. Equally striking is his return to positioning himself as a nonperformer: someone who loved producing plays for the people he loved. Although Vawter had starred in *The Marilyn Project* just two months earlier, he now seemed reluctant to entirely relinquish his initial role as someone who supported TPG administratively. Meanwhile, in a journal entry dated 29 February 1976, Schechner set down his belief that Vawter was the only TPG member (besides himself) who had earned the right to make managerial decisions:

> Ron and I deal with the outside in terms of running TPG business, fundraising, public relations. This pattern of specialization isn't likely to change—because this kind of work needs people who like to do it, and most TPG members don't like to do it. [...] [T]he person who does the administrative work actually controls the Group. And I am not willing to share administrative decisions except with those who do administrative work. At present, only Ron does this kind of work.

Schechner's provocative claim that those who did the behind-the-scenes office work actually ran the Group provides a useful entry point for my study of Vawter's remarkable rise to influence, first in TPG and later in The Wooster Group.

Vawter was seen as an outsider on multiple levels, but especially in relation to TPG's politics. First, his role as a business manager placed him outside of TPG's central power struggle, which was between the performers and the director. Schechner filled his India journal with reports of that conflict. On 29 February 1976, he wrote: 'Liz and Steve especially, but others too, want their own groups. [...] They don't want to be known as "members of Schechner's Performance Group"'. On 14 March 1976, he chronicled Joan MacIntosh's desire to 'make the commercial rounds and play a Broadway role if she could'. After a TPG meeting that same month, Schechner quoted Spalding Gray's equally

---

13 All journal entries discussed in this chapter can be found in 'Mother Courage: India', Box 167, Folder 4, Richard Schechner Papers.

individualistic goals: ' "I want Liz to work with me [. . .] as my outside eye. And I want Ron and Steve to work with me too. It's a combination of personal therapy and art that I've wanted to get for a long time" '. Meanwhile, Schechner admitted on 11 February 1976 that he himself wanted 'what (I suppose) Robert Wilson and Richard Foreman have: the ability to listen to all opinions but myself to make all decisions'.

In contrast to those competing bids for autonomy, attention and control, Vawter, as Schechner recounted, simply wanted to keep producing plays for the people whom he loved. Vawter's self-positioning as a neutral figure with a mission to hold TPG together and LeCompte's positioning of Vawter as untrained in conventional theatre, just as she was untrained as director, linked them as outsiders. In the fall of 1976,, Gray and LeCompte asked him to join them in improvisations that would lead to a piece about Gray's mother and her suicide.

There are two major reasons why Gray, LeCompte and Vawter began working together at the Performing Garage. First, Schechner stayed in India on a Fulbright scholarship for the rest of that year. As Gray explained during our interview, 'We had the space to ourselves and we wanted to utilize it, so we did' (2004). Second, as Gray later recounted to David Savran in *Breaking the Rules*, his mental health crisis proved a fertile creative mindset:

> *Rumstick Road* grew out of a need on my part [. . .] to con-
> cretize some of the fears I had after getting back from India:
> that I was identifying with my mother so much, that I had
> inherited the genetic quality of manic-depressiveness. And
> those fears provided a terrific drive for me to make that piece,
> to get that out in the open, to explore. (1988: 74)

Vawter's desire to 'hold onto the pieces' if TPG fragmented found a more urgent outlet than anyone might have predicted as a result of Gray's breakdown and Vawter's relationship to both Gray and LeCompte at that time: Vawter was a friend who wanted to help Gray pull himself back together. As had often been the case in his history with TPG, Vawter stood in an ex-centric place, in the shadow of the crisis that affected Gray. Additionally, he was not sexually involved with Gray or LeCompte, who were in a relationship. For these reasons, as well as his perceived distance from various forms of company turmoil, Vawter became a figure of trust, emotionally and politically. As the three worked together, LeCompte developed great confidence in Vawter's aesthetic judgment. He became someone whose opinions about her ways of working mattered. Thus, *Rumstick Road* marked a turning point in Vawter's approach to performance, in his own self-definition and in his role within the group as a centre of trust.

FIGURE 1. Ron Vawter as Jean-Paul Marat in Jarka Burian's *Marat/Sade* (1972). Copyright Jay Rosenberg. Courtesy of the Jarka M. Burian Papers, M.E. Grenander Department of Special Collections and Archives, University at Albany Libraries.

FIGURE 2. Ron Vawter as Jean-Paul Marat in Jarka Burian's *Marat/Sade* (1972).
Copyright Jay Rosenberg. Courtesy of the Jarka M. Burian Papers. M.E.
Grenander Department of Special Collections and Archives, University at
Albany Libraries.

FIGURE 3. Ron Vawter and Spalding Gray interview a member of the audience in a piece titled *What Happened on the Way Here*. Copyright Paula Court.

FIGURE 4. *Rumstick Road* (1977). Actors (LEFT TO RIGHT): Libby Howes, Ron Vawter, Spalding Gray. Copyright Bob Van Dantzig. Courtesy of The Wooster Group.

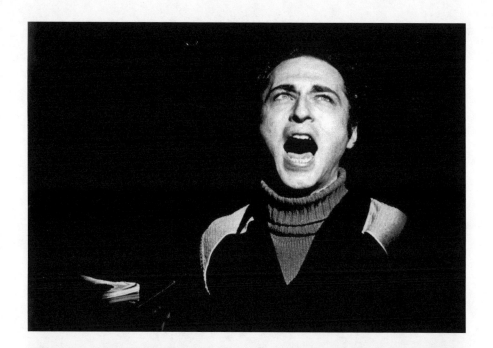

FIGURE 5. *Point Judith (An Epilog)* (1979). Actor: Ron Vawter. Copyright Bob Van Dantzig. Courtesy of The Wooster Group.

FIGURE 6. *Route 1 & 9* (1981). Actor: Ron Vawter. Copyright Nancy Campbell. Courtesy of The Wooster Group.

FIGURE 7. *Frank Dell's The Temptation Of St. Antony* (1987). Actors (LEFT TO RIGHT): Ron Vawter and Peyton Smith. Copyright Louise Oligny. Courtesy of The Wooster Group.

FIGURE 8. *Frank Dell's The Temptation Of St. Antony* (1988). Actors (LEFT TO RIGHT): Kate Valk, Anna Köhler, Ron Vawter, Jeff Webster, Michael Stumm, Peyton Smith. Copyright Paula Court. Courtesy of The Wooster Group.

FIGURE 9. *Frank Dell's The Temptation Of St. Antony* (1988). Actor: Ron Vawter.
Copyright Paula Court. Courtesy of The Wooster Group.

FIGURE 10. *Frank Dell's The Temptation Of St. Antony* (1988). Actor: Ron Vawter.
Copyright Paula Court. Courtesy of The Wooster Group.

ROY COHN / JACK SMITH

CONCEIVED AND PERFORMED BY

RON VAWTER

May 1st – June 7th

The Performing Garage • 33 Wooster Street, New York, NY
Reservations: 966-3651 • Tickets $20

Co-created by Gregory Mehrten, Clay Shirky, Ron Vawter, and Marianne Weems
Directed by Gregory Mehrten • Lighting by Jennifer Tipton • Costumes by Ellen McCartney
"Roy Cohn" written by Gary Indiana • "Jack Smith" text courtesy of The Jack Smith Archives
Photos: Paula Court, Sigrid Estrada, and Jack Smith

ROY COHN/JACK SMITH co-commissioned by Creative Time Inc., The Fan Fox and Leslie Samuels Foundation, The Museum of Contemporary
Art in Los Angeles, San Francisco Artspace, the University Art Museum and Pacific Film Archive at the University of California at Berkeley, the
Walker Art Center, the Wexner Center for the Arts, and The Wooster Group

FIGURE 11. *Roy Cohn/Jack Smith,* The Performing Garage, New York City, 1992.

FIGURE 12. Ron Vawter as Roy Cohn and Jack Smith; Photograph by Paula Court. Courtesy of Paula Court.

CHAPTER 4

'Standing In'

Vawter's Early Collaborations with Gray and LeCompte

Finding a Place, 1976–1978

Compared to the rest of Ron Vawter's work with Spalding Gray and Elizabeth LeCompte, a vast amount has been written about *Three Places in Rhode Island*.[1] The four pieces comprising this series—a trilogy plus one—are *Sakonnet Point* (1975), *Rumstick Road* (1977), *Nayatt School* (1978) and *Point Judith (An Epilog)* (1979). Although *Three Places* is widely viewed today as staged by the early Wooster Group, each show was in fact a production of The Performance Group as the former did not officially exist until 1980[2]. LeCompte officially became the new group's director, though her distinct aesthetic had already begun to define *Three Places* during their time at TPG, just as Gray's stories of growing up on Rhode Island also shaped this early work. This chapter will cover Vawter's contributions to the new working methods that began to emerge during the making of *Rumstick Road*— specifically the notion of the performer as a 'stand in' for absent others. I will also document the increasingly significant professional

---

1 For a sampling of writings on this topic, see James Bierman (1979); Robert Coe (1978); Florence Falk (1978); Elizabeth LeCompte (1978); James Leverett (1978); Spalding Gray (1979); Gray and LeCompte (1978); and David Savran (1988).

2 The TPG members who stayed on after Schechner's resignation adopted the 'Wooster Group', TPG's legal name, as their new moniker.

relationship between Vawter and LeCompte, and its lasting impact on The Wooster Group.

Vawter began collaborating with Gray and LeCompte in September 1976, while they were all still technically members of TPG. However, *Rumstick Road* was made entirely without creative input from Schechner, who was still in India after the company's tour of *Mother Courage*. Schechner acknowledged during one of our interviews that Vawter's artistry emerged in his absence: 'Ron's gifts as an actor were really discovered by Elizabeth LeCompte, or used by Liz and Spalding' (2006). Bruce Rayvid also recalled the remarkable shift from scripted roles to self-presentation that characterized Vawter's performances in *Rumstick Road*:

> In *The Marilyn Project*, Ronnie was efficient and he played one character. He got it, and that was what he was. But in *Rumstick Road*, you started to see the range and subtlety coming out. You could see *Ronnie* coming out! It wasn't something layered on him, like a character. This was really Ronnie, shining in his own brilliance (2004).

As Rayvid's quote suggests, this chapter is about new ways of working and performing. Although Schechner previously had encouraged Gray's development of a character named 'Spalding' in TPG's group-devised piece, *Commune* (1970), his roles in that show were still characters in a traditional sense. 'Spalding' shared Gray's first name, but was a character based on how Schechner saw Gray: as an observer commenting on the action.[3] Schechner adapted this observer perspective to fit into a drama exploring two key events that shook and transformed American life during the late 1960s: the My Lai Massacre, and the murder of Sharon Tate by members of Charles Manson's cult.

By contrast, *Rumstick Road* marked a small group's turn away from dramatizing America's dominant political and human interest narratives to more self-referential and seemingly more personal ways of devising performance. Even as LeCompte and her collaborators still

---

3 See Neil Casey, 'Spalding Gray's Tortured Soul' (2013).

used TPG's corporate name and performance space to advertise, rehearse and stage their projects, they deviated from TPG's usual working methods.

For instance, instead of starting with a dramatic text or a major historical event, they began by listening to personal conversations that Gray had tape-recorded over the years. Most were Gray's interviews with family members about his mother's mental illness and 1967 suicide; there was also a phone conversation with a psychiatrist who had treated Bette Gray, which Spalding Gray recorded without the doctor's consent. After listening to these oral testimonies about Gray's New England family and their largely reticent grief, LeCompte invited Vawter and another performer, Libby Howes, to improvise scenes from the audiotapes with Gray. Although the voices on tape discussed events that affected Gray, other members of LeCompte's group soon began relating to this life material in their own ways, thus reframing and transforming its import.

As noted in the preceding paragraph, *Rumstick Road* seemed to stage a profoundly personal story. Of course, on one level, it did: how does someone get more intimate with an audience than by sharing oral reflections on one's own mother's suicide? On other levels, however, *Rumstick Road* marked the start of a performance aesthetic rooted in various forms of intervention. This new approach to seemingly autobiographical material would quickly demonstrate the layers of mediation involved in presenting lived experience, including one's own past. In addition to the mediations effected by having performers improvise theatrical scenes about the actual loss of a family member, *Rumstick Road* introduced another form of distancing at the level of acting. Specifically, Vawter did not try to 'become' any of the people in Gray's recordings, even as he performed in two scenes where he stood in place for Gray's father and grandmother. Instead of developing these roles on a psychological level—which would involve trying to imagine what Gray's family would have thought or felt upon learning of Bette Gray's death—Vawter developed his scores around physical actions and tasks.

Just as Vawter's focus on perfecting a task-based score helped shape a new approach to staging life material, his own multifaceted 'coming out' as a performer was rooted in LeCompte's focus on objects and physicality, a notable shift from Schechner's more narrative-based approach. Under Schechner, Vawter had often performed in physically restricted situations. Photos of *Mother Courage* show him playing the snare drum in a small corner of the space. When Vawter performed his duties as TPG's business manager on stage, he mainly sat behind a desk and counted receipts. Even his role as the Director in *The Marilyn Project* required what Schechner described as 'highly controlled film-acting movement'—where the actor has to convey more with less since every gesture is amplified when filmed. By contrast, *Rumstick Road* facilitated Vawter's return to creating roles with his body—a surface-level mode of performing he had originated in college—which he seemed to favour over imagining a character's depths.

This preference brought him closer to Elizabeth Le Compte during *Rumstick Road*, bringing their commonalities to the surface. And in the course of fleshing out another man's family stories, Vawter transformed from stand-in, to go-between, to finally, a confidante who gained LeCompte's absolute trust.

'Standing-In' for the Gray Family

'Playwright's Notes', published in *Performing Arts Journal*, is Gray's account of the process of assembling *Rumstick Road*. That process began in 1975, when Gray interviewed his grandmothers about their lives: 'I had no particular reason for doing this. I just found that it was a way in which I related well to them' (1978: 89). The next year, after TPG's tour of India and Gray's ensuing mental and physical collapse, he interviewed his father about his mother's own breakdown and eventual suicide. These early interviews were made without plans for turning them into art: 'I was not conscious of doing anything [...] other than asking questions as they came up' (89). Notable, however, is his reference to the tape recorder as a 'witness': even as he was himself a literal witness to his family's oral histories, Gray said he found it was 'more fun to talk with a witness, the tape recorder' (89). For Gray, the recording device seemed to stand in for an imagined future audience.

LeCompte became the next audience when she listened to Gray's tapes. In 'Playwright's Notes', Gray recalled how they initially used the unedited tapes as 'background for theatrical improvisations at the Performing Garage with Libby Howes, Ron Vawter, and myself, with Liz acting as the director' (90). Later, LeCompte designed 'structured improvisations' to explore specific 'situations recorded on the tapes' (90). Formal rehearsals for *Rumstick Road* began in September 1976.

When I interviewed Gray almost 30 years later, he gave a straight-forward account of Vawter's entry into the world of *Rumstick Road*: 'I think Liz just chose him to work with us. And the process was impro-vising around certain material—tapes and slides—and things that I brought in'. LeCompte echoed Gray's sense that the collaboration emerged from their everyday relationships: 'I think it was kind of a natural thing, and I don't remember making any choice. We were socially involved all of the time'. LeCompte added that because Schechner stayed in India for 'another six months, maybe even longer', she and the others, in the director's absence, began utilizing the Per-forming Garage on their own.

In *Rumstick Road*, Gray played himself, known by his childhood name of 'Spud'. Vawter and the other cast members (originally Libby Howes and Bruce Porter) were identified only as Man (Vawter), Woman (Howes), and Operator (Porter). Porter sat in a booth at centre stage and controlled the lights, records, and audio tapes played during the piece. In *Breaking the Rules*, David Savran explains the non-representational manner in which the figures of Man and Woman functioned:

> They are never identified as members of the Gray family [...] Rather than impersonate one of the Grays, the Man or Woman simply allows the voice or features of one to be superimposed over him or her. The Man, for example, mouths the words of Rockwell Gray, Sr. in a recorded interview

performed in lip-sync. Shortly thereafter, for a recorded conversation between Spud and Gram Gray, he dons a mask of
an old woman. (1988: 80–81)

During our 2004 interview, Gray clarified that Vawter had
brought in a mask of an 'old person'. He did not know how or where
Vawter got it, but recalled Vawter playing and improvising with that
mask. Gray added that his own habit of gathering objects bearing personal value (and bringing them on stage) prompted others to develop
their own attachments: 'I brought them in first of all, for *Sakonnet
Point*. Then Liz got interested in objects as a form of relationship, and
the people who have objects to relate to. [. . .] Being a graphic artist,
she started reusing them as totems'.

Jim Clayburgh, LeCompte's co-designer throughout most of
Three Places,[4] told me that *Sakonnet Point* 'used the skeleton of the
Mother Courage set' (2004). Staged in the same physical space, it shared
aspects of the environment used in Schechner's production. On top
of an aluminium structure that obliquely referenced Courage's wagon,
LeCompte placed a red tent that Clayburgh referred to as 'Red Tent
Healing Number One' (2004). This red tent that first appeared in
Sakonnet Point became for LeCompte a 'totem' that she would go on
to reuse in varying contexts in other parts of the trilogy as well. In
Sakonnet Point, that tent gave shelter to Spalding, a Boy and four
Women. In *Rumstick Road*, it became a space in which older male figures interacted. It also appeared in *Nayatt School*. Outside of the per-
formance, the tent actually belonged to Gray and LeCompte. Porter
recalled the object's functional history during our interview:

> Spalding was a great outdoors person, at least at that point
> in his life, and I thought it was actually the tent they used to
> go camping in. [. . .] I just remember it being their tent. And
> I think we used the same tent the whole time; I don't think
> we ever bought another tent (2004).

---

4 Clayburgh did not work on the design for *Nayatt School*, and Bruce Porter
was often a co-designer during *Three Places*.

LeCompte recycled other props, as well. For example, the white sheets hung from clotheslines at the end of *Sakonnet Point* came back as sheets worn by ghostly figures in *Rumstick Road*. These sheets also draped the seats in which Gray and Vawter sat during the 'Interview with Dad in Chairs' scene in part 3 of *Rumstick Road*. Here, recycled objects accrued layers of associative meaning, especially for viewers who had watched LeCompte's previous work. Part of the pleasure and mystery of watching these shows was that viewers could make their own connections. Of course, the impulse to share new objects also proved vital to *Rumstick's* collaborative process. Porter explained that even technicians brought in things to use: 'I remember buying the mirror for the chase scene, laminating it to the doors, and getting that fun-house-mirror effect' (2004).

Of interest here are Vawter's specific contributions to the production. In *Breaking the Rules*, Savran interviewed LeCompte about the idea to project an image of Gray's mother onto Libby Howes' face during the 'Letter from Mom' scene. LeCompte replied that Vawter had initiated this superimposition: 'We had these slides that Spalding brought in and one day when we looked at that picture Ron tried it on Libby. Ron brought the slide projector [to rehearsal] and put the slide over Libby's face' (1988: 82–4).

Vawter's integration of the static slide and the performer's live body recalls an aesthetic experiment he had undertaken seven years earlier, in the production of *Rashomon* he directed at Siena College in 1970. Vawter had asked his crew to design a special curtain so he could project a silent home movie during the live performance. The vinyl curtain that stagehands built, with the top-to-bottom slits through which performers could step, allowed the stage actors to intermingle with the celluloid bodies featured in Vawter's silent film. Along the curtain's agile plane, two distinct casts and temporalities became part of a shared performance event. In *Rumstick Road*, Vawter went further to stage a meeting of bodies, times and states. Howes' face became an animate surface onto which was projected the slide of Gray's dead mother—the two women from different times and places seeming to inhabit the same body. This superimposition created an optical illusion: Bette Gray appeared to speak, to come back to life, if only fleetingly.

In 'Playwright's Notes', Gray recalled a second situation around which he and the cast had improvised: 'the mention of my mother's visitation from Christ and her subsequent healing' (1978: 90). This time, instead of using technology to resurrect an image of Gray's mother, Vawter embodied the Christ role:

> We worked on the situation of Vawter being a Christ figure and Howes the mother figure. We read from *Acts* in the Bible and one image, the image of Christ healing a sick person by spitting in his ear, captured our imaginations. This led to Vawter becoming more directly physical with Howes and expressing a desire to tickle her stomach. (90)

Gray added that Vawter later 'dropped the role of Christ, and began to improvise a mad Esalen[5]-type doctor-healer who both healed and tickled his patient to the point of very real and uncontrolled laughter' (90). Not unlike the Christ who spits in his supplicant's ear, Vawter's doctor-healer worked in shockingly visceral ways. Near the end of his examination of the mother-patient, Vawter mounted the table and got on top of Howes. She could not stop laughing and he continued to tickle her until her laughter led to screaming.

Vawter's fascination with intersections of religion, theatre and transgression is nowhere clearer than in Savran's *Breaking the Rules*. There, Vawter recounted a passion play that he and his fellow seminarians had staged one Good Friday. He described watching in awe as another young seminarian strapped to a cross (performing as Christ) came crashing down to the floor when the wire supports holding up the crucifix snapped:

> Everyone on the stage froze because the cross does not fall in the crucifixion. That's not how the story goes. Then it

---

5 The Esalen Institute is a well-known retreat centre in Big Sur, California that focuses on personal growth activities such as meditation, massage and yoga. Many notable artists, philosophers and religious thinkers have led workshops at Esalen over the years, which may explain Gray's reference to an 'Esalen-type'.

tipped all the way forward and he fell [. . .] and it was CRASH!! You could hear the unmistakable sound of bone being crunched. There was silence on the stage. No one moved a muscle. The audience was quiet. And finally, from under this bloody mass came a nasal voice that said, 'Holy shit!' [. . .] That theatre experience has always impressed me as an odd and wonderful rendering of the Passion. And I've always sought to repeat experiences like that in the theatre. (1988: 129)

Of course, the most interesting detail about Vawter's graphic account is that none of the Franciscan students who attended Siena College with him remember it. Former members of the Little Theatre also fail to recall staging a passion play. Regardless of whether Vawter's narrative is true or invented, his joy about the seminarian's life-affirming profanity is obviously genuine. 'Holy shit' marks a verbal collision of the sacred and the profane. Furthermore, the miracle of Christ's resurrection is perversely embodied by the human seminarian who survived a real fall. At least on the stage, the man slated for death can live.

Mindful of Vawter's assertion that he always sought to recreate such experiences in the theatre, I imagine that part of his impulse in projecting a slide of Gray's mother onto Howes' face was precisely to contravene the rules of death. Richard Eder recognized this impulse in his 1978 *New York Times* review, 'Spalding Gray's Youth'. Eder wrote that 'Lazarus is not simply being recollected; he is being revived and made to walk among us' (1978: C7). Although Savran's insights about The Wooster Group's later forms of hybridity are not rooted in *Rumstick Road*, they still apply, at least in part, to Vawter's 1977 experiment: 'In *Route 1 & 9* the relationship between life and death, black and white, man and woman, live and recorded media is defined less as a static polarity than as an insistent crossing over' (1988: 35).

Like Howes standing in for Bette Gray through the slide that Vawter projected onto her face, Vawter in the old person mask enacted a form of crossing over, a kind of temporal drag. During 'The Second

Examination', the penultimate scene in *Rumstick Road*, Vawter/Man donned the old person rubber mask and opened Gray's mouth to inspect it, while a tape-recording of Gray's paternal grandmother praised her grandson's teeth: 'Oh, I never saw such beautiful teeth. They look 'sif you had a false set in there' (Savran 1988: 113). Of course, Vawter's costume bore no resemblance to the real Gram Gray. Atop his young male torso, the wrinkled mask seemed surreal, even grotesque. And yet, the Man's silent, quasi-erotic stroking of Spud's face successfully evoked a tender and complex relationship. In short, Vawter's physical gestures allowed him to 'pass' as a believable (if unexpectedly sexual) substitute for the woman whose elderly voice was recorded on tape, even as his monstrous mask signalled a refusal to represent Gram Gray in any realistic way.

While the incongruities between Vawter's physical tenderness and his hideous mask had an inexplicably moving impact, LeCompte stressed a clinical approach to staging Gray's family stories. Using performers to emanate or rouse emotions was not her goal. On the contrary, her method involved using performers almost as objects, as visual aids or props:

> I was working with the idea of a lecture-demonstration, a science lecture. I was trying to present the material as clearly as possible, with as little interference from other people's egos, other people's personas ('characterizations'), as possible. What would be best? When would it be best just to listen to the tape and when would you need someone to 'sit in', to show you, for example, how far away the speakers sat at the time of the interview? (Savran 1988: 75)

In *Rumstick Road*, Vawter literally sat in for Gray's absent father and grandmother, but without acting 'as if' he were them. Although this approach may sound Brechtian, one key difference is that Vawter did not start by playing a role from which he later stepped away to expose as artifice. Instead of critiquing illusions, he physically filled an absence. He approached such absences with both technical rigour and the psychological distance sought by LeCompte in order to convey a credible sense of their presence. In fact, Vawter stunned Gray by studying the audiotape of Gray's interview with his father so closely that he could replicate how Gray Sr. breathed and moved his lips: 'One night I looked across at Ron and heard my father's voice coming out of his chest' (Savran 1988: 98).

Gray saw Vawter's precision as 'the perfect illusion' (98). Again, Gray's reaction complicates any effort to view this type of performing as Brechtian. While Brecht sought to distance audiences from emotional involvement in a given play through jolting reminders of the artificiality of theatrical performance, Vawter's seamless virtuosity abetted Gray's illusion. Nevertheless, Rayvid took some magic out of Vawter's approach by describing a physical philosophy of acting that differed greatly from Gray's more inward-focused training and belief system:

> Ron was amazingly choreographed. He understood that it was *exactly* the same [score], night after night. Spalding fought against that because he worked from Stanislavsky where he had learned, 'You get the feel of it and then your body will do the part'. Ron worked from, 'I learn exactly the steps; I go through it, and then I'll feel it from the steps' (2004).

Vawter explained how he perceived the practical work of presenting Gray's father: 'I never tried to act older, or like I thought his father would be. I always saw myself as a surrogate who, in the absence of anyone else, would stand in for him' (Savran 1988: 114). Vawter's inference that others might stand in for Gray Sr. implies that he saw his performance as task-based and transferable, as opposed to psychological and/or limited to one unique actor.

Vawter shared this vision of performance as surrogacy with LeCompte, who first applied it in a practical way when she charged Kate Valk with learning the arduous physical scores created by Libby Howes.[6] In *Rumstick Road*, for example, Howes repeated a demanding

---

6 This technique found its ultimate expression in *Poor Theatre* (2003), where LeCompte's American cast stood in for the Polish actors that Jerzy Grotowski

cycle of motions for an extended period of time. She began bent at the waist, head near the floor. Then, using the strength in her upper body, she abruptly lifted herself upright, long hair flailing against a projected image of Gray's mother. Over and over, Howes raised herself up with her torso from bent to erect, all the while whipping her hair back and forth against the wall. Over time, many of The Wooster Group's matchless originators, including Vawter, were replaced by new performers.[7] Yet long before those surrogates began drawing upon an audiovisual archive of gestures and steps, LeCompte used Vawter to show his contemporaries what she wanted.

With the advent of *Nayatt School* in 1977, Vawter literally became the go-between who passed information to and fro between Gray and LeCompte. At first, LeCompte gave irritable responses to Gray's idiosyncrasies. Later, she simply asked Vawter to direct his peer. Porter explained: 'She would say, "Ronnie, *you* show Spalding how to do that!" Liz wanted it done a certain way, so she increasingly turned to Ronnie as her sounding board' (2004).

In addition to mediating the fraying relationship between Gray and LeCompte, Vawter gradually emerged as LeCompte's public go-between. He explained her tough directorial style to other company members, and presented a more likeable side of her to outsiders. Ironically, those outside her circle would soon come to include the founder of TPG.

---

had directed in *Akropolis* (1962), going so far as to learn their lines in Polish. Performance as surrogacy was also apparent in *Hamlet* (2006), where The Wooster Group performed alongside (and consciously out-of-sync with) Richard Burton's 1964 film version of *Hamlet*.

7 For Valk's account of how she acquired the upper-body strength needed to perform rigorous actions formerly executed by Libby Howes in *Nayatt School* and *Point Judith*, see Savran (1988: 146). *Sakonnet Point* also had a slightly different cast each time it performed. And in both *Nayatt School* and *Point Judith*, performers other than Howes came and went.

Go-Between: From TPG to The Wooster Group

Schechner returned to New York from India in early 1977. His long-term plan was to stage Seneca's *Oedipus* (adapted by Ted Hughes) that winter. His immediate goal was to generate money. Schechner told the critic Thomas Lask in a *New York Times* interview, 'A Place to Pick up New Theatre Ideas', that the costs of mounting *Oedipus* would be considerable: 'It will be a very physical production, in a dirt arena with real earth, like a bull ring' (1977: C2). In that same article, dated 25 March 1977, Schechner announced yet another revival of *Mother Courage*: 'Starting next week, *Rumstick Road* will be offered in tandem with Brecht's *Mother Courage* (though there will be two admissions)' (C2).

Rumstick Road opened at the Performing Garage in April 1977. Gray and LeCompte did not welcome doing *Mother Courage* alongside their new and acclaimed show. Even at the time, critics recognized *Rumstick Road* as a watershed event in American avant-garde theatre.[8] By contrast, as Porter put it, '*Mother Courage* was tired work'. TPG had worked on that play since 1975, and many performers felt the material was old and worn out. Nevertheless, the company accepted doing Brecht's play as a fiscal necessity.

Oedipus was a different story. Porter noted the problems wrought by what was widely perceived as Schechner's immoderate project: 'I think *Oedipus* was one of the breaking points. It was a costly and exhausting show to mount. [. . .] *Oedipus* filled the whole downstage space to the point where you couldn't do anything else. It was very much Richard in command of the budget, and of his creative vision' (2004).

Vawter initially functioned as a peacemaker when tensions arose between Schechner and LeCompte. Rayvid said that most company members went to Vawter when they needed to work out a problem: 'Ron was extremely rational, and people listened to him' (2004). Porter

---

8 See Adcock, '*Rumstick Road* Is Superb' (1978); Breuer, 'Guest View: The Actor Evolves' (1977); Harris, 'Looking at One's Self' (1977); and Sainer, 'The Courage Not to Know' (1977).

agreed that Vawter was 'the guy you could go to' in times of duress: 'It wasn't like he didn't have feelings, but he always had the interests of everybody in mind—not only his own interests, but the company's interests, and your interests as a person' (2004).

Rumstick Road and *Mother Courage* ran smoothly together in the spring of 1977. Meanwhile, by reviving *Mother Courage*, Schechner raised the funds he needed for *Oedipus*. Joseph Mydell's review, 'Performing Garage Digs Environmental Dirt as Seneca's *Oedipus* Buries Sophocles',' described the project's imposing set: 'Clayburgh has designed a remarkable environment,' Mydell wrote, 'A tight circular theater, on sharply rising tiers, […] encloses a 16-foot diameter stage of dirt, which the performers dig into and otherwise use' (1977: 19). Meanwhile, David Sterritt (1978a: n.p.) noted that Clayburgh's miniature amphitheatre required 27 tons of dirt!

The rivalry began in earnest in October 1977, when LeCompte began rehearsing *Nayatt School* a month before Schechner's previews of *Oedipus*. Both projects required money and manpower. 'It was definitely "choose a side"', Rayvid said, 'This was not one company anymore' (2004). Schechner had Steven Borst (Oedipus), Joan MacIntosh (Jocasta) and Leeny Sack (Manto) as his principal actors and Rayvid was his technical director. In addition to that core group, Schechner cast Caroline Ducrocq (Tiresias), Ron Guttman (Creon) and John Holms (Chorus) from outside of TPG. LeCompte had Gray, Howes and Vawter as her core performers. Joan Jonas, Erik Moskowitz, Ursula Easton, Tena Cohen and Michael Rivkin were brought in from outside. Shortly before *Oedipus* premiered, MacIntosh gave birth to Samuel, her son with Schechner. Two months later, she and Schechner separated. Schechner said this added immeasurable tension to TPG, since he and McIntosh could no longer be in the same company (2003).

Besides the struggle for resources, the two camps were divided on aesthetic issues, which was obvious when LeCompte's *Nayatt School* opened alongside Schechner's *Oedipus*. Gray outlined the stylistic differences dividing these directors: 'Liz was much more concerned with form, whereas Schechner was interested in narrative, character and explorations of the psyche' (2004). Porter added, 'There was a philological basis to a lot of Schechner's work. And Liz didn't care for that. It was all pretty academic, if you will' (2004). Yet it was ultimately LeCompte the visual artist, not Schechner the vanguard theatre person, who devised what Porter defined as 'a new and truly experimental way of performing' (2004).

Rayvid spoke lovingly of Schechner, but acknowledged that the director often provoked dissent by pushing people past their limits: 'For me, Richard was like the father figure [...] He manipulated me into doing these things that I didn't even understand, and he brought out great things in me because of it. But ultimately, it was like, 'I'm going to *rebel!*' You felt that with Richard—you just had to rebel against him at a certain point'. (2004)

An equally precarious side of Schechner's approach to leading a company was his call for political conversion, which enlisted members' beliefs and even their livelihoods. Schechner did not, for example, support MacIntosh's desire to perform in commercial theatre. He did, however, expect people to pack their bags and tour *Mother Courage* in India.

By contrast, LeCompte did not ask her performers to adopt a political stance in relation to theatre. Her only requirement was for people to do onstage exactly what she wanted. Still, Clayburgh argued that LeCompte's more narrow focus was not only principled, but also deeply affecting: 'Richard's mode of directing espoused greater socio-cultural concepts, and ideas in relationship to the work, that he was asking people to share with him. Liz's work, at that point, it was upstairs, it was small, and it was perhaps overly aesthetic—but it captured something'. (2004)

Part of what LeCompte captured was a rising postmodern awareness that individual lives matter as much as master narratives. 'It was such a big change!' Rayvid explained. 'All of a sudden, we weren't telling stories someone else had written; we were telling *our* stories' (2004). Perhaps more accurately, they each participated in telling and recontextualizing a specific group member's stories. Gray performed as himself, sharing a real family trauma in the process. Yet LeCompte's ways of framing that experience for others were neither literal, nor what Clayburgh called 'hopelessly metaphorical. You know: when different emotional tracks are made parallel in a visual form' (2004). Clayburgh added that LeCompte's staging of Gray's personal stories was 'aestheticized to the perfect degree', where Vawter and Howes did not attempt to portray Gray's family onstage, but simply played with objects, interacted with other performers, and followed a precise score.

'Standing in' for Gray's family members gave Vawter a tremendous sense of fulfilment. More egotistical actors might have resisted thinking of themselves as a substitute. Yet as Vawter told Savran, he felt gratified and transformed by this:

> I took a lot of pleasure from performing in a new way [...]
> And even now, when I'm in front of an audience and I feel
> good, I hearken back to that feeling that I'm standing in for
> them [...] That's the feeling I have about any character I
> play, that I'm there in the place of the real thing or of anyone
> who's watching it. [...] This feeling came out of the Trilogy
> because I behaved in those pieces in place of people who
> were important in Spalding's life, or members of his family.
> (1988: 114)

Vawter's testimony about standing in for 'the real thing' initially implies that he aligned himself with the fake, the copy, the inauthentic double. Yet his account of behaving 'in place of people' also connotes a sense of altruism, even sacrifice. Without claiming that Vawter actually *felt* like a sacrificial figure, I suggest he did, in fact, serve a redemptive role. By standing in for Gray's loved ones, Vawter helped Gray to salvage and reexamine a part of his life that had passed, but had not yet been resolved.

Equally important was Vawter's recognition that the pleasure he experienced in performing came from presenting surfaces, as opposed to representing depths. Perhaps this 'new way' of performing—external, task-based, and highly disciplined was rigorous enough that it felt to him like legitimate work should feel: difficult. This allowed the former soldier to give himself permission to embrace his love of acting.

Consolari: From Company Middle Man to LeCompte's Centre of Trust

During our interview, Bruce Porter recalled how Vawter gradually realigned himself during the power struggle that began with *Oedipus*. While Schechner was using the entire downstairs space, those who worked with LeCompte took over what little room was left: 'We huddled upstairs and did our thing. And Ronnie stuck with it as a mediator for as long as he could, but eventually he drifted towards Liz', a decision that Porter reported as 'very painful' for Vawter to make (2004).

Vawter's shift in allegiance proved crucial to LeCompte's enduring success. 'The reason I mention this', Porter explained, 'is because he was very much a front for her in terms of giving her a softer edge. He would explain Liz to a lot of people' (2004). Despite her ample artistic talents, LeCompte was not known for her people skills. Porter recalled how Vawter often tempered LeCompte's abrasive words or clarified her instructions: ' "Oh she didn't really mean that". Or, "Oh, here's what she really wants". He would be her front man. He was very good at that, and he loved her. He just worshipped Liz'. (2004).

Porter's provocative term, 'front man', has several meanings. The *Oxford Dictionary* defines it as: 1. 'a person who leads or represents a group or organization'. The *Oxford American Dictionary of Current English* adds another meaning: 'a person acting as a front or cover'. Vawter loosely functioned in both these senses. First, he represented The Wooster Group favourably at various social events. At parties, fundraisers, after performances and even in the course of routine conversations, Vawter attracted talented people who were in positions to help the young company. Secondly, Vawter aided LeCompte in creating and maintaining friendships that were often guided by ulterior motives. His personal warmth and charisma made people feel valued even as LeCompte used them for the skills she needed from them to foster her work.

Porter maintained that LeCompte's various friendships 'were not shallow ones, but certainly you got a sense that you were part of Liz's vision. She definitely had her own objectives in mind' (2004). Meanwhile, Rayvid suggested what he and Porter brought to the table at the time: 'To this day, audio is revered by The Wooster Group. They have amazing audio capacities; and they hire really good people to do the mixing and playing. I remember the audio being hugely important to *Rumstick Road*. Bruce Porter and I worked very hard on that system' (2004).

Willem Dafoe joined TPG in 1977 after meeting Schechner at the New Theatre Festival in Baltimore and asking to work with the company. When I interviewed Dafoe, he noted that Vawter had skills that surpassed the everyday work of running a theatre business: 'He wasn't a particularly good businessman, but people *liked* him, which wasn't so true of Liz' (2008). Dafoe essentially restated what Porter said: 'To know [LeCompte] is something else, but she's not socially loose. So [Vawter] was very important' (2008). Spalding Gray agreed. He recalled speaking to LeCompte shortly after Vawter's death: 'She was very devastated about it. She didn't know if she could go on and have a company without Ron' (2004). When I asked why LeCompte felt so disabled by Vawter's loss, Gray replied thoughtfully: 'Ron was the facilitator of her vision' (2004).

Yet Vawter was more than LeCompte's low-key front man, the friendly, likeable guy who explained her to others. Most reviews published in the 1970s credit him only as a performer in *Three Places*. However, a Wooster Group programme from 2004 posthumously acknowledges Vawter as an assistant director in both *Rumstick Road* and *Nayatt School*.

In January 2004, Spalding Gray committed suicide, likely by jumping from a ferry into the frigid waters of New York harbour. Gray's long battle with depression had intensified after a 2001 car accident left him with severe mental and physical disabilities. In

September 2004, The Wooster Group hosted a tribute commemorating Gray's work on *Three Places*. A programme from that event, 'Selections from the Archive in Honor of Spalding Gray',[9] identifies Vawter as an assistant director in *Rumstick Road* and *Nayatt School*, but does not explain what he did in this capacity.

His unpublished master's thesis, submitted on 17 May 1979 to the Department of Graduate Drama at New York University, offers more detailed clues, titled 'Piero della Francesca: An Analysis of His Paintings' Performance Documentation'. In a preface to that manuscript, Vawter recounted his introduction to medieval art. Curiously, he avoided any mention of Siena College, where he took art history courses with Father John Murphy, a Franciscan who had a PhD in medieval studies. Instead, Vawter described his independent study of an early Italian painter, explaining how this research informed his later collaborations with LeCompte:

> In 1969, I was a student of the Italian language in Perugia, Italy. There, at the National Gallery of Perugia, I began an acquaintance with the paintings of Piero della Francesca. I traveled to his native town, San Sepolcro, and became further involved with his work. In 1976, I began to work with Elizabeth LeCompte. Together, we spent hours looking over art history books which contained Piero's work. As we worked on two performance pieces, *Rumstick Road* and *Nayatt School*, concepts from Piero's painting began to surface in the design, use of space, and selection of the colors to be used in the performance. In 1978, we began work on a new piece, *Point Judith*, and again went back to Piero. (1979: 1)

Nowhere does Vawter claim a role as LeCompte's assistant director. Nevertheless, when asked about the visual design for *Rumstick Road*, Porter recalled the books that Vawter brought to rehearsal: 'Certainly we looked at the triptychs, and at books of medieval religious art. Piero della Francesca, and also Francis Bacon. Ron would bring a

---

9 A tribute commemorating Gray's work with The Wooster Group was held at the Performing Garage on 16 September 2004.

lot of books from that period while we were talking about the set' (2004). Porter added that a 'strong religious thread was still there' for Vawter 'in terms of his philosophy of life', even though he had cut ties with *organized* religion by the time. Finally, Porter recounted how LeCompte satisfied her architectural needs in the course of looking at religious images that she and Vawter brought in:

> I remember Liz actually pointing to a particular triptych and saying, *'That's* what we're looking for here'. It had a center panel, which is where I sat, the 'godhead', if you will, the heavens: a handing down of life to the two scenes on either side of the center panel. And then, in the front, was something like an examination table. (2004)

Clayburgh confirmed that 'the vision of a central panel, with the idea of a manipulator up above, was [taken] directly from one of the medieval triptychs' that either Vawter or LeCompte brought in. He added that the term 'godhead' was a joke, not intended to position the Operator (the technical director who controlled the sound) at the heart of the Trinity (2004). Yet mindful of Rayvid's comment about how much LeCompte valued audio, it seems fitting that she literally elevated her soundman above the rest of the action, in a glass booth. The gesture reads both ways.

Vawter's sense of himself as a stand-in shared this functional/ symbolic interplay. He was at once a literal substitute for people who could not be present onstage, and a vaguely emblematic figure. Vawter's awareness of himself as an object in space informed his interactions in the trilogy, and his decisions about how and where to move gradually became a kind of compass for LeCompte. LeCompte's interview with Andrew Quick, published in *The Wooster Group Work Book*, sheds light on her trenchant trust in Vawter's physicality: 'He wasn't one of those performers who made it up to get attention. He had an idea in his brain, and I don't think it was a psychological idea so much, I don't know what it was, but when he moved you believed it' (2007: 110). LeCompte never fully understood why Vawter 'just picked things up and [. . .] did them with such authority' (110).

Nevertheless, the director came to trust in his instincts so completely that she 'kind of put everything around that' (110). In this way, her approach to directing Vawter became an everyday act of faith.

Vawter began as a stand-in who took LeCompte's rules for improvisation seriously. As a result of his exactitude, he became a go-between who showed others what she wanted to see onstage. Later, Vawter took on the role of a front man and publicly represented The Wooster Group. Finally, however, he evolved into what Porter called a *consolari*, a Latin word meaning to comfort or to console:

> He adored her. He gave her all the turf she wanted. There was never any struggle between Liz and Ron in those years. And Spalding was less and less involved. [. . .] It was Liz's vision, and she would consult with Ron because she trusted his artistic sense greatly. Whether it was the right thing? Whether we were headed in the right direction? She would really consult with Ron in a very personal kind of way (2004).

Where Gray had been LeCompte's lover and eventual rival, Vawter was more like her brother. And just as LeCompte's unmitigated trust in Vawter's actions and judgments gave rise to a new company dynamic, her approval empowered Vawter to take new risks and flourish as an actor.

Most everyone who knew Vawter describes *Three Places in Rhode Island* as a turning point for Vawter in his capacity for spontaneity. As Rayvid put it in reflecting on Vawter's performance in *Rumstick Road*: 'He was directing himself; he was reaching down deep and pulling out stuff that was emotional. And everybody was doing that' (2004).

This communal process of sharing and staging content charged with personal meaning slowly infused the work of LeCompte and her performers. During the late 1970s, onstage references to real circumstances affecting the group were often submerged or covert. Audiences outside of the group's immediate circle of friends and followers would likely miss its subtle, ironic allusions to the offstage lives of its members. Nevertheless, the origins of an ongoing and self-referential group mythology were emerging—particularly in *Point Judith*, a piece discussed in the next chapter.

CHAPTER 5

Ensemble Autobiography
From Individual to Group Life Material

Introduction

As noted previously, Wooster Group productions of the late 1970s began exploring the important life events of specific company members. This chapter explores the gradual transition from creating pieces based on Gray's life stories, to developing works that that can be theorized as 'ensemble biography'—which the Wooster Group refers to as 'Group autobiography':

> The Group has used both personal and Group autobiography, and existing texts as organizing principles for their work. Sometimes the autobiography is foregrounded (*Poor Theater*) and sometimes it is submerged (Ron's illness as source material for *St. Antony*) (2014).

Most famously, *Rumstick Road* (1977) arose directly out of Spalding Gray's need to confront his mother's suicide. Schechner's theatre was also informed by life events during this period. During a 2002 lecture, Schechner described TPG's violent staging of Terry Curtis Fox's *Cops* (1978) as 'therapy' for the end of his marriage to Joan MacIntosh, a founding member of TPG. Both Schechner and LeCompte engaged in aspects of what I call 'ensemble autobiography': their productions referenced, re-contextualized, or otherwise engaged with actual circumstances impacting each company.

116

However, there were notable contrasts in their approaches to using life material. One difference between Schechner and LeCompte was how each director dealt with the performers' offstage lives. Even as Schechner acknowledged that *Cops* came on the heels of his divorce, the actual production made no mention of MacIntosh or their split. The same was true of *The Balcony* (1979), explored in chapter 6. Although Schechner's cast shared their sexual experiences and fantasies in workshops and rehearsals, Schechner never attributed those details to actual people during the show. Instead, he used them to develop Genet's characters, thus maintaining a distance between the world of the drama and performers' lives.

By contrast, LeCompte's pieces began referring to performers by their real names, blurring the lines between their onstage and offstage selves.[1] For example, Gray was called by his childhood nickname 'Spud' in *Rumstick Road*. And at the start of *Point Judith* (1979), a piece discussed in this chapter, Gray addressed Vawter as 'Ron' (even though his character's name was Dan Silver), and asked Ron about the state of his health. Later in *Point Judith*, Ron/Dan disclosed to another character, Stew (Willem Dafoe), that he may have acquired a sexually transmitted disease from a new lover, who treated Dan's STD comically and even vulgarly in this scene. In retrospect, however, it arguably presaged the then-unknown AIDS epidemic of 1982. Ron/Dan's concern about his sexually transmitted 'pox' would also prove relevant to Vawter's own HIV-positive diagnosis, roughly a decade later. By contrast, Schechner's use of his performers' life material was far more private: apparent to the group, but not to the audience.

Despite these differences, Schechner and LeCompte shared a fascination with fringe communities: convents, communes, sex workers, manual laborers and other socially marginal groups. Even here, however, The Wooster Group soon diverged from TPG by inserting their

---

1 This practice actually began with TPG's *Commune* (1972), where Schechner allowed his performers to choose a stage name for the characters they developed. While Schechner did not revisit this naming experiment again, the practice of using performers' real names onstage continued in pieces directed by LeCompte.

specific company and its interpersonal and social dynamics into the texts they staged. *Point Judith*, a piece about three ex-centric groups (rig workers, a dysfunctional family, and reclusive nuns), alluded to The Wooster Group's own forms of precariousness within New York's theatre circles; .in the late 1970s, LeCompte's fledgling company lacked money, reliable audiences and connections beyond the down-town scene. A few years later, in *Route 1 & 9* (1981), The Wooster Group donned blackface to reconstruct a Pigment Markham comedy routine. In adopting these African American-inspired performance traditions, the all-white company implied their personal affinities with another culturally marginalized group. However, their decision to invoke the problematic history of blackface set off heated debates about racism, white privilege and the appropriation of race—issues that will be explored at the end of this chapter. As a lead-up to Vawter's central role in the self-referential group stories staged in *Point Judith* and *Route 1 & 9*, it is useful to start by reviewing his perform-ances in Schechner and LeCompte's more subtle gestures toward 'ensemble autobiography'.

Cops (1978) and Nayatt School (1978)

Cops, written in 1976 by Terry Curtis Fox, opened at The Envelope Theatre, next to the Performing Garage, in March 1978.[2] The play begins when two plainclothes detectives (Steve Borst and Timothy Shelton) enter George's, an all-night diner. They bully a waitress (Eliz-abeth LeCompte), harass a customer (Dafoe), and talk about work. A uniformed officer named Czerwicki (Gray) joins them while another man (Vawter) enters the diner to use the restroom. Unknown to the cops, this man is on the run from the law. He exits the restroom just as Czerwicki narrates the climax of a recent arrest: 'Hold it right there' (30). Startled, Vawter's character panics at being discovered, and rashly shoots Czerwicki. The detectives shoot back, accidentally killing the

---

2 Named for its past use as an envelope factory, The Envelope Theatre was located at 35 Wooster Street, next door to the Performing Garage. TPG briefly used this second performance space to stage *Cops*.

118

waitress in the crossfire. Vawter's character takes the Cook (John Pynchon Holms) as a hostage, and a standoff ensues until the detectives, promising not to harm the Killer if he surrenders, fatally shoot him when he does.

As previously noted, Schechner said during a lecture that his anger and disappointment over his split with MacIntosh shortly after the 1977 birth of their son, Samuel, informed his staging of *Cops*: 'I liked this play because there were a lot of gunshots in it. I got a gun license and we used two .38s. It was fabulous therapy for the break-up of my marriage' (2002). In performance, real disarmed bullets (firing caps without the lead slug) made for a terrifying theatrical experience. Each night, Schechner and at least one other person made sure the bullets in the real guns were safe.

While Schechner found personal catharsis in the mayhem of *Cops*, several critics described the production as an attack on TPG's aesthetic and political traditions. Richard Nason noted the play's lack of meaningful narrative, which had always been central to TPG's projects: '[*Cops*] is barren of all complexity [. . .] unburdened by philosophy, uncluttered by [. . .] characterization, indeed even devoid at times of authorial attitude or outlook' (1978: 15). Meanwhile, Michael Feingold proposed in the *Village Voice* that *Cops* was an elaborate prank staged by another New York director with a far more mainstream reputation, since it was so unlike Schechner to embrace realism:

> Naturally, Marshall Mason's production of *Cops* for the Circle [Repertory Company] is impeccably accurate at every moment—though, in an effort to add a layer of aesthetic comment to the event, the Circle is playing a curious game. They have actually moved their theatre down to Wooster Street and are pretending to be The Performance Group; Mr. Mason is billed on the program as Richard Schechner. This is just plain silly. Nobody can imagine Mr. Schechner, Grand Keagle of the pseudo-avant-garde [. . .] directing something like *Cops*, which looks bright and shiny and bourgeois enough to transfer to Broadway or film [. . .] (1978: 73).

119

Several prominent theatre people, including Marshall Mason, chastised Feingold via angry letters to the *Village Voice*. Ted Hoffman, an NYU drama professor, argued that '*Cops* is faithfully environmental and not a naturalistic exercise' (1978: 13). Yet despite the backlash, Feingold made a valid point: *Cops* was highly atypical of anything TPG had staged before.

The timing of Schechner's experiment is also notable: *Cops* coincided with MacIntosh's bid to launch a career in commercial theatre, a genre whose realist illusions Schechner had long disparaged and deconstructed. Yet now, as if to upstage MacIntosh's intended transition, he appropriated those veneers wholeheartedly. Schechner recalled being delighted when passersby took his set for an actual restaurant: 'TPG purchased an actual diner going into receivership. We bought all the fixtures in the diner. We got a real gas stove. We called the phone company, said we're opening a diner, and they put in a real phone. People would actually come in thinking it was a diner and order something' (2002).

MacIntosh's departure was not the only group conflict underlying *Cops*. By 1978, it was doubtful that TPG could survive the power struggle between Schechner and LeCompte. The Schechner Papers include no rehearsal notes about the show's development, which is unusual compared to other productions. However, interviews with performers who worked on the show reveal that interpersonal tensions were near a crisis point. Willem Dafoe recalled that his own entry into TPG coincided with Schechner's breach of a promise he had made to Vawter about a lead role in *Cops*: 'Richard brought me in and told me, privately, that I was going to play Ron's role [the Killer]. Then I went to a Group meeting where he said that, and everybody was so angry. Liz turned to me and said, "I don't know who the fuck this guy is, but get him out of my house!"' (2008)

Without being sure of Schechner's motives, Dafoe assumed the director's change of plans was payback for Vawter's allegiance to LeCompte: 'Ron was always seen as working around Liz [. . .] so it was a weird, political sort of slap in the face to bring in a young actor to play the role he had promised to Ron' (2008). Fortunately for Vawter, TPG's other members refused to let a newcomer take the lead role he had waited years to play.

Vawter and LeCompte appeared to triumph over Schechner in the lead-up to *Cops*, but the show's action tells a different story. The play features three violent deaths: Czerwicki, the Waitress and the Killer all get fatally shot. These terminated characters were played by Gray, LeCompte and Vawter: performers who posed the greatest threat to Schechner's future as TPG's director. Steve Borst, a veteran TPG member who remained loyal to Schechner throughout his clashes with LeCompte, played the cop who gunned down LeCompte's Waitress as well as Vawter's Killer. In drawing attention to this dynamic, I do not mean to say that Schechner deliberately cast Gray, LeCompte and Vawter in roles that were killed off. Nevertheless, there was perhaps a symbolic—if unacknowledged or even uncon-scious—level on which *Cops* enacted one 'solution' to Schechner's problems: dramatically eradicating the people who stood in his way.

In terms of group autobiography, Schechner suggested during an interview that another important aspect was Vawter's relationship to his role. Vawter's convincing performance as the Killer came from his firsthand understanding of 'passing', and the terror inherent in being found out:

> In the structure of the play, the cops are just passing time; they're talking [. . .] but as soon as the Killer comes in and goes to the bathroom, he knows he's being hunted. Then when he comes out and sees these cops, he immediately leaps into action. Ron was like a spring: all wound up, and boom! (Schechner 2003)

Prior to this explosive moment, Vawter's fugitive presented him-self as a customer: he politely ordered coffee before asking to use the restroom. On the surface, his character fit in. Had he not reacted to Czerwicki's punch line, 'Hold it right there', the police would never have viewed him as a threat.

Unlike his doomed character, who failed to conceal a secret, socially discredited identity as a wanted man, Vawter presented several successful fronts in his offstage life. His highly masculine demeanor allowed him to pass as straight in situations where coming out as gay was a risk. He also passed in New York's theatre circles as having entered that world as a nonperformer, even though he had starred in numerous campus productions before joining Schechner's TPG. And although Vawter ultimately revealed his allegiance to LeCompte when she challenged Schechner's leadership to form what became The Wooster Group, he had long maintained a neutral role in TPG: a man on the margins, a friend to all. In *Cops*, Vawter played an outsider, a status he understood well. 'That was a very good role for Ron', Schechner acknowledged in 2003, despite having tried to cast Dafoe in the part.

Cops premiered at the Envelope from 23 March to 4 June 1978 while *Nayatt School* ran next door at the Performing Garage from 6 May to 11 June that same year. Directed . by LeCompte, she and Gray are identified in the programme as the show's composers. And although Vawter is typically remembered for his work as a performer, LeCompte credited him as her assistant director, as she had done in the programme for *Rumstick Road*.[3] *Nayatt School* was also the last of LeCompte's productions to use Gray's past as a basis for the action, working largely with his individual life story, rather than the group autobiography that would distinguish *Point Judith* and subsequent Wooster shows.

Nayatt School was divided into six parts, each one called an 'Examination of the Text'. Vinyl records were the 'texts' most prominently examined. In parts I and II, Gray sat at a long table and introduced various records that had a personal meaning for him. After saying a bit about each choice, he dramatized the record with other performers. Gray and the sound operator (first Bruce Porter, later Jim Clayburgh) played a total of 15 records during the show, both musical and

---

3 A program for *Nayatt School* (published by TPG in 1978) is held in The Wooster Group archive and credits Vawter as LeCompte's Assistant Director.

nonmusical. In Part VI, 'The Sixth Examination of the Text', Gray, Howes and Vawter ferociously destroyed Gray's chosen records.

As in *Rumstick Road*, Gray, Howes, and Vawter each played more than one role in *Nayatt School*. However, they were simply identified in the programme based on what they wore. Vawter was described as 'Man in Black Striped Shirt'. Gray was 'Man in Grey Suit', and Howes was 'Woman in Purple Dress'. Even in Part V, when performers took on specific roles from *The Cocktail Party*, they did not try to become those characters in a Stanislavskian or a psychological sense. For example, Vawter played Edward Chamberlayne, an awkward yet image-conscious lawyer hosting the party. Yet his persona largely became visible through a restless and repetitive physical score. Likewise, Howes performed as a silent but physically riveting maidservant. Task-based actions were the most expressive elements of their performances.

Throughout most of his article, 'About Three Places in Rhode Island', Gray described the losses staged in *Nayatt School* as the familiar ones of *Rumstick Road*—his curtailed childhood and his mother's suicide. At the very end of the essay, however, Gray recounted a more recent and unsettled loss. He told of how *Nayatt School* had forced him to surrender control of his personal approach to performing: 'The three scenes in the soundproof room and the use of phonograph records were developed by Liz. In the scenes, I functioned only as an actor and was not involved on any conceptual level. I gave myself over to "playing" the doctor"' (1979: 42).

Group improvisations around Gray's life story had guided LeCompte's approach in *Sakonnet Point* and *Rumstick Road*, but *Nayatt School* marked a turning point. Gray struggled with her call for a more tightly choreographed, more action-based style of performing. In our 2004 interview, Gray recalled how Vawter outdid him in handling the records and other props used in *Nayatt School*: 'It was Ron who liked handling the objects the most. I didn't. Personally, I could do without too many props'. Gray added that Vawter's attention to the physical details of performance prompted LeCompte to use him as a model: 'I was less precise in my moves, in the way I handled props.

And Liz would use Ron as a go-between to tell me to shape up [. . .]
she would infuriate me by speaking about me in the third person to
Ron (2004).

Gray called *Rumstick Road* 'therapeutic' precisely because it
reflected his life back to him as 'ART' (1979: 39). He saw *Nayatt School*
as belonging to a different genre: 'For me, *Nayatt* was a kind of illogical
dance, a celebration—as when the music breaks into full swing during
a New Orleans jazz funeral' (42). That he perceived it as a 'dance', indicates how far the final production departed from Gray's original vision
for the piece, which was simply to talk about his attraction to *The
Cocktail Party* in front of an audience (Savran 1988: 110–11). Gray's
analogy was also prescient, since music and dance would recur as overt
strategies for introducing racial and/or cultural forms of otherness in
subsequent Wooster Group shows. *Hula* (1981), *Route 1 & 9* (1981),
L.S.D. (. . . Just the High Points . . .) (1984), and *Brace Up!* (1991) are
productions in which music and dance were used to signal the company's interpretations of foreign performance traditions.[4]

Despite its new directions, *Nayatt School* did retain aspects of
Gray's early vision. In Part I, he played a recording of the Broadway
production of *The Cocktail Party*, and narrated his personal history of
involvement with the play. In Part II, he and Joan Jonas performed a
reading of Eliot's second act. Here, Gray revealed that he associated
the role of Celia Copplestone (a troubled woman seeking spiritual
guidance) with his dead mother. Little by little, however, *Nayatt School*
set aside Gray's narrative-based focus on his past. Savran described
the work as 'an explosion of texts, performers, images, props, and
media' (1988: 102). Savran added that it was 'the first Wooster Group
piece to use a wild assortment of texts and the first to incorporate
excerpts from a classic play' (102). These new dynamics slowly took
center stage.

Self-referential gestures and images recalling earlier pieces staged
by this ensemble also played a notable role in *Nayatt School*. In Part
III, which utilized Arch Oboler's 1962 comedy-horror sequence, 'A

4 Opera arguably served that function in *La Didone* (2007).

Day at the Dentist', Gray played a dentist and Howes played a dentist's aide. Vawter played a man seeking a check-up, but he ended up chasing Gray around the set with a sheet draped over his head, visually ghosting the chase scene from *Rumstick Road*. Next, both men groped Howes' breasts after covering her body in butcher paper. 'The Breast Examination' record that played during this scene reinforced Howes' torso as the primary 'text' being examined. This disturbing examination of a woman by male figures also ghosted an earlier scene from *Rumstick Road*, in which Vawter played a doctor-healer who climbed on top of his patient (Howes) and tickled her stomach until she screamed. Yet whereas *Rumstick Road* conveyed clear disappointment with doctors who had failed Gray's mother, the targets of *Nayatt School's* gendered critique were broader and less explicit.

Part V of *Nayatt School*, titled 'The Cocktail Party', transformed the sophisticated soiree in Eliot's play into a rowdy club party. Ken Kobland filmed this segment, which begins with Gray introducing the children who played Eliot's other characters[5]: These child performers wore adult wigs, hats, and coats. They wasted no time rushing the bar at centre stage, which Vawter stood behind, performing as the party's host. He opened a giant, display-sized bottle of vodka and filled the children's plastic glasses as disco music played in the background. Throughout this scene, an alarm bell signaled dramatic changes of pace. Each time the alarm rang, party-goers turned from calmly reciting Eliot's lines to enacting manic rounds of drinking, dancing and fighting. All the while, Vawter continued to refill guests' glasses with his ridiculously large bottle. Vawter's performance in Kobland's film recording of 'The Cocktail Party' scene recalls an account by Father Vianney Devlin, Vawter's college director, who described his behavior at actual parties thrown by Siena College seminary students:

> If you were at a cocktail party, Ron would not be able to sit
> still very long. He would have to be active, either by his voice,
> projecting something that would attract your attention, or he

---

5   Ursula Easton as Lavinia Chamberlayne, Tena Cohen as Julia Shuttletwaite, Michael Rivkin as Alex MacColgie Gibbs and Erik Moskowitz as Peter Quilpe.

would be getting up and asking if you wanted a refill, even if
he had already served you crackers and cheese.

Vawter displayed this excessive energy throughout Part V. He was
always on the move, in the middle of doing something. When he was
not busy pouring drinks, he picked up Ursula Easton, one of the child
performers, like a rag doll and carried her around the set. He shook
Tena Cohen as she spoke: whispering lines into her ear, or quickly saying them for her. This was arguably the first time the company used a
form of live audio feed—only with Vawter acting as a human audio
device. His cocktail party persona was at once generous, obnoxious
and electrifying—arguably Vawter performing an amplified version of
himself.

Near the end of Part V, the alarm bell rang a final time. Performing as a psychologist named Sir Henry Harcourt-Reilly, Gray
descended from the Performing Garage's upper level and joined partygoers to offer his take on Celia Copplestone's mental state before
her violent demise in Africa: 'It was obvious that here was a woman
under sentence of death'. Vawter and other guests shook their heads
in vigorous unison, applauding Gray's diagnosis. The cocktail party
ended.

In his article for *Soho Weekly News*, 'Mapping Rhode Island', James
Leverett praised the ironic manner in which LeCompte's performers
deconstructed Eliot's high art: 'It is the genius of *Nayatt School* that it
destroys the play-within-a-play using the original cast recording'
(1978: 71). Yet more than just Eliot's drama was destroyed in the end.
Like the tapes and slides shared in *Rumstick Road*, the vinyl records
played throughout *Nayatt School* held memories of people and events
that had shaped Gray's life. Mindful of this affective function, *Nayatt
School's* closing scene is even more shocking. The critic Robert Coe
described the cast's literal destruction of the records, an act that sym-
bolically desecrated the archive of Gray's past:

> Gray, Vawter, and Howes squat [. . .] on the three record
> players [. . .] in front of the audience, all naked or nearly so,
> gnashing their teeth, contorting their faces, even masturbating

as they run the arms of the record players over the records. (1978b: 121)

Coe called this scene 'apocalyptic' (121). David Sterritt described the burning of records as 'an orgy of destruction and a rite of exorcism' (1978b: 22). Schechner recalled Vawter using his penis as a phono-graph needle and 'trying to play the records with his cock' (2008b).

LeCompte's *Nayatt School* departed in shocking ways from the retrained aesthetics of Eliot's *The Cocktail Party*. But if her ensemble's obvious sacrifice was the elevated, verbose, adult world of Eliot's play, its more subtle casualty was Gray's custom of performing as himself, with his biography at the center of the action. Gray identified with his mentally ill mother so deeply that his perceived similarities to her became an enduring focus of his work. By contrast, LeCompte began looking beyond that formative relationship. *Point Judith*, her next piece, was preoccupied with staging the intimate yet at times brutal interac-tions of three small groups.

Point Judith (An Epilog) (1979)

Point Judith (*An Epilog*) (1979), the final piece in what became known as *Three Places in Rhode Island*, was actually the fourth production in that group of works, and itself comprised of three parts. Part I is 'Rig', another play by Jim Strahs[6] about a foreman and his crew on an oil rig in the Gulf of Mexico. Part II, 'Stew's Party Piece', is a 13-minute dance version of Eugene O'Neill's *Long Day's Journey into Night* (1956). Part III, *By the Sea*, is the silent film by Ken Kobland, shot on the Long Island Sound. Whereas Gray's life had been the basis of the earlier *Trilogy* pieces, the new personae developed in *Point Judith* were more diffuse and not as clearly linked to real people or events. They were more like small, theatrical puzzles of self-presentation within the

---

6 James Strahs died in October 2011. He was a playwright and novelist who collaborated on several occasions with experimental theatre ensembles like Mabou Mines and The Wooster Group. Strahs was married to Ellen LeCompte, Elizabeth LeCompte's sister.

larger drama. These personae invited viewers to recognize their resemblance to actual Wooster Group performers, yet at once signaled their
staged nature, making it hard to decipher what was real and what was
just 'part of the act'. Some of the performance personae created for
'Rig' would recur in subsequent Wooster Group shows. The dysfunctional family and spiritual community respectively featured in the
O'Neill-inspired parody and the closing film section would also return
and evolve in future productions. By 'standing in' for different types
of isolated groups, the company found ways to reflect, dramatically
and publicly, on its own interrelationships, obstacles, and values.

Every part of *Point Judith* demonstrates an engagement with what
I call ensemble biography. However, the show's opening section is
where the most overtly self-referential performance personae emerge.
Strahs wrote 'Rig' after watching improvisations that featured Dafoe,
Gray, Vawter and two teenagers, Michael Rifkin and Matthew
Hansell. The men and teens played cards, pretended to drink and
talked about sex. In 'Point Judith', a published documentation of the
various collaborations involved in making *Point Judith*, LeCompte
remarked on the nature of improvising for Strahs: 'We made up ourselves in front of him, and he made up the words' (1981: 20). Her
quote suggests the fusion of reality and theatricality that informed this
process. Strahs developed his play script using the social personae that
performers presented during their improvisations, as opposed to creating entirely fictional characters.

At the start of 'Rig',[7] Gray introduces his own role as Stew
Diamond, 'the foreman, a master of ceremonies' (1981: 17). He
describes Dafoe's character, B.B. Nettleson, as 'a bit of a hothead' (16).
Kid, played by the teens, Rifkin and Hansell, who took turns with this
role, is 'a bit of an intellectual' (16). When Gray introduces Vawter,
however, he uses his real name:

---

7 All subsequent quotations from Strahs' play, 'Rig', come from an article documenting the development of *Point Judith*. See LeCompte, 'Point Judith', *Zone*
(Spring–Summer 1981): 14–27.

GRAY. Hi Ron; how are you this evening? Feeling better?

VAWTER. Pretty good. (17)

After exchanging these pleasantries, Gray tells the audience that Vawter plays Dan Silver. 'Are you in character?' Gray abruptly asks. He goes on to say: 'I never know whether to call you Ron or Dan' (17). Vawter replies that he is 'Dan', but this exchange generates confusion about whether it is Vawter or Dan who feels better this evening, and, by implication, whether it is Vawter or Dan who has recently been ill.

This kind of deliberate attention to the proximity between performers and their onstage personae soon became a regular feature of Wooster Group shows. Some scholars identify it as a Brechtian influence, via Schechner's TPG. However, I contend that The Wooster Group's approach to character is more complex than the *Verfremdungseffekt*. Brecht's alienation effect requires actors to step away emotionally from their characters, demonstrating them with detached self-criticism. Yet Vawter does not step away from his character in this exchange with Gray/Stew, nor in subsequent exchanges. Rather, he seems to step *towards* his onstage persona. He is, as he tells Gray, 'in character', but viewers familiar with Vawter's biography will soon realize that the role of Dan Silver relates to Vawter's personal life in very provocative ways. As the action unfolds, our uncertainty about whose story we are watching makes Vawter's onstage persona as suspenseful and compelling as the overt drama of 'Rig'.

In 'Rig', a central device used to advance the action is a 'party piece' that each worker carries out at the behest of the other men on the oil rig. In the world of the play, these 'party pieces' help the rig workers pass time and entertain each other. According to Dafoe, LeCompte came up with this task-based motif when she asked cast members to create 'some sort of fantasy performance piece' (2008). While he did not indicate if LeCompte required these fantasy pieces to be musical in nature, each performer seemed to come up with a number involving music. The teens who played Kid sang the ballad 'Danny Boy'. As B. B. Nettleson, Dafoe sang Elvis Presley's 'Peace in the Valley'. 'Stew's Party Piece', the 13-minute condensation of *Long Day's Journey into*

Night that comprises Part II, was Gray's and group's response to the assignment.

The context leading up to Ron/Dan's party piece is a private conversation with Stew. In the presence of the other workmen, especially Dafoe's B.B., Ron/Dan is full of homophobic bravado. He accuses B.B. of being a 'punk shit cocksucker' (LeCompte 1981: 19). Alone with Stew, however, he lets down his guard. When Stew expresses concern about Dan's appearance, Dan reluctantly admits he may have 'a touch of the pox' (21). Dan never names the specific disease he has contracted, but it is clearly a sexually transmitted one. When Stew asks if he caught the pox at Miss Teresa's, a brothel, Dan rejects that option and names an even more surreptitious-sounding place: 'No, this was different. I met her in Chunky's Hide-Out' (21). Moreover, he offers an unusual description of his lover: 'Name a Tammy. Tam. Not too big. Not too small. Soft brown hair. Nice little feet' (21). Stew responds with alarm to the name of Dan's sex partner: 'Not Tammy Poxy, used to be called Judy: that old whore? Jeez, Dan, even if you didn't go in the stink-hole and get the sewer rot, a rim job and you got cavities on your sphincter' (21). Stew's graphic image of anal sex implies that Tam could be a man, a possibility that seems misaligned with the tough, macho milieu of the rig (though viewers familiar with Vawter's gayness would recognize it as consistent with his personal life). This particular reference to anal sex is striking not only because of its queerness, but its emphasis on the vagina-like mouth of the ass. It is not Dan's penis that Stew worries about, but the body part that marks him as a 'bottom', having the more passive or 'subservient' sexual role. Finally, we learn that Dan is so smitten with Tammy/Tam that he wants to leave the rig: 'I know it ain't right. I know I ain't supposed to [. . .] I can't help it. I just love her [. . .] I gotta get back to her' (21).

Dan's effort to leave the rig marks a critical point in the action. Stew restrains him, issuing a jarring order: 'You're going nowhere, squawface. You hear?' (22). Stew's epithet is both startling and puzzling. It seems to come out of nowhere in this context. However, I learned through interviews with Vawter's colleagues that around this time, in the early 1980s, he began making claims about his own Native

130

American heritage. The term 'squaw' also appears in a later interview with Ross Wetzsteon, published in the *Village Voice*. This was a rare occasion where Vawter spoke publicly about his family's Choctaw lineage, and about his forefathers' pattern of buying women: ' "Both my grandmothers were purchased," says Vawter in his characteristically somber voice. "My father's father bought himself a squaw off a Choctaw reservation, and my mother's father [. . .] sent back to Italy for a mail-order bride." ' (1989: 38). Greg Mehrten, Vawter's life partner, also recalled Vawter's accounts of a mysterious union between his white paternal grandfather and a Choctaw Indian woman: 'It was some kind of arranged marriage with this Indian woman. Ron used to tell me stories about this Indian woman. He had known her slightly when he was young, and couldn't remember too much about her, but the main thing was that she was very silent. She didn't ever say anything' (2002a). While the basis of Stew's racial slur is unclear, its dramatic effect is a kind of unmasking (and shaming) that exposes Dan as different from other men on the rig. For those in the audience familiar with Vawter's stories about his Choctaw heritage, it is hard to detach that knowledge from the scene's emotional force.

The practical effect of Stew's speech act is to subdue Dan and stop him from leaving the rig. After calling him 'squawface', Stew tells Dan what to do: 'Just sit tight, Dan boy, and I'll do you up brown. Now you do your party piece. Do your party piece, Dan' (LeCompte 1981: 22). Since there is no video recording of this scene, I asked Dafoe about the phrase 'do you up brown', which comes directly before Stew's order for Dan to do his party piece. Did Stew offer to paint Dan's *face* brown, perhaps as a visual allusion to 'squawface?' Dafoe chuckled at my suggestion that *Rig* marked the group's first reference to a form of blackface. He offered a different explanation: 'No, I think "Do you up brown" was—like so much of the language from *Point Judith*—just coded sex-talk. I don't even know what some of it meant' (2008). Dafoe went on to share some peculiar details of Dan's party piece, which is described briefly in a stage direction: (*Stew plays record of* ' "Dead Man's Curve" ' [by Jan and Dean] and Dan yowls choruses in falsetto, building to screams. B.B. enters right, Kid left.)' (1981: 22)

'Thinking back on it', Dafoe recalled, 'Ron's party piece is sort of revealing. Ron was an incredibly committed performer, but he didn't really have the traditional actor personality', and did not 'always feel like he had to perform for people'. Dafoe explained that performers like him, who came from conventional acting backgrounds, treated their party pieces like an audition. Their goal was to wow the audience. However, instead of singing, Vawter opted to scream. 'He brought that gut-wrenching commitment to anything he did', Dafoe said. 'And I think his party piece is literal. It's basically a primal scream. And it reflects Ron's untraditional performability' (2008).

Although there is no complete video of *Rig*, there is an existing sound recording of *Point Judith* made by the Wooster Group in 1980.[8] Here, the listener experiences Dan's 'party piece', a powerful and haunting track mingled with a sample of Jan and Dean's 1963 hit song, 'Deadman's Curve'. From the opening beats of song where trumpets blare to announce a drag race, Jan and Dean's All-American brand of vocal masculinity enters into strange competition with Dan's high-pitched yowling. On the one hand, Jan and Dean narrate their fatal crash with an eerie, deadpan calm:

> I know I'll never forget that horrible sight,
> I guess I found out for myself that everyone was right
> Won't come back from dead man's curve [...]

By contrast, Dan does not sing along at all, but instead cries out repeatedly during the chorus. Over time, Dan's yowls grow louder and increasingly out-of-control. His falsetto mimicry of the song's upbeat chorus builds to screams during the final verse:

> Dead Man's Curve, it's no place to play
> Dead Man's Curve, you best keep away
> Dead Man's Curve, I can hear' em say
> Won't come back from Dead Man's Curve

---

8 The *Point Judith* sound recording is held in The Wooster Group's archive at the Performing Garage.

In terms of group history, Vawter's screams recall a scene from an earlier piece that featured the same performers (except for Dafoe). His screams recall the reaction of the Woman medically examined in *Rumstick Road*, whose laughter turned to terrified shrieks when the Vawter as the doctor character got on top of her and tickled her. However, in Dan's case, there is no obvious explanation for his distressed engagement with Jan and Dean's classic Surfer Boy hit. Nevertheless, Dan becomes an especially visible subject precisely because of his differences from other men on the rig. He sings in falsetto, is called 'squawface', and is implied to have had anal sex with Tam/Tammy. All of the factors that cause Dan to stand out also complicate the distance between Vawter and his character.

As in *Nayatt School*, the tensions staged in *Rig* are never fully resolved. First, Dan's struggle to rejoin his infected lover ends abruptly, without further discussion. Stew's edict—'You're going nowhere, squawface'—causes Dan to cry out, 'No, Stew, no!' (1981: 22), but nonetheless serves in stopping him from leaving the rig. We never hear about Tam/Tammy again. Second, Dan's party piece begins as a forced confrontation with otherness, but the nature of that otherness is never really explored; moreover, although Stew hails Dan as 'squawface,' Vawter's performance persona comes across as conventionally white. In a photograph of the 'Deadman's Curve' scene, Vawter's Dan wears a sporty V-neck sweater, looking young and clean-cut in a Jan-and-Dean way. Only his falsetto screams betray an unstable relation to the white male icons of 1960s American culture. Do Dan's closing screams protest Stew's effort to confine him in the brutal male community of the rig? Do they signal a repressed homosexuality (suggested in the earlier dialogue about Tammy/Tam)? Or do they signal an unseen connection to race? Perhaps 'squawface' serves as shorthand for several distinct yet intersecting forms of difference that separate Ron/Dan from other men on the rig.

In the article documenting 'Point Judith', LeCompte wrote that Strahs 'made the subtext of our lives manifest in his verbal imagery' (1981: 21). This insight signaled a new trajectory in her approach to staging life material. Whereas she had previously focused on re-imagining scenes from Gray's childhood and youth, the director now began to introduce personal histories and interpersonal dynamics that affected other members of the company as well. Therefore, *Point Judith* arguably marked the first time that group autobiography became an organizing principle for a Wooster Group piece.

As previously noted, LeCompte recycled images and props from piece to piece. She also returned in later productions to dramatic challenges she could not solve during earlier shows. LeCompte's directorial notes for *Point Judith*, published in the 'Point Judith' article, reveal a seemingly minor concern: that Vawter/Dan had a very different relationship to Dafoe/B.B. on the oil rig than in a scene where the workers built a house together. Although LeCompte had never before seemed interested in developing consistent characters, she now posed a curious question: 'Character and continuity. Is this important?' (1981: 23). Unable to reconcile the workers' open hostility in *Rig* (Dan finally stabs B.B. with a knife after B.B. calls him 'queer-bait') with their friendly exchanges as house builders, the director wondered whether 'BUILD-ING and RIG [are] two separate sections?' (23). She eventually cut the building scene from *Rig*. Two years later, in 1981, it became part of *Route 1 & 9 (The Last Act)*. *Rig*'s cryptic references to race and racism also became profoundly more visible and relevant in *Route 1 & 9*.

Route 1 & 9 (The Last Act) (1981)

Though titled *Route 1 & 9 (The Last Act)*, this piece marked a new beginning for The Wooster Group, without Gray. The ensuing discussion will not rehearse the many arguments published about *Route 1 & 9* due to its provocative use of four white performers (Dafoe, Vawter, Peyton Smith, and Kate Valk) in blackface.[9] Instead, the focus is on the show's function in connecting as well as revising some of the group's prior autobiographical gestures. In *Route 1 & 9,* The Wooster

---

9 Readers interested in debates about the show's racism may refer to Savran 1988: 9-45; see also 'Gray Areas: More Angry Words on *Route 1 & 9*', *Village Voice* 27 January 1981.

Group used Thornton Wilder's *Our Town* (1938) as a jumping-off point for their iconoclastic vision of another American microcosm: New York City. Part I: 'The Lesson' featured Vawter addressing the audience on video monitor, presenting a reconstruction of a educational film by Clifton Fadiman, a well-spoken media celebrity of the 1950s. In a deadpan manner that was both comic and credible, Vawter satirized Fadiman's didactic style while explaining the plot and symbolism of Wilder's classic play. His clever winks and knowing smiles about the themes we would encounter soon proved ironic, however, since the rest of *Route 1 & 9* radically upended Wilder's depiction of small town American life.

Shifting from the lecture mode of Part I, Part II: 'The Party', opened with two labourers (Vawter and Dafoe) stumbling around the stage, comically trying to assemble the skeletal frame of a house while wearing glasses painted black so that neither man could see. Both performers wore blackface. An audio tape of Dan and Stew matter-of-factly discussing the 'cold' people who lived in these airy, unfinished structures played in the background.

At the level of ensemble autobiography, this scene reworked an interpersonal dynamic first seen in *Point Judith*. *Rig*, the opening section of that earlier piece, ended with Vawter/Dan stabbing Dafoe's B.B. in reaction to B.B.'s homophobic slurs. The two characters competed for attention and openly despised each other. To some extent, their rivalry touched upon real conflicts affecting the group (I previously cited Dafoe's account of how he joined TPG at Schechner's request, and unwittingly was pitted against Vawter for the Killer's role in *Cops*).

While *Rig* squared off Dafoe's and Vawter's personae against each other, presenting the labourers as impulsive adversaries, 'The Party' scene from *Route 1 & 9* transformed Dafoe's Stew and Vawter's Dan into affable coworkers. No longer crude or hotheaded, the pair seemed older and aware of their precarious status in a world run by powerful people. Perhaps the two-year gap between *Point Judith* and *Route 1 & 9* did more than help LeCompte resolve her questions about character continuity. It also gave Vawter and Dafoe time to get to know each other. Dafoe said that his role in *Rig* as B.B. Nettleson was shaped by his actual status as 'the new kid on the block' in LeCompte's company, whereas Vawter was 'the reliable old hand' (2008). In *Route 1 & 9*, the growing friendship and respect that came with Dafoe's duration in the group also seemed to inform the changed relationship between their onstage personae.

As 'The Party' continued, The Wooster Group presented a community not unlike the tight-knit, provincial one found in *Our Town*. However, they replaced the white, middle-class folk of Grover's Corners, New Hampshire, with performers in blackface who lived or worked in New York. In doing so, their production addressed certain racial and class divides effaced by Wilder's 'universal' truths. For example, as Vawter/Dan and Dafoe/Stew struggled with the task of assembling houses for wealthy suburbanites, Kate Valk/Willie and Peyton Smith/Ann talked on the phone about an upcoming party. Like the male labourers, both women wore blackface. Video footage of this scene and a script for *Route 1 & 9*, published in magazine titled *Benzene*, indicate that they spoke with slang inflections presumably intended to sound urban and black:

ANN. Hello.

WILLE. Hi girl, how you doin?

ANN. Uh-huh.

WILLE. I can hardly wait, so I got an idea: why don't you get all your stuff together, come on over my house and we get dressed together, you know, have a little pre-party . . . whatya say?

ANN. Uh-huh.

WILLE. Hey, you gonna wear that gold dress, aren't ya?

ANN. Uh-huh.

WILLE. Oh, great, honey. So hurry on over, OK?

ANN. Uh-huh. (1981: 7)

Later in the piece, Valk/Willie called actual fried chicken places trying to order fried chicken for delivery to her party, and giving the address of the Performing Garage. Her phone conversations with restaurant workers were amplified so that audiences could hear them. At the end of many calls, Valk/Willie found out that the Harlem restaurants she had dialed did not deliver to the downtown neighborhood of Soho. The repeated difficulty of getting her fried chicken exposed not only the physical distance but also the race-based divisions separating upper and lower Manhattan.

'The Party' did more than demonstrate the city's racial/spatial divides. This section also appropriated black modes of performance in arguably racist ways. Several prominent critics argued that The Wooster Group crossed the limits of acceptable parody by wearing blackface while reconstructing a Pigmeat Markham comedy routine originally performed by black actors at the Howard Theatre in Washington, D.C. (circa 1965). Shifting from Dan the workman to a new persona named 'Pig', Vawter enacted a number of scenes that played into harmful stereotypes about black men. First, Pig gambled away the money he had saved to buy gin for Willie's party. Next, he briefly considered pawning his suit, but decided instead to break into a drugstore. Since it was dark, Pig accidentally stole a bottle of castor oil rather than gin, and unwittingly poured the laxative into Willie's punch bowl. 'The Party' section ended with Pig 'sending a telegram' (a euphemism for defecating in his pants).

Although they belong to different constellations of works, The Wooster Group's use of blackface in *Route 1 & 9* should be studied as a continuation of the racial imagery first glimpsed in *Rig*. References to race that were peripheral in *Rig* abruptly moved to the forefront in *Route 1 & 9*. On one level, Stew's puzzling threat to Dan, 'I'll do you up brown', became literal. Vawter's 'Pig' embodied the gross ineptness and simple-minded criminality that racists often associate with black men. On another level, the early 1980s marked a growing fascination with the complexities of racial otherness. Books and college courses theorizing race proliferated during this period. Indeed, several TPG members began exploring (and perhaps inventing) their own racialized stories of origin.

In TPG's programme for *The Balcony* (1980), Stephen Borst listed his first name as 'Esteban[10]', which he had never done before.[11] When asked about his veteran performer's abrupt change to 'Esteban', Schechner replied: 'I do not think that was Steve's real name. I think that was a "fancy name" he took a fancy to—a European version of Stephen' (2013).

Perhaps Borst was not alone in fancying exotic names and ancestors. Kate Valk (who joined The Wooster Group during *Point Judith*) described her affinity for passing as black in several interviews.[12] Even LeCompte hesitantly voiced her gender-based identification with 'blackness'. Moreover, according to Celeste Vawter Fonda, Ron Vawter's younger sister, the Choctaw grandmother that he remembered from childhood may also have been more rooted in desire than in genetics. These statements position *Route 1 & 9* as rooted in the risks and challenges of exploring cultural 'others' via the self. However, the white company's experiments with their individual and collective relationships to blackness came at very high costs. One major consequence was a decision by the New York State Council on the Arts (NYSCA) to rescind The Wooster Group's funding by 43% the next year (more than *Route 1 & 9* had cost to produce).[13]

---

10 I could not track down Borst's birth certificate, but did find a newspaper article about him, 'NFA Graduate Returns with Theatre Group,' published in the *Norwich Bulletin*. The author, Roberta Burke, celebrated his homecoming to Norwich, CT, where he had graduated from a fine arts high school in 1962. Burke referred to Borst as 'Stephen' throughout (1974: 6). She added that Borst's father was a 'retired Naval commander', and his mother a 'social worker' (1974: 6). There was no mention of an Esteban Borst in this detailed human interest piece about the performer.

11 See Richard Schechner papers, Box 165, Folder 1.

12 See David Salle and Sarah French, 'Kate Valk,' *BOMB Magazine* 100, 2008.

13 For more on this loss of funding and the Wooster Group's failed efforts to restore it, see Savran 1988:10.

This chapter on The Wooster Group's turn from Gray's life to group autobiography closes with members' thoughts on the sociopolitical issues that compelled them to stage the jarring world of 'The Party.' Vawter's goals were of an activist nature, albeit an activism rooted in a sense of superiority: 'It was all about pulling the rug out from people's secure, liberal, and righteous feelings about racism, their own and their society's. We were agent provocateurs' (Savran 1988: 14).

Vawter added that wearing blackface allowed him to examine his own forms of prejudice. He concluded that the order to cease such self-based inquiry affected the company more than other forms of backlash: 'We were told that you can't confront, not only the audience, with such volatile possibilities, but you can't confront yourself with it publicly either, as artists. That was even more damaging than the problems we had with the audience: that we were being punished for exploring our own attitudes'. (Savran 1988: 45)

During her conversation with critic Don Shewey, originally published in the *Village Voice* in 1981 with the title 'Elizabeth LeCompte's Last Stand?', LeCompte responded somewhat evasively to the question about whether *Route 1 & 9* is racist: 'You may consider yourself not subjectively racist, but objectively if you exist and make money in a culture that is obviously living off a third world people, you must be. In that sense, I'd say yes, this piece is racist. Straight down the line'.[14] LeCompte's use of the second person voice positioned racism as an inevitable byproduct of American life, but sidestepped any direct responsibility for staging offensive caricatures of black people. Instead, she suggested (too simply) that America's larger, structural racism informed her company's work on this piece, just as racism informs all other forms of production and consumption in America.

Near the end of her conversation with Shewey, LeCompte finally spoke more personally about her perceived relationship to blackness:

---

14 Shewey's 1981 *Village Voice* article, 'Elizabeth LeCompte's Last Stand?' appears on his personal website: www.donshewey.com. A transcript of his 1981 conversation with LeCompte is also published there: https://bit.ly/2zDWsiM (last accessed on 17 June 2020).

I use the color black very literally: if you mix all colors, you get black. I thought of mourning, too, this being the last piece. And I thought of our relationship to those workers that Ronnie and Willem play; something in that building scene with those black men has some feeling for me. I hesitate to say this, but I identify. I identify with the color black as well as with cultural blackness.

Shewey explained LeCompte's identification with cultural blackness as a sense of being marginalized: 'the way the contributions of blacks and women are often overlooked in our culture'. LeCompte was more specific about her experience of being overlooked: 'I always had illusions that people saw the woman making the work. They didn't. They saw Spalding. [. . .] because he's male and I'm female, I would find people thinking that he conceived of the structure, that he wrote those lines'. Today's readers would rightly contest and reject LeCompte's comparison of her lack of recognition as a female director with the oppression and segregation experienced by blacks. On a basic level, LeCompte was clearly recognized early on as a remarkable director. As demonstrated in previous chapters, many professional theatre critics (mostly male) took her vision seriously from the start.

LeCompte told Shewey *Route 1 & 9* would be the 'last act' in a series she began directing in 1975, with *Sakonnet Point*. Yet despite its fierce polarization of audiences and the loss of NYSCA funding, *Route 1 & 9* ultimately proved to be a potent catalyst for a second trilogy, *The Road to Immortality*, which would eventually include *Route 1 & 9*, *L.S.D.* (1984) and *Frank Dell's The Temptation of St. Antony* (1988). Known to very small audiences just a few years earlier, the Wooster Group was suddenly both famous and infamous, and would continue to find itself mired in controversy throughout the early 1980s.

This new decade also ushered in a very turbulent period in Vawter's life, and in the overlapping histories of TPG and The Wooster Group, including several major events that would change Vawter and both companies for ever.

CHAPTER 6

Major Drama

Vawter's Foremost Roles in an Era of Crisis

Taken literally, 'major drama' applies to those performances that are arguably the most challenging and weighty. But in popular culture, 'major drama' indicates excess: too much commotion, too much spectacle, too many things going on at once. Faced with these pejorative connotations, I began to reconsider the term's suitability in the context of a study of Ron Vawter's foremost dramatic roles, in plays that are indeed major dramas. Nonetheless, each production studied here bears an indisputable relation to the theatrical excess outlined above. Alongside the turmoil that abounds in these works at the level of dramatic plot, each production was strongly shaped by upheavals that Vawter and his colleagues experienced in their lives.

The Performance Group's 1979 adaptation of Jean Genet's *The Balcony* (1956) explored the failures of a revolution just as TPG, a revolutionary ensemble of its time, was about to collapse. The Wooster Group's epic project, *Frank Dell's The Temptation of St. Antony* (1988), staged a feverish quest for meaning that coincided with the onset of Vawter's serious health problems. Finally, Vawter's last two roles with The Wooster Group—performed live in *Brace Up!* (1991) and played on a video monitor during *Fish Story* (1993)—were fraught with the knowledge of his imminent death. My analysis of Vawter's 'major dramas' will encompass both the serious and histrionic elements of these shows, as well as the behind-the-scenes circumstances of their production.

Major Shakeups: *The Balcony* (1979–1980) and *Point Judith* (1980)

Richard Schechner opened his essay, 'Playing with Genet's *Balcony*', by acknowledging the 'many problems with the show' (1985[1982]: 261). For the first time since 1973, TPG held open auditions in early 1979: 'These were necessary because only a fraction of the people in TPG wanted to work on *The Balcony*' (261). Elizabeth LeCompte was busy developing what would become *Point Judith* (1980), and other core members had left the group to try new initiatives.[1]

Vawter stood by Schechner during this turbulent period. He agreed to perform in *The Balcony*, along with Stephen Borst (the Police Chief), Willem Dafoe (Arthur), Spalding Gray (the Bishop), and Libby Howes (Carmen). Vawter took the central role of Irma, the proprietor of a French brothel. However, at the same time, all of these performers except for Borst made it clear that they would also work on *Point Judith* with LeCompte.[2] Schechner was hurt by their divided loyalties: 'Directors, like the Old Testament God, are jealous and want no other directors before them' (1985[1982]: 262). In addition to the personal conflicts, there were problems with sharing space and scheduling. Finally, there was a lack of money to pay the performers: 'And what was missing in cash was made up for in bitterness' (263).

Dafoe said *The Balcony* was 'a struggle' for Vawter because 'his heart was very close to Liz's work' (2008). Yet Vawter also coveted playing Irma in *The Balcony* because he had 'never got to do big roles with Richard' until that point. Dafoe's claim is partly accurate; Vawter had played the Director in *The Marilyn Project* and the Killer in *Cops*, but neither was the lead role. After six years with TPG, he relished a chance to finally be the company's headliner. Dafoe added that Vawter took him to see several drag performances and was fascinated with

---

1 Joan MacIntosh was trying to put together a commercial career. Leeny Sack left to develop her own interests in the combination of performance and therapy. Bruce Porter built the set for *The Balcony*, but left before the show opened to start a stage scenery business with Bruce Rayvid.

2 Shortly after *The Balcony*, in 1982, Borst died of leukaemia.

drag queens at the time: 'It's another kind of mask that's tinged with sexuality, so I think the idea of playing Irma was very attractive to him' (2008).

In addition to playing the role of Irma (a.k.a. the Queen), Vawter helped Schechner to conceive the environment for this production. Although Genet's *The Balcony* is set in a heterosexual brothel, Schechner recalled via email a gay men's venue that he and Vawter visited in 1979:

> Ron took me to 'Men's Country', a gay sex club in a townhouse on, I think, West 12th Street. I was—what word is right?—'taken' by how casual the sex was, a lot of it totally silent. No names, no nothing, just blowjobs and whatever. [I was] also [taken] by the very theatrical quality of the settings. I remember clearly a room that looked like the cab of a 16-wheeler. And the glory hole room, etc. It was really *The Balcony*, without the revolution or politics of any kind (2008).

Fantasy is an integral part of *The Balcony*, because Irma the madam sells more than raw sex. She takes time to learn each client's most private desires, and customizes her brothel accordingly. For the man who wants to be a Bishop, Irma supplies a mitre and a young woman whose sins he forgives. For the more sadistic client who fancies himself a Judge, she provides a thief whose crimes he must weigh and punish. Irma's toughest client, however, is the Chief of Police. He longs to be the object of other men's fantasies, but no one seems interested in pretending to be him. *The Balcony* ends when a client finally asks to play out a scene about being the Chief of Police. In a brothel theme room resembling a tomb, the new client violently castrates himself and then commits suicide.

As LeCompte remarked in Chapter 3, Vawter got naked at the start of every rehearsal period. Schechner's idea that the role of the Queen should emerge from a performer's naked state gave rise to one of Vawter's most famous scenes of nudity and self-transformation. In 'Playing with Genet's *Balcony*', Schechner described his queer metamorphosis into the brothel's monarch: 'The audience sees him first as a man in jeans but shirtless, like so many advertisements in magazines and on TV: the 'Jordache' look. Then he strips naked. Next, step by step, scene by scene, he makes himself up into a queen in both senses: royalty-in-drag'. ([1982] 1985: 266)

It is hard to imagine a character called Irma the Queen as anything other than feminine. Yet according to a review by John B. Gordon, Vawter retained his core masculinity: 'Ron Vawter plays the role of Irma, not as a drag queen but as a strong male actor doing a role in a woman's costume. The audience watches his performance aware of two levels of reality—Ron Vawter, the male actor, and the words of a female character' (1980: 264).

Schechner said he cast Vawter as Irma and Borst as the Chief of Police because they were both gay men. In 'Playing with Genet's *Balcony*,' the director expressed his desire to 'make public' what he saw as Genet's closet drama, or 'the gay love affair between Irma and the Police Chief' (272). Schechner also emphasized how the stormy relationship between these characters reached its climax in his play: 'When they fight, the Chief of Police rips off Irma's wig [. . .] revealing her, for one pathetic moment, as an early middle-aged drag queen' (266). Vawter was only 30 in 1979, but he experienced premature balding. Thus, when Borst yanked off Irma's wig, he not only exposed Vawter's thinning hair, but surely roused the spectre of the 'old fag' that Vawter reportedly feared and hoped to avoid in his future.[3]

Vawter, Borst and two other actors from the New York cast accompanied Schechner to Connecticut College that summer, where they helped him to teach a workshop using student actors in a version of *The Balcony*. Vawter took turns playing the role of Irma with

---

3 In May 1979, Vawter completed a Master's thesis in the Department of Graduate Drama at New York University (renamed the Department of Performance Studies in 1980). A former Wooster Group associate said Vawter went back to school again, in the early 1980s, because he hoped to teach when he became too old to play leading men. According to my source, Vawter told friends that he 'didn't want to end up an old fag'.

students.[4] 'He really got enamoured with the role up there', Schechner said in 2003.

Vawter also became enamoured with Nancy Reilly, a young woman who auditioned successfully in New York to play the General and went to Connecticut for the workshop. Like Vawter's Irma, Reilly's role involved crossdressing; her character entered Irma's brothel as a high-powered female executive who dressed in drag as a teenage boy. Her/his sexual fantasy was to be a powerful grown-up man. Reilly's hair for the play was a military crew cut and for her costume she wore boxer shorts, combat boots, and a tank top under which her breasts were bandaged flat against her chest. Reilly's natural voice was quite deep: many in the audience thought they were looking at a male actor. Onstage, Reilly's roleplaying was multilayered: she was a female actress playing a woman playing a boy who fantasized about being a man. Offstage, Reilly also displayed a far more masculine look than other female TPG members. During a 2008 interview[5], Reilly suggested that her boyish style was part of what attracted Vawter, who was at a personal crossroads in 1979. On the one hand, he had been in a gay relationship since roughly 1973. On the other hand, he still sought on some deep level, perhaps, to follow the path of his deceased father. For instance, Reilly said Vawter often voiced a fantasy (even after they broke up) in which he married her and they joined the Armed Services together. Vawter's own parents met during World War II while serving in the U.S. Navy. Despite his homosexuality, he sporadically romanticized the idea of reproducing a military family.

Vawter's work on Irma roughly coincided with another drag performance that he did in *Point Judith*. In chapter 5, I discussed Part I of *Point Judith*: 'Rig', a play by Jim Strahs about an all-male work crew on an oil rig. Here, I will briefly focus on the making of Part III,

---

4 Rebecca Schneider, now Chair of the Department of Theatre, Speech, and Dance at Brown University, was one of the students with whom Vawter took turns playing Irma.

5 All quotes attributed to Nancy Reilly are taken from this interview with the author (20 December 2018).

'The Convent', which featured Ken Kobland's silent film, 'By the Sea', about what happens when the men leave the rig. The film was shot in July and August 1979, while TPG completed a residency at Connecticut College. The cast included Dafoe (Sister Muriel), Gray (Mother Elizabeth), Howes (the Postulate) and Vawter (Sister Margaret), all of whom were dressed as nuns. The action took place around a house-like structure that designer Jim Clayburgh built out of plywood on the Long Island Sound, near New London, which was in close proximity to Connecticut College.[6]

Meghan Coleman,[7] who worked at the college that summer as an arts administrator, recalled her striking first encounter with Vawter and Gray: 'Ronnie and Spalding were walking up the main road of conservative Connecticut College in nuns' robes!' (2008).[8] Later, Gray came to her office looking for a space in which to workshop his first monologue, *Sex and Death to the Age 14*. 'Spalding was this deeply tanned Mother Superior. I said, "I can give it to you Sunday". He said, "Well, I'm busy on Sunday." I laughed, and we kind of got each other'. Meanwhile, Coleman said that Vawter presented a far more officious persona: 'Ron came in sounding like Richard Nixon. When he got into being Ronnie, he did adopt this "guy-in-a-suit" approach'. Unlike Gray, who wanted a venue for solo work, Vawter came asking permission so that LeCompte's collective could film *By the Sea*. Coleman, a resourceful administrator, secured a spot for the filming near campus.

Savran writes that *By the Sea* explores 'Mary Tyrone's experiences as a girl, her education in a convent, and her dream of becoming a nun' (1988: 138). He argues that when audiences figure out that 'all except one of the nuns are being played by men in drag,' they simultaneously

---

6 It was also very close to the Monte Cristo House—the actual house that the O'Neill family lived in during the summer—who became the Tyrones in *Long Day's Journey into Night*.
7 Meghan Coleman was Meghan Ellenberger when she worked at Connecticut College; for the sake of consistency, she is referred to as Meghan Coleman throughout.
8 All references in this chapter to Coleman's remarks come from our 9 November 2008 interview.

remember that Mary's dream is 'the vision of a male playwright' (138). Indeed, *Long Day's Journey into Night* was Eugene O'Neill's autobiographical masterwork: a man's violent vision of a day in the life of his family at their seaside Connecticut home. Yet B*y the Sea* was also part of LeCompte's emerging group autobiography. It was her farewell to Spalding Gray, whom she had been involved with for 13 years, and it was her send-off to Gray's performance persona (also named Spalding), which she had helped bring into being.

By June 1979, Gray was headed in a different direction than either Schechner or LeCompte. Gray befriended Coleman and they worked together that summer on developing a new autobiographical monologue, *India and After*, staged at the Performing Garage in November 1979. Meanwhile, LeCompte and Willem Dafoe started seeing each other. When the summer ended, Dafoe moved into the Wooster Street loft that Gray and LeCompte still shared. About that same time, Gray began his affair with Renée Shafransky; it is difficult to say whose actions dealt the final blow to the relationship between Gray and LeCompte. To add to the unrest, Vawter broke up with his longtime boyfriend, Jon. For roughly five years, they had lived together at 14 Pierrepont Street in Brooklyn.[9] It's not exactly clear when they got together, but Gray recalled in a 2004 interview that Jon had accompanied Vawter to *The Tooth of Crime* as early as 1973.[10]

Nancy Reilly shed light on one unexpected factor that led Vawter to leave his boyfriend: 'When Ron was leaving Jon during *Point Judith*, he decided that he was in love with me, which completely threw everybody. He liked that. [. . .] It made Jon go ballistic. It's one thing to say you're in love with a man, but it's totally insulting to say that you love a girl' (2008). Apparently, Vawter felt so guilty about the breakup

---

9 Vawter's Brooklyn address appears in a letter sent to him on 16 March 1977 by Jeremy Nussbaum, who was TPG's legal advisor. See 'Mother Courage: Correspondence', Schechner Papers, Box 167, Folder 3.

10 Gray described Jon as the more accommodating partner: 'Sweet, tolerant. He obviously loved Ron, but it was a lot to put up with. They broke up. And Jon moved to Boston' (2004).

that he gave his ex-lover everything he owned: numerous books, furniture, valuable carpets and other items.

Reilly became intimate with Vawter in 1981: 'It was still the hangover of free love, and I was very flattered that I had become the one that Ron saw as his girlfriend' (2008). Reilly loved Vawter and wanted to spend her life with him, but he gradually scared her away with a maxim he often repeated: 'Honey, longevity is not in the cards'. While Vawter meant that men in his family tended to die young,[11] Reilly came to view his saying as a self-fulfilling prophecy. Vawter did not expect to grow old, so he made few long-term plans.

Schechner likewise struggled with an imminent loss that season—namely, the loss of his company. He invited Meghan Coleman to join TPG as an administrator after watching her perform as Gray's timekeeper in *India and After*. Coleman later recalled that Schechner had the foresight and generosity to let LeCompte keep the Performing Garage once he realized that his time with TPG was ending. 'I respect him utterly for that', Coleman said, 'There was a bit of a fight, and Richard held the lease. He could have refused to do it, but he graciously said, "The tide has turned. You and Spalding and Ronnie are the company now. Here's the lease"'. Schechner corrected Coleman's memory via email, explaining that what he gave to LeCompte, Gray and Vawter in late 1979 was much more than a lease:

> We owned the Garage. It was shares in the Grand Street Artists Co-Op which I held in trust for The Wooster Group (always TPG's legal name, from the very beginning). I turned over these shares. Later, to tell the truth, I regretted it and tried to get some kind of arrangement so that I could use the Garage for my own work. That didn't work out (2009b).

After turning over his shares and his key to the Garage, Schechner briefly visited Korea and Japan in December 1979, just as *The Balcony* opened at the Performing Garage. When he returned to New York in

---

11 Vawter's father died of a heart attack at age 47. His paternal grandfather died at 57. His maternal grandfather also died young while working at his automobile garage.

January 1980, the show had already closed because performers lacked the will to go on. At this beleaguered moment, Schechner decided that he himself would leave TPG, the ensemble he had founded in 1967. 'Within a year', he wrote in his essay on *The Balcony*, 'those who remained renamed it The Wooster Group' ([1982] 1985: 293).[12]

Major Love: Gregory Mehrten and *Pretty Boy* (1984)

The road to The Wooster Group's major dramas included transforming personal developments. A pivotal force entered Vawter's life during that period: the actor, director and writer Gregory Mehrten. Vawter and Mehrten became lovers in November 1979 and had a 14-year relationship. The two also collaborated professionally on several performances. They remained a couple until Vawter's death in 1994.

Mehrten moved to New York in 1975 to work with Mabou Mines, and soon started going to see theatre by other companies. Among the first shows Mehrten saw was TPG's *Mother Courage*. One night, after attending another production at the Performing Garage, Mehrten lingered outside when Vawter came over and invited him to a house party in Brooklyn. At the time, Mehrten was there with his girlfriend, a fellow artist, and they jumped at the invite: 'We got into a van that Ron was driving, and I thought it was so glamorous that I was going to this big theatre party, because I hadn't been to too many' (2002).[13]

After that party, Mehrten continued to attend TPG's shows; Vawter also went to see Mehrten's performances with Mabou Mines. However, it was not until 1979, close to Thanksgiving, that the two of them became lovers:

> I had broken up with my girlfriend. I'd had some affairs with men, and I was living alone. One time, I just decided to go

---

12 Schechner remained on The Wooster Group's Board of Directors for about a year after leaving TPG.

13 All references in this chapter to Mehrten's remarks, unless otherwise indicated, come from our 14 June 2002 interview.

out. I went to this gay bar called The Bar, on 4th Street and
2nd Avenue. I walked in, and there was Ron. He said 'Hi' to
me, and we started talking […] We stayed at the bar talking
for hours. And then I went home with him.

By late 1979, Vawter was living alone in a small Manhattan apartment on Sullivan Street. Soon, he and Mehrten began 'having an
affair', as Mehrten described it. But Mehrten found Vawter's tiny
apartment confining, so Vawter began spending more and more time
at Mehrten's place on Bleecker Street. Vawter eventually moved in
with Mehrten in 1983.

Even as the young men fell deeply in love, Mehrten explained,
they were both in theatre, a profession that doesn't lend itself to
monogamy: 'We were always travelling, always touring. Half the year,
we weren't even in the same city together'. Vawter had a reputation
within The Wooster Group for his frequent sexual encounters while
on tour. Meghan Coleman told me about a particularly harrowing
incident that happened in 1981, while Vawter was going out with
Mehrten, but before they had moved in together. The Wooster Group
was in Amsterdam; Coleman was in New York managing their office.
One night, Coleman dreamt that Spalding Gray had been beaten.
Shaken, she called Gray overseas to make sure he was OK and learned
that it was Vawter who had been violently assaulted by another man.
Gray told her that Vawter had gone home with a stranger in Amsterdam, who beat him up for reasons that are not fully clear. Yet despite
his bruises and the emotional shock, Vawter went back to performing
just a few nights later.

Mehrten and Vawter's first collaboration featured a climactic
scene of gay-on-gay violence. In 1984, they staged *Pretty Boy*, a drama
that Mehrten wrote, directed, and in which he performed. Vawter
played a supporting role, made a film sequence used in the show, and
helped to compile the soundtrack. Mehrten created the piece for
Mabou Mines, but they staged it at the Performing Garage.

In his *New York Times* review, Mel Gussow wrote that *Pretty Boy*
'deals with the homosexual experience, the first time Mabou Mines

has produced a play on that subject' (1984: C3). Indeed, the gay issues that Mehrten and Vawter tackled in *Pretty Boy* were a departure from their usual work within their respective ensembles. Mehrten described his play as 'an updating' of the Lulu story found in Frank Wedekind's play, *Die Büchse der Pandora* (*Pandora's Box*) (1904), which traces the decline and fall of a young woman. In the final act, Lulu becomes a sex worker in London, where she meets Jack the Ripper, who murders her. Mehrten changed the play's time period to the 1970s and Wedekind's uninhibited Lulu into a handsome gay male, Peter, the 'Pretty Boy' character, who was played by a different actor in each act.

Act 1, set in Berlin in 1975, opens with 19-year-old Peter resisting his army colonel father's efforts to enlist him. A fight breaks out when Peter's father catches him disco dancing with an older male soldier. Peter wounds his father with scissors and flees. In Act 2, Peter moves to Paris, where he manipulates a wealthy older woman while sleeping with questionable men behind her back. Act 3 is set in 1979 New York. In this act, Mehrten played the protagonist and Vawter played Wolf, Peter's German lover. Gussow singled out Vawter's performance as 'the most vivid' one of the show: 'Mr. Vawter is bitterly amusing as his demanding and volatile lover, a man who seems to have a rabid disrespect for all convention' (1984: C3). The play ended with a stunning murder. Besieged by Wolf's verbal and physical abuse, Peter escapes to the piers to find a one-night stand. But when his date also begins acting aggressively towards him, the 'Pretty Boy' snaps and strangles him.

Pretty Boy addressed a range of issues affecting gay wellness: substance abuse, promiscuity, concerns about whether to come out or remain in the closet, and gay-on-gay violence. Mindful that Mehrten staged his play in 1984, when the gay community in New York was already well aware of the HIV epidemic, I was initially surprised that AIDS was not mentioned. Yet the prospect of meeting a bad end as a result of one's sexual practices recurs in every act. In act 2 of Mehrten's final script,[14] Helene, the older Parisian woman, asks Peter not to

---

14 The Ron Vawter Papers also contain an earlier version of the *Pretty Boy* script, with markings and notes. See Box 3, Folder 7.

touch her. When he asks if something is wrong, Helene replies cryptically, 'No, nothing's the matter. I don't think. Peter, when was the last time you were at the doctor?' (1984: 28). Later, Helene cautions Peter that sleeping with 'these men' is 'dangerous' (29). Given the time period when the play was created and its derivation from a text in which the protagonist's death is tethered to her deviant sexuality, it makes sense to ask if AIDS functioned as an unspoken subtext in *Pretty Boy*.

Mehrten and Vawter took a professional break after this difficult collaboration. Mehrten said the problem was proximity; he was too involved with the play, and it was exhausting to work with an intimate partner day in and day out. Although they did not join forces again onstage until Lee Breuer's gender-reversed *Lear* (1990), Mehrten and Vawter continued to live together through the height of the AIDS epidemic in the US.

Major Speed: *L.S.D. (. . . Just the High Points . . .)* (1984)

In 1986, The Wooster Group began promoting their second trilogy, *The Road to Immortality*. This was also the title of a four-month retrospective cosponsored by the Kitchen, and scheduled to open in November 1986. It was supposed to include *Route 1 & 9*, *L.S.D. (. . . Just the High Points . . .)*, and a work-in-progress titled *Frank Dell's The Temptation of St. Antony*, but did not unfold as planned because Vawter fell gravely ill that same month. Having previously discussed *Route 1 & 9*, we will briefly cover Vawter's roles in *L.S.D.* before addressing his illness.

An early, incomplete version titled *L.S.D. (Part One)* ran at the Performing Garage in late 1983. A more finished production titled *L.S.D. (. . . Just the High Points . . .)*, featuring all four parts of the show, 'Newton'[15], 'Salem', 'Millbrook' and 'Miami', opened at the Boston Shakespeare Company in April 1984. As research for the play,

15 'Newton' was named for the Boston suburb where Dr Timothy Leary lived while he taught at Harvard and gave psychedelic drugs to some 300 graduate students, professors and local writers.

the cast read texts by William Burroughs, Allen Ginsberg, Jack Kerouac, Arthur Koestler and others who had associated with Leary. They later selected excerpts from these texts and read them out loud during performances. Some readings were planned out; others were chosen in the moment by readers. Each show was a bit different.

A reviewer named John Bush Jones described the show's jury-like set-up: 'On a raised scaffold, up to twelve actors sit behind a long table [...] Microphones, a turntable, books, and other artifacts are scattered along the table's length. The house lights stay on, making the audience an integral part of the proceedings. (1984: 13)

Bush Jones added that 'Newton' opened with Nancy Reilly delivering a 'spaced-out monologue' (13) as Ann Rower, a babysitter in Leary's home.[16] Reilly's Rower functioned as a kind of narrator/MC: she provided a historical context for the ideas that other characters debated.

In Boston, Vawter read texts by Arthur Koestler, the Jewish-Hungarian author who joined in Leary's experiments with magic mushrooms. According to Carolyn Clay's review, Act 1 ended dramatically yet comically when Vawter, reading as Koestler, 'freaked out at the discovery of Ginsberg in bed with Peter Orlovsky' (1984: 6). Clay described this scene as 'a mock-technical reenactment, with Vawter's deadpan Koestler running blankly in place to an excited narration' (6). Bush Jones also noted the low-affect delivery of emotionally charged texts: 'It's all very quiet, very natural—almost as if the company isn't acting at all' (1984: 13).

After a brief pause to set the stage, 'Salem' began. A critic named Jo Ann Augeri Rowe noted excerpts in that section from Arthur Miller's McCarthy-era play, *The Crucible* (1953):

Using the theme and dialogue from Miller's play, the actors, again strung out along the table and miked for sound, re-enact the Salem witch trials. Emotion builds with increasing

16 The programme from the 1986/87 retrospective at the Kitchen states that the Babysitter's text was 'composed from letters, interviews, and text given to The Wooster Group by Ann Rower'.

hysteria, reinforced by mind-wrenching electric guitar music played at full volume (1984).

In 'Salem', Vawter played the inquisitorial Reverend Hale. He famously sped up Hale's dialogue, causing the reputed witchcraft expert to sound like he spoke gibberish. Augeri Rowe noted in 'Salem' an unsettling nonchalance toward the victims of mass hysteria: 'The act culminates in a strange, macabre, funny "dance," as young women in long skirts move to dance music as disembodied feet dangle beneath them' (1984). In a post-show discussion, LeCompte said she included this image 'because she thought it was funny, and only later saw that the effect was of hanging bodies' (in Augeri Rowe 1984). Reviewer Joan Lautman agreed: 'The work is funny. How else can you view the witches' hanging bodies doing a dance to "Tico-Tico" and "You Belong to my Heart" as striped-stocking legs, belonging to other actors, perform their own unison dance?' (1984). When the production returned to the Performing Garage in September 1984, Arthur Miller's lawyers sent The Wooster Group a cease-and-desist order to stop performing *The Crucible*. In response, the company replaced Miller's script with scenes from *The Hearing*, a play written by Michael Kirby in November and December 1984.

'Millbrook'—the name of the upstate New York estate where Leary and others convened in the late 1960s—dealt with the years after Leary was forced out of Harvard for his experiments. Here, Reilly narrated Ann Rower's explicit anecdotes about the kinds of parties that Leary threw, interspersed with live rock music performed by the cast. Vawter revived his talent for drumming (last seen onstage in TPG's *Mother Courage*). Michael Stumm, Anna Köhler, Jeff Webster, Steve Buscemi and Willem Dafoe were the other musicians.

Most critics saw 'Millbrook' as a wry commentary on the displaced utopian promises of the 1960s. Clay recounted how a woman 'hallucinates that the birds on the bathroom wallpaper are swooping down to "steal my shit"' (1984: 6). Skip Ascheim argued that Act 3 was an indictment of religious and political counter-cultures: 'The thematic connection is both cemented (in each case, a deviant ideology is

officially condemned), and satirized (chemically induced hallucina-
tions replace the visions of "witches")' (1984: 24).

'Millbrook' also featured a video by Ken Kobland called 'The Man
in Miami', in which Vawter played The Man, a figure who spent much
of his time walking around Miami. The lines between drama and
group autobiography again became blurry in this section. At one point
during the live performance, Vawter's Man persona 'telephoned' the
other cast members (who were presumably in New York) and reported
that by impersonating a band called *Donna Sierra and the Del Fuegos*,
The Wooster Group 'might find a gig for the next night'. His phone
call suggested that The Wooster Group was more than a theatre company: they also sought other ways to generate income, such as passing
as musicians. This notion of a shadow company behind the legitimate
one would soon become a prominent trope in the group's self-referential mythology. In addition to scouting for ways to make money,
The Man's other activities involved prowling the beach and looking
for drugs dropped on the floor of a motel bathroom. According to
Norman Frisch, who was The Wooster Group's dramaturge during
L.S.D., the drug-addled figure of Lenny Bruce informed Vawter's
'Miami' persona, which he developed in partnership with LeCompte
and Kate Valk. Frisch said the Lenny Bruce material 'was just under
the surface the whole time [in *L.S.D.*], and exploded into *St. Antony*'
(2002a).

Major Trauma: *Frank Dell's The Temptation of St. Antony* (1988)

In an interview with Andrew Quick, published in *The Wooster Group
Work Book*, LeCompte identified Vawter as one of the agents behind
her collaboration with another director, Peter Sellars, on Gustave
Flaubert's novel, *La Tentation de Saint Antoine* (1874). 'I think it started
with Ron and Peter Sellars', LeCompte said. 'Sellars picked the
Flaubert book. He thought we could get some arts funding if [...] he
co-directed it with me' (2007: 56). The Wooster Group and Sellars
worked together for a relatively short period of time, but *Frank Dell's*

The Temptation of St. Antony took LeCompte and her company almost four years to complete. According to The Wooster Group's online 'Production History', the show's development spanned from January 1985 until September 1988.

Part of what initially drew Vawter to *La Tentation de Saint Antoine* was its similarities to a passion play. Flaubert's drama is based on the story of the fourth-century Christian hermit who lived in the desert and resisted great temptations. Marianne Weems, who replaced Frisch as The Wooster Group's dramaturge in 1988, agreed this was a perfect role for Vawter: 'The idea of being tormented by the flesh [was] so completely illustrative of Ron's life'. Weems added that Flaubert's text was 'an epic closet drama', explaining that 'it was never meant to be performed because it's insanely difficult' (2003a).

Preliminary work on *St. Antony* began in January 1985, and early rehearsals took place at MIT in Cambridge, MA. That spring, The Wooster Group began a wholly different joint venture with Richard Foreman, director of the Ontological-Hysteric Theater. Work on *St. Antony* resumed that August. In November 1985, The Wooster Group began a three-month residency in Washington, DC, at the Kennedy Center for the Performing Arts. During that time, LeCompte directed a video shoot starring naked company members. The resulting video, parts of which were later screened during St. Antony, became known as Channel J because it parodied an actual TV programme that had aired on Manhattan's public access cable channel (Channel J) in the early 1980s. The programme, titled 'Interludes at Midnight', featured explicit sexual discussions between a nude talk show host and his guests: exotic dancers, porn stars and so on. LeCompte cast Vawter as a send-up of the lurid talk show host. His persona became known as 'Frank Dell', which was also the name of a character in an early Lenny Bruce monologue. Vawter and other performers (Willem Dafoe, Anna Köhler, Peyton Smith and Kate Valk) improvised the nude talk show scenario to a reading by Nancy Reilly of Flaubert's play.

In January 1986, The Wooster Group staged open rehearsals of *St. Antony* at The Kennedy Center to conclude their Washington residency. They continued working on Flaubert's play in New York. Yet as LeCompte told Quick, she could 'hardly imagine [the text] in [her] head, let alone stage it (2007: 56). The director soon realized she needed 'some other language' (56) to help her concretize the action. She selected Ingmar Bergman's film, *The Magician* (1958). Set in Scandinavia during the 19th century, *The Magician* follows Dr Vogler, a mesmerist and conjurer, and his medicine-show performers. Forced to flee Denmark in a stagecoach, the troupe arrives in Sweden only to be detained by the police. The town's elite demand a performance to prove that supernatural powers exist. After local officials try to humiliate Vogler as a fraud, he exacts a shocking revenge.

In an interview with Quick, LeCompte and Valk briefly addressed his questions about a motif that recurs in many Wooster shows: the undercover theatre troupe. For example, *L.S.D.* ends with a 'Shoe Dance' by a troupe of dancers impersonating Donna Sierra and the Del Fuegos. *Brace Up!* and *Fish Story* feature what Greg Giesekam described in an online review as an 'itinerant troupe of traditional Japanese geinin performers reduced to putting on ropey productions for tourists' (2008). Frisch, the dramaturge for *Route 1 & 9* during the 1986/87 retrospective, said this show ended with what most people viewed as a porn video: 'But in fact, underneath it, there was a whole story that The Wooster Group had made up about a down-and-out experimental theatre company trying to develop new forms of income' (2002b).

These performances-within-performances have a fascinating function as doubles. The company presents a troupe (dancers, geinin, actors turned pornographers, etc.) that is not *simply* The Wooster Group, but also an exotic alter-ego epitomizing what Savran describes as 'the "other" within the self' (1988:64). As Frank Dell, the designated leader of still another Wooster Group shadow company (the traveling medicine-show troupe from Bergman's *The Magician*), Vawter became *St. Antony's* multilayered centre.[17] He was at once the sleazy talk-show

---

17 An unpublished 'Glossary' for *St. Antony* traces the origins of Vawter's persona back to 1981: 'The Wooster Group's Frank Dell first appeared in *Route 1*

host, the tempted saint, the persecuted magician and a kind of Master of Ceremonies who kept the action moving.

LeCompte assembled these disparate lines of material, but could not get them to gel into a coherent stage structure. Frustrated, she shelved *St. Antony* and began rehearsing *Route 1 & 9* for the retrospective scheduled to open at the Kitchen on 17 November 1986. Yet shortly before that date, Vawter fell seriously ill.

According to Greg Mehrten, he suffered a seizure and then slipped into a coma. Mehrten was not actually present when Vawter lost consciousness, so he did not witness Vawter's seizure, but he repeated what doctors told him at the time. Recounting the events leading up to his hospitalization, Mehrten recalled that Vawter 'had been at rehearsal with The Wooster Group, and fell ill and came home' (2002b). Mehrten returned to their apartment after his own day out and found Vawter in bed, unresponsive. There was blood on the pillowcase: 'I called an ambulance and it was a horrifying situation' (2002b), and phoned Dafoe and LeCompte after. Dafoe recounted what happened next: 'I remember really specifically that they mistreated what it was, and they were confused about his state. It was a big mess, getting him to the hospital; we thought he was going to die' (2008).

Vawter was initially treated at St. Vincent's Hospital in Greenwich Village, and then moved uptown to Lenox Hill at Mehrten's urging, where doctors had several theories about the cause of his seizure. One theory involved an accident dating back to the late 1970s, when Vawter had fallen backwards from a high platform during *Nayatt School*; he'd landed on his head, lost consciousness and suffered a serious concussion. Initially, the doctors at Lenox Hill proposed that there had been some scar tissue that eventually had broken loose and caused the seizure. According to Mehrten, a more ominous hypothesis was that Vawter's sudden health problems were the first major symptoms

---

& 9, as the driver of a van who stops to pick up two hitchhikers'. Original programs for *Route 1 & 9* confirm that the driver in 'Act Four: Route 1 & 9' was named Frank, but his connection to Frank Dell was not yet explicit.

of an HIV infection: 'At the time, the doctors did say, "Well, it might be HIV-related". But we hadn't been tested, neither of us by then, and they couldn't test him right then for some reason' (Mehrten 2002b).

Ironically, the dire wait for Vawter to regain consciousness finally helped *St. Antony's* tangled storylines to coalesce. Frisch said The Wooster Group gathered around Vawter's hospital bed, and their vigil suggested the stage architecture for *St. Antony*: 'Ron in a bed, with everyone running around behind him' (2002b). Weems described what members did at his bedside: 'read him plays, talked to him and tried to bring him back to this world. That space—that level of dream life, and the social imagination of the company—influenced the rest of *St. Antony* very vividly' (2003a). At last, LeCompte began to imagine in concrete terms what Flaubert's 'un-performable' closet drama might look like. At the level of group autobiography, it was about Vawter's sudden collapse and near death. It was also about the company's struggle to come to terms with significant changes that accompanied his health crisis.

Although Mehrten said his lover could not be tested during his 1986 hospitalization, Vawter's mother told me she was informed at this time of his HIV-positive status: 'It was a blow, because there was no cure whatsoever. It was basically like the plague: a death sentence' (2004). Several Wooster Group members recalled that Vawter left the hospital a changed person. However, they offered diverse accounts of exactly what changed.

Dafoe said the adjustments made to *St. Antony* were minimal, and largely due to Vawter's diminished physical strength: 'If I remember right, the piece was basically made. It was just that Ron couldn't perform with the same vigour' (2008). By contrast, LeCompte identified his recovery as the most difficult phase of their professional history: 'I had to make *St. Antony* by myself, without him being able to speak. And that was very hard. I wasn't used to that; I was used to him contributing something. And he didn't. I could tell he was very sick' (2005). LeCompte's testimony conveys the painful complexities of Vawter's illness. It not only disabled his body, but also deprived her of what she relied upon most as a director: his incomparable ability to invent. LeCompte added that Vawter's altered state forced her to create material on his behalf: 'I made him front and centre of the piece, and he had to just memorize stuff that I made up, which is not my usual way of working with him' (2005). Reilly recalled the coma's aftermath as devastating for Vawter. After leaving the hospital, Vawter went on to face frightening new medical problems: 'He had all this stuff, like blisters on his mouth. His energy was so dark. His life was in mourning, going somewhere else, I can't even explain it' (2008).

The October–November 1987 programme notes for *St. Antony* (performed as a work-in-progress at the Performing Garage) broke the production down into six 'episodes', each one united by a morbid narrative about Frank Dell's impending demise:

EPISODE ONE (*the monologue*). During the last year of Frank Dell's life, the mood in the hotel room mysteriously changed.

EPISODE TWO (*the household*). He didn't look like Frank or sound like Frank or have any of the interests of the old Frank . . .

EPISODE THREE (*five hours later*). He was surrounded by a bunch of weirdos who acted like they were his personal slaves, and all he did from one end of the day to the other was to sit in his room and go over the tapes of his old shows . . .

EPISODE FOUR (*the show*). He didn't work and he didn't earn, and God knows how he put food on the table . . .

EPISODE FIVE (*post mortem*). . . . and once you had seen it, you never wanted to go back and see it again.

EPISODE SIX (*the next morning*). [no text]

By 16 September 1988, when the finished version of *St. Antony* finally premiered at the Performing Garage, the titles and summaries of these episodes had changed dramatically. The focus was no longer on Dell's failure to be productive in the final year of his life, but on tasks that Dell performed with other troupe members. For example, Episode I was now described in the programme as 'Frank works on an adaptation of a French closet drama targeted for Cable TV. He takes a call from L.A. on the videophone'.

Dell's adaptation referred to the company's spoof on the 'Channel J' nude talk show filmed in Washington. Dell's call from L.A. was actually Dafoe on video monitor. Dafoe played Cubby (a.k.a. Hilarion the Devil), who periodically called Dell from California to tempt him with his glamorous life. In real life, Dafoe spent much of 1987 in Los Angeles, working on a film by Martin Scorsese, *The Last Temptation of Christ* (1988). At the time, Vawter was also trying very hard to succeed in Hollywood and played minor and supporting roles in a number of films from that period, including *Sex, Lies, and Videotape* (1989), *Fat Man Little Boy* (1989) and *Silence of the Lambs* (1991), but had yet to get his big break like Dafoe. The notion of Dafoe/The Devil tempting Vawter/Dell with images of Dafoe's lead role as Jesus Christ was, on one level, rooted in the real and very disparate life circumstances of these two specific performers.

On the whole, *St. Antony* has a strangely disassociated tone. For example, the dialogue exchanged between Dell and other characters often juxtaposes poignant thoughts on death and the afterlife with wisecracks or bawdy talk. LeCompte did not write the dialogue, but she took credit for 'making up' some of the things that Vawter's persona had to say. During our interview, Reilly reflected on LeCompte's new role:

> It was the first time that Liz took on her own psyche, which I think can be very cruel. It was the first time we saw that; we see it again in *House/Lights*. She was trying to work that out. And I think it's great; it's honest. But I left that show. I was so cross and freaked out (2008).

Reilly quit *St. Antony* for several reasons, including her weariness of watching LeCompte struggle with Flaubert. Additionally, Reilly and Vawter had a terrible falling out while on tour in London. Without going into detail about what caused the rift, Reilly explained that the loss of his friendship was the last straw: 'He wasn't even talking to me at rehearsals, and I hated *St. Antony*, so I quit' (2008).

The production's 'major dramas'—sirens, blackouts, fights, bloody pillows—are painful to watch precisely because of their connection to events that Vawter suffered through in real life. In the NYPL video recording of a 1993 performance at the Performing Garage, *St. Antony* ends in chaos: Frank Dell attempts a final speech, but cannot tie it together; Onna announces the King of Sweden (who, in Bergman's film, saved Dr Vogler's troupe from disgrace); the Soviet National Anthem starts to blare. Suddenly, everything grows quiet. Even Cubby (Dafoe), the play's demonic figure, is alarmed. Cubby calls out for Dell using phrases that recall Mehrten's testimony about finding Vawter unconscious: 'Frank! Frank! Speak to me!' Dell huddles mutely at centre stage as Cubby's panic intensifies: 'Frank! Come on, Frank. Something's wrong!' Vawter/Dell abruptly leaves the stage without explanation. The lights fade to black. An exhausted-looking company, with Vawter at its centre, returns to take their bows. There is no resolution, no happy ending (1993).

And yet, for some viewers who were familiar with the show's offstage circumstances, *St. Antony* offered inspiration. Weems recalled Vawter's final performances in November 1993, when The Wooster Group staged the piece one last time with him in it: 'Ron could barely walk before the show some nights, and then you see him hopping around with his pants down in the third part. *That* was really transcendent!' (2003b).

St. Antony was reprised in March 1995, with Dafoe taking over Vawter's role. Dafoe said one of his 'greatest pleasures' was getting the chance to play Frank Dell. Significantly, Dafoe also linked this occasion to a seminal shift in Wooster Group methodology—the advent of live audio feed:

> We had a tour in São Paolo in 1995. That was the first time we started working with things in our ears. And I learned his speeches and rhythms, first by necessity, just to learn the show, but also to get the flavor to kind of reconstruct the performance. […] As we rehearsed it, I always had the tape of Ron in my ear (2008).

LeCompte had recycled discrete objects (props, images, bits of set) as early as *Rumstick Road*, but Dafoe's comments recall this moment as the beginning of a high-tech era for The Wooster Group, when entire scores were reused: 'That was one of the first times we directly stole from one performance in order to make another'. Dafoe described the experience of reconstructing Vawter's original score as 'very chilling, because certainly he was around, but he wasn't able to perform then'. Dafoe learned the part of Frank in March/April 1994, because the company was contracted to do the show in Berlin. Vawter was still alive, but too sick to perform in *St. Antony* again. Dafoe learnt the part, but before the Berlin tour began, Vawter died. Dafoe performed the part the following year, in São Paolo. His reliance on Vawter's recorded voice suggests that it functioned an embodied archive of sorts: transmitting knowledge, enduring as an audible presence, and somehow transcending death.

Major Sorrow: *Brace Up!* (1991) and *Fish Story* (1993)

In *The Wooster Group Workbook*, Andrew Quick reproduces several pages from a rehearsal workbook kept by Marianne Weems during the making of *Brace Up!* In that document, Weems reflects on a basic reason why Wooster Group shows often confuse critics:

> The error of almost all critical writing in relation to the work is the *identification* of the bearer of the message (i.e. Spalding in the first trilogy, Ann Rower, Ron, etc.) with the 'story'. [LeCompte's] history and many other elements are lain [*sic*] over the *top* of these storylines but the naturalistic elements are done *very* convincingly, which throws people (in Quick 2007: 69).

In a 1989 article by Daryl Jung, LeCompte offered her own perspective on the focus of her company's work: 'What we do is about my life' (1989: 20). Given LeCompte's statement that all of her work is about her, and Weems's account of layering 'history and many other elements' on top of a story line to create each Wooster Group piece, it seems counterintuitive to launch a study of *Brace Up!*,(a project based on Paul Schmidt's translation of Anton Chekhov's *Three Sisters*) by focusing on Vawter's role as Vershinin. On the other hand, based on interviews with Vawter's colleagues, it is clear that the gradual onset of AIDS and his decision to leave The Wooster Group had a profound impact on LeCompte's life and work. The title is itself an imperative to get ready, to makes plans, to summon one's strength: to 'brace up!'

The Wooster Group's online production history states that rehearsals for *Brace Up!* began in spring of 1989. According to Mehrten, Vawter learned his HIV status at about the same time:

> In 1989, Ron went to Los Angeles to do a film called *Internal Affairs* [. . .] and got ill with pneumonia. Anyway, he got tested there and was positive. He didn't tell me right away, but when he got back. So I got tested, too. [. . .] And out of some miracle, I was negative (2002b).

Meanwhile, Vawter's mother said doctors shared her son's diagnosis with her in 1986, during his hospitalization. As noted earlier, Mrs Vawter was in the early stages of Alzheimer's when we spoke, so her memory may not be reliable. Either Vawter's mother was mistaken, or it is possible that Vawter concealed his HIV diagnosis from everyone else, from November 1986 until early 1989: more than two years.

Regardless of when Vawter found out, part of his reluctance to disclose surely had to do with the stigma of HIV and AIDS. However, there was also his longstanding role as The Wooster Group's caretaker. For instance, Linda Chapman, who joined the company in 1983 as an administrator, noted Vawter's selfless concern for her feelings: 'Ronnie took me out privately and said, "I hate to tell you this because I know you've lost so many people already, but I'm HIV-positive". He was very apologetic' (2003). Chapman's life partner, Lola Pasholinski, a performer who worked for many years with Charles Ludlam, agreed: 'We were the ones who were supposed to console him, but there *he* was, trying to make it better for *us*' (2003).

When rehearsals for *Brace Up!* began, Vawter may have already been contemplating a break from The Wooster Group. LeCompte told Quick that she gradually came to view Chekhov's *Three Sisters* as Vawter's premeditated exit strategy:

> I think Ron knew he was very sick and, in his way, he was kind of preparing the group. [...] He wanted to do a piece where he wasn't the central focus, so that he could leave [...] and also because he wanted a piece that had more women in it. [...] So, as I recall, he suggested reading Chekhov. I'd never read any Chekhov [...] He must have known he was going to play Vershinin, but he didn't say anything. [...] I didn't know what happened to Vershinin in the play, I didn't know that he left or said goodbye at the end. (2007: 106–10)

In his final piece with the company, Vawter returned to the self-presentation that had framed his earliest appearances at the Performing Garage. He played a military man, Colonel Alexander Ignatyevich Vershinin. In a sense, Vawter left The Wooster Group as he had entered TPG. On a symbolic level, his early response to his HIV status seemed to involve a kind of onstage return to the closet: Vawter embraced the formal, rigid, emotionally reticent demeanour that had shaped his performances in *Mother Courage* and *The Marilyn Project*.

According to Weems, who was LeCompte's assistant director during *Brace Up!*, the production began as an experiment: '*Three Sisters* was something we came back to several times before it became apparent that that would be the direction to go in' (2003a). While researching the play, Weems found an auspicious photograph of Chekhov with his own sisters: 'The caption below the photo was "The Temptation of St. Antony". So it was this great transitional moment. And there were lots of little signs along the way that made Liz excited about it' (2003a).

Reilly and Vawter repaired their friendship privately. She initiated that reconciliation while touring alongside the company (but now performing her own work). Apart from Reilly, there were other women in The Wooster Group to whom Vawter needed to say goodbye. Early on in the video recording of *Brace Up!* held at Lincoln Center, Vershinin reflects on his relationship to the Prozorov sisters: 'Well, well. How you have grown. I remember three sisters, three little girls'. Romantic music and the sounds of birds chirping accompany Vershinin's remarks, both adding to and undercutting their poignancy. This subversive moment—so representative of The Wooster Group's aesthetic strategies—led me to reflect on Vawter's actual ties to the women of The Wooster Group: Liz LeCompte, Peyton Smith and Kate Valk. He had literally watched them grow up as people and as artists. In the play, Vershinin tells the sisters that people once teased him: 'They used to call me The Lovesick Major. I was young and in love. Now, I am not. I'm almost 44'. This was, in fact, Vawter's true age when the performance was videotaped on 23 April 1992.

The Wooster Group initially had planned to end *Brace Up!* with Vershinin's famous Act 4 'goodbye' speech to the sister whom he secretly loves: Masha. Yet in the Lincoln Center video recording, Vershinin's urgent bid to see her one last time before his departure is inexplicably deferred. In that video, Vawter's Vershinin earnestly addresses Olga (Peyton Smith), who plays Masha's older sister: 'I wish you all the best, the very best'. Then, he remembers the crucial reason why he came: 'Where's Maria Sergeyevna?' At this point, the Narrator (Kate Valk) abruptly whispers into Vawter/Vershinin's ear. 'That's all for tonight', she announces. He says nothing more.

Brace Up! ends without warning or resolution. Vawter/Vershinin's goodbye is interrupted and deferred. By contrast, *Fish Story*, first presented as a work-in-progress in Spring 1993, then continued and lengthened in the winter of 1993–94, is based on the final scene of *Three Sisters* and provides a more conventional sense of closure. When Quick asked LeCompte about her reason for doing *Fish Story* after *Brace Up!*, she replied that the latter project was again strongly influenced by Vawter:

> I was having so much trouble trying to figure out the style for *Brace Up!* and the text was so huge [. . .] So, we didn't really do the last act. When it came to *Fish Story*, Ronnie tried to get me back to what I had done before, which was to take either the last act, or a section, and make a little thing around it. (2007: 112)

Fish Story rehearsals spanned from February to April 1993. Yet despite his advocacy for a last act, Vawter only appeared on video in *Fish Story*, in the final scene. LeCompte acknowledged that he could have performed live in *Fish Story*: 'But, I wanted it to be like *Point Judith*—that was a goodbye piece as well' (112). LeCompte explained her reasons for saying goodbye to Vawter: 'Something had changed. First of all, he was making his own work outside of the Group and he was very ill' (112).

From the perspective of group autobiography, it seems significant that both 'By the Sea', the silent film that ended *Point Judith*, and 'I Came to Say Goodbye', the video concluding *Fish Story*, are mediated farewells. Film and video technologies capture live moments of performance, yet also transpose them into new contexts and temporalities, altering how and what they signify. In addition to the mediating effects of such media, other factors intrude on Vawter's goodbye in *Fish Story*.

In July 2008, I watched a video recording of *Fish Story* at the Performing Garage. Although I had read the script in Quick's *Wooster Group Work Book*, nothing prepared me for the manifold difficulties of Vershinin's final scene. Most notable is the deliberate ambiguity between Vawter's character and his own self-presentation. 'Olga Sergeyevna, we're leaving right away. I have to go', Vawter says in the video, abruptly followed by, 'I think it's time for a cigarette'. The latter line is not found in Chekhov, yet everyone who worked with Vawter recognized his ingenious ways of sneaking a cigarette onstage while in character. The question of who is speaking—Vershinin? Vawter? A hybrid of both?—becomes even more complicated when Vawter addresses the camera directly: 'The town gave us a sort of farewell lunch, champagne, the mayor made a speech, and I ate and listened, but my heart was here. I kept thinking of you. I'm going to miss this place . . . probably not' (Quick 2007: 155). At this point in the video, there is an unexpected pause. For a split second, Vawter's eyes appear to water. But then, he abruptly reaches into his pocket and pulls out a plastic vial: 'Let's try, uh, some, uh, glycerin. Oh shit [. . .] Yeah—all set' (155).

The tears that seemed real are quickly masked and upstaged by the highly visible fake 'tears' produced by the glycerine. As every Wooster Group aficionado knows, glycerine is was the in-house staple for simulating a tearful affect. In fact, Vawter had been the first performer to use glycerin onstage in *Nayatt School*: Performing as The Man, he played a sad record, applied glycerin to his eyes, and then 'cried'. Vawter presented a realistic emotional response, yet who would believe that his character actually cried after watching the performer apply fake tears?

In *Fish Story*, the relationship between fiction and reality, performer, character and persona grows even more perplexing. If glycerin is part of the script, why does Vawter pause to comment on his inept application of the drops: 'I think I put too much glycerin in. [. . .] Too much in one eye and none in the other [. . .] Do you have any Kleenex?' (155). From behind the camera, someone hands him a tissue. Quickly, as if embarrassed, Vawter wipes his face. Vershinin's poignant goodbye scene becomes perversely comic. Tears stream out of one eye, while Vawter's other eye remains dry.

Indeed, it is almost as if the gravity of the life material informing *Fish Story's* fiction demands sacrilege. Vawter had AIDS by the time of this recording, and would die in under a year, in April 1994. Fusing the sacred and the profane was an aesthetic strategy that he had embraced while still a student at Siena College. Irreverence toward classic texts was also a frequent tactic of The Wooster Group, so perhaps it made sense to honour and flaunt that approach when leaving the company. Or perhaps, like video itself, it was another distancing strategy, a way to ward off and mediate what was actually happening to him. In *Fish Story*, Vawter's Vershinin follows the *Three Sisters* script when he asks Olga not to 'think badly of me' (155). When Vawter performs Vershinin's lines, he does not look at the camera: 'Life isn't always easy', he says to Olga, 'sometimes it must seem stupid and hopeless, but we have to remember that it is getting constantly brighter, and I don't think the time is far off when it will be completely bright' (155–6). Yet Vawter the performer quickly undercuts this sentimental dialogue and grounds the scene in the materiality of video-making by chatting with the cameraman and looking at the camera: 'Am I moving in and out too much?' Vawter/Vershinin finally ends his speech: 'Well, now I must go . . . I came to say goodbye' (156).

In the video, Vawter/Vershinin and Karen Lashinsky/Masha exchange a prolonged, theatrical kiss. Their lips barely touch. Lashinsky looks more at the camera than at Vawter, who looks uncomfortable with his head tilted sideways. In contrast to Vawter's strangely heartfelt and heartrending speech, there is no passion here. 'Now, now, that's enough' (156), Olga says. With Olga's ironic comment, straight from Chekhov's play, the video fades out and *Fish Story* ends.

At the end of my interview with LeCompte, I asked how she remembered Vawter. She replied by referencing several forms of media that keep Vawter alive for her, as more than a memory:

> When I remember him now, it's always just as my brother who died. I remember him all the time because he's so present in all of our work. And he's around all the time, in pictures and videos. It's kind of hard for me; he's still very present for me. I think he's still kind of *in* the present for me.

LeCompte mourns Vawter's literal death. Yet her attention to how photos and videos of him live on in the company archive compels a rethinking of the relationship between media and mediation. At least for LeCompte, the media forms that preserve Vawter's work with The Wooster Group do not distance him from her, but rather make him feel present to her: through these technologies, he remains an integral part of the company. Vawter supported her unreservedly, and devoted a central part of his performance career to her vision, which included the use of multimedia, multiple texts, and multilayered storylines.

In late 1991, however, Vawter at last began a theatre project that did not involve LeCompte or The Wooster Group. *Roy Cohn/Jack Smith* (1992) marked a profound transition for the actor. Responding to Jack Smith's AIDS-related death, Vawter ended a two-decade career as a core member of group-based theatre to undertake a solo performance memorializing Smith's style and persona. In Chapter 7, I discuss the people and methods involved in Vawter's reconstruction process. I also assess the implications of his turn from The Wooster Group's traditions of mediation and obfuscation, to a piece that explained his motives and identified him as a person living with AIDS.

Reconstructing *Roy Cohn/Jack Smith*

In 1991, for the first time in his history as an actor, Vawter took a break from group-based theatre to develop a solo performance called *Roy Cohn/Jack Smith* (1992). In doing so, he slowly yet appreciably departed from The Wooster Group's traditions of media and mediation. Vawter's ultimate achievement in *Roy Cohn/Jack Smith* (hereafter abbreviated as *RC/JS*) was to perform as himself onstage. In what eventually became a three-part show, Vawter disclosed he was living with AIDS, explained several factors that led him to engage theatrically with the figures of Cohn and Smith, and took an unambiguous stand on a larger political issue that he saw as contributing to the AIDS crisis: society's repression of gay men. In what follows, I trace the evolution of *RC/JS* alongside notable changes in Vawter's working methods, starting with his reconstruction of Smith, turning to his portrait of Cohn, and ending with Vawter's addition of a personal address to the audience: his 'Introductory Remarks for the Performance of *Roy Cohn/Jack Smith*'.

Reconstructing Jack Smith

In 1989, Jack Smith died of AIDS at the age of 56. Born in Ohio and raised in Texas, Smith moved to Manhattan in 1953, making him a transplant like Vawter, who came from a small town as well. Estranged from his biological family, Smith found a new home on the Lower East Side: a gritty, eclectic and artist-friendly neighbourhood in those days. There, Smith became a costume maker, performer, photographer and pioneer of American underground cinema, best known for *Flaming Creatures* (1963), a film seized by the police at its premiere and judged to be obscene by a New York Criminal Court. Charles Ludlam, founder of the Ridiculous Theatrical Company, is widely quoted as saying 'Jack Smith is the daddy of us all',[1] referring to Smith's status as an early, openly gay performer who inspired many other gays and lesbians to express their sexualities via experimental theatre.

Despite Smith's reputation as a multitalented iconoclast, he also led a life burdened by poverty, paranoia and volatile relationships. For example, he was once close to Jonas Mekas, an influential filmmaker and archivist who screened *Flaming Creatures* at his Film-Makers' Cooperative, and also invited Smith to publish in his journal, *Film Culture*. Smith later turned on Mekas, repeatedly disparaging the older man in his performances, and accusing Mekas of exploiting him and his art. Having alienated many former supporters, Smith died poor and obscure, although fame would find him posthumously.[2]

Vawter began performing standalone tributes to Smith as early as 1990. However, those initial pieces underwent many changes, and Vawter did not complete the larger show called *Roy Cohn/Jack Smith* until 1992. That same year, during an interview by Richard Schechner, 'Ron Vawter: For the Record',[3] the actor hinted at why Smith's death had prompted him to interrupt his work in ensemble theatre, and instead branch out on his own:

> You know, I never wanted to have a career doing solos like Spalding [Gray]. I was very content to work with The

---

1 The quote attributed to Ludlam is readily accessible via Internet search engines. The late José Esteban Muñoz also references it in the 'Preface' to his *Disidentifications: Queers of Color and the Politics of Performance* (1999): xiii.

2 An account of the battle over Jack Smith's estate is found in C. Carr, 'Flaming Intrigue' (2004).

3 Schechner interviewed Vawter on 31 July 1992. That interview, published in *The Drama Review* a year later, is titled 'Ron Vawter: For the Record' (1993): 17-41.

Wooster Group, but after Jack Smith died in September of '89, I thought, jeez, I'd like to make something that memorialized him in some way. (1993: 17)

According to the OED, *memorialize* means 'to preserve the memory of; to be or supply a memorial of; to commemorate'. Yet given the one-off, undocumented nature of much performance art of the 1980s, what does it mean for one performer to 'memorialize' another performer's work? And why did Vawter feel that commemorating Smith was something he needed to do apart from The Wooster Group?

Perhaps part of the answer lies in Gray's statement that *Rumstick Road* offered 'no attempt to reconstruct the past' or 'in anyway create a gesture of memory' (1978: 87). LeCompte's focus on theatre's structural and audiovisual aspects led her to assemble multilayered scores that greatly exceeded Gray's remembered relationship to his mother. By contrast, Vawter's goal of preserving Smith's memory required a more concrete commitment to the historical past. Although Vawter began his research by working externally (looking at surviving vestiges of Smith's performances), what motivated him in the first place were the 'queer' (odd, intense, gay) details of Smith's personality. Vawter's effort to understand Smith as a fellow gay man and artist ultimately led to a more introspective process than the external, task-based work of standing in for others that he had undertaken with The Wooster Group.

In 'The Death of the Avant-Garde', David Savran credits Vawter with helping LeCompte to develop, perfect, and disseminate a 'house style of performance' (2005: 15). Savran argues that Vawter and his Wooster Group colleagues remade acting 'not by attempting to become characters but merely by standing in for others (to borrow Vawter's phrase), the ones who could not be present' (15). From 1977 until 1991, Vawter stood in for a broad range of others: real people such as *Rumstick Road's* Rockwell Gray Sr. and Gram Gray; performance personae originated by other artists (Lenny Bruce's Frank Dell); and many fictional characters. Yet even with classic roles such as Chekhov's Vershinin, Vawter did not attempt to inhabit those characters in a psychological sense. Savran argues persuasively that

Wooster Group pieces 'represent not impersonations, but, to borrow Joseph Roach's term, acts of surrogation' (2005: 15).

Vawter's portrait of Smith shared several features in common with his surrogate acts as a member of The Wooster Group. One basic similarity was Vawter's reliance on audiotapes and audio technology: tools that had previously facilitated (and mediated) his ability to 'stand in' for absent others such as Gray's father and grandmother. According to a programme note for an event titled *Jack Smith Revisited*, staged in November 1990, Vawter performed his original portrait of Smith at a May 1990 tribute in Amsterdam, both without the Roy Cohn section. *Jack Smith Revisited* was a second Smith memorial held at the Walker Art Center in Minneapolis. Vawter's contribution to the Minneapolis memorial was titled *Death of a Penguin* (1981). According to Sally Banes's 'Junk Alchemy', a *Village Voice* review of Smith's *Death of a Penguin*, Smith actually performed this piece at Millennium Film Workshop on 9 and 10 February 1985, and not in 1981 (89). The inaccurate date found in the title of Vawter's tribute suggests he may have confused *Death of a Penguin* with *What's Underground About Marshmallows?*, which Smith presented at Theatre for the New City on 9 and 10 October 1981. Penny Arcade, a longtime friend of Smith's, tape-recorded *What's Underground* on one of those nights, thus creating a rare audio document of Smith's largely ephemeral performance art. Significantly, Vawter used Arcade's audiotape of *What's Underground* as a starting point for his tribute to Smith.

During a 2003 interview, Arcade offered an important supplement to published accounts of *RC/JS* that largely ignore her contributions to Vawter's project.[4] Arcade said Vawter called her 'out of the blue' shortly after Smith's death. At the time, she was fighting to save Smith's body of work, housed in his Lower East Side apartment. When Arcade took Vawter to see the apartment's contents, he told her he wanted to foster Smith's legacy by means of performance. She welcomed his interest. 'Jack's never-to-be finished film was *Sinbad in a Rented World*', Arcade explained, 'and Ron had all these ideas about

---

4   All quotes attributed to Penny Arcade are from this 25 May 2003 interview.

building a ship'. Vawter's enthusiasm convinced Arcade to share Smith's archive with the acclaimed Wooster Group actor: 'I finally said, "Here". I photocopied a whole bunch of stuff for him, and [duplicated] a tape that I'd made of Jack's performance in 1981' [of *Marshmallows*]. In addition, Arcade entrusted Vawter with some of Smith's ashes: 'I had asked Jack if it would be okay to give his ashes to people whom he knew. And then I figured, well here's Ron Vawter, and Ron Vawter is Ron Vawter, so okay'.

Arcade's explanation implies that Vawter did not actually know Smith, but he was such a gifted performer and special person that she felt justified in gifting him Smith's remains. Arcade said she was wholly unprepared for what happened next:

> Jim Hoberman,[5] my associate in the Jack Smith archive, calls up and asks, 'Do you realize Ron Vawter is mixing Jack Smith's ashes in his eye makeup?' And I'm like, 'That's really bizarre. But it's not *that* bizarre. Yeah, that's not exactly what I had in mind'.

Despite her deep respect for Vawter, Arcade felt conflicted about assisting him in a project that others viewed as a transgression: 'I gave him that tape so he could familiarize himself with Jack Smith—not *do* Jack Smith!' Furthermore, she felt that Vawter's portrait distorted Smith's voice and persona: 'Anybody who knew Jack Smith knew he was *not* effeminate [...] Ron did this without knowing Jack Smith, and without ever having seen a Jack Smith performance!' Arcade's criticism points to an ironic yet overlooked aspect of Vawter's painstaking effort to 'memorialize' Smith—namely, its participation in the processes of mediation, transposition and representation that have always characterized The Wooster Group. Even as Vawter took a break from that company to immerse himself in the details of Smith's work, The Wooster Group's long tradition of transforming life material into theatre still influenced him. His attempt at preservation was criticized as an overly theatrical intervention by Hoberman and Arcade.

---

5   J. Hoberman began working at the *Village Voice* in the 1970s, and was their senior film critic from 1988 until 2012.

In his interview with Schechner, Vawter acknowledged his reliance on the audiotape, but did not say he got it from Arcade: 'I took a tape recording I had of a 1981 performance of *What's Underground About Marshmallows?* […] and I took a slide show which was separate and put them together' (1993: 17–18). Vawter added that he wore a Walkman, listening to the tape of Smith's *Marshmallows* whenever he performed the portrait. He described it as kind of a 'metronome' to help him maintain Smith's protracted pace of performance: 'Jack performed with a sense of time that I would never try to pull off in front of an audience. I can't imagine performing without the audiotape. Once, my machine didn't work and I stopped the show and got another one brought on stage for me' (24). In short, Vawter possessed technology that should have allowed him to replicate Smith's vocal rhythms. And yet, the general effect of drawing attention to this technology during his portrait (by clicking on the Walkman) was similar to The Wooster Group's emphasis on Gray's taped conversations with his family: it demonstrated 'the incapacity of the theatre to capture or restore that to which its signs refer' (Kaye 2007: 167).

It is impossible to say for sure whether Vawter ever saw Smith's work live. Mehrten recalls Vawter telling him about Smith's performances, and believes that Vawter witnessed some of Smith's work in person. Vawter attended scores of New York performances, and Smith's offbeat shows may well have appealed to him. That said, however, there is compelling evidence to suggest that Vawter's familiarity with Smith's aesthetic came from a range of outside sources: his conversations with those who knew Smith, the materials Arcade gave him as well as an unpublished dissertation by Uzi Parnes, titled 'Pop Performance: Four Seminal Influences, The Work of Jack Smith, Tom Murrin-The Alien Comic, Ethyl Eichelberger, and the Split Britches Company' (1988). I contend that Parnes's research also played an instrumental role in Vawter's ability to reconstruct Smith's work.

In the preface to his dissertation (completed in the Department of Performance Studies at New York University) Parnes drew a central distinction between 'performances documented and the reconstructed performance' (xvii). By *documented*, Parnes meant performances he had 'recorded on videotape' and for which he could create 'an exacting transcript' based on 'repeated observation of the tapes' (xvii). By contrast, Parnes identified Smith's *I Was a Male Yvonne De Carlo for the Lucky Landlord Underground* (1982), as an example of a *reconstructed* performance, meaning there was no complete audio or visual record of the piece:

> The author [Parnes] 'reconstructed' Smith's performance based on an audio tape. In part, this was due to this writer's lack of access to video equipment at the time. In addition, because the writer was also participating in that performance, he was not able to tape-record the entire four or five hour show in one complete sequence. As such, what is presented [. . .] is a reconstruction [which] attempts to fill in the lacunas in the recording through cross references to a tape of an earlier performance. (xvii)

In extant programs and interviews, Vawter never directly acknowledged Parnes' dissertation as part of his own research. Yet he clearly knew about Parnes' two chapters on Smith; a copy of them is held in the Ron Vawter Papers. In the first chapter, Parnes chronicles Smith's rise as an artist. In the second one, he undertakes the aforementioned 'reconstruction' (95) of Smith's *I Was a Male Yvonne De Carlo for the Lucky Landlord Underground*.

In Vawter's copy of Parnes' dissertation, someone underlined many details concerning Smith's stage practices. As if drawing on Parnes' vocabulary, Vawter began to describe his project as a 'reconstruction' in the program for his November 1990 Minneapolis tribute: 'Next year, portions of this reconstruction will be joined with materials concerning Roy Cohn [. . .] this double portrait will be entitled *Jack Smith/Roy Cohn*'. Moreover, Vawter applied Parnes's focal contrast between reproduction and reconstruction to his own approach: 'I'm not doing an impersonation, it's not a copy. I've created another little portrait off the surface of Cohn' (Schechner 1993: 24). In essence, Vawter recognized the non-mimetic yet externally focused qualities of reconstruction, and seemed at home with this method of developing a persona.

Of course, if Vawter never actually saw Smith perform in person, this makes Parnes' research even more significant. Having completed his dissertation in 1988, Parnes said he gave Smith a copy of the relevant chapters in early 1989, along with some slides that Smith requested: 'Since I documented *I Was a Male* extensively, there were many images of Jack performing that play in his slide archive' (2008).[6] Parnes added that he 'spent many years working with Smith and shooting countless photos of Jack from 1982–89', could be why Parnes copied chapters from his unpublished dissertation for Smith, After Smith's death, Arcade let Vawter access his archive and copied numerous documents for him. This may explain how Parnes' chapters came into Vawter's possession.[7]

Whatever the case may be, Parnes deserves credit for his scholarly role in Vawter's reconstruction.[8] The Ron Vawter Papers reveal that Vawter's May 1990 Amsterdam tribute was called *Rehearsal for the Destruction of Atlantis*. Like *Death of a Penguin*, which Vawter staged a few months later, the title came from a prior performance by Smith. In 'Junk Alchemy', Banes writes that Smith performed *Death of a Penguin* (1985) in a room full of youngish people (1985: 89). In short, Vawter could have seen this show. But he could not have seen Smith's *Rehearsal for the Destruction of Atlantis* (1965) because it predated his arrival in Manhattan by seven years. Parnes quotes at length from Banes' review of *Death of a Penguin*, and from Jonas Mekas's review of *Rehearsal*.

---

6 The email correspondence attributed to Uzi Parnes in this chapter was sent on 2 June 2008.

7 Parnes also lent his dissertation to the organizers of a Jack Smith tribute staged in 1990 at Lincoln Center. 'Arcade provided most of the material for that show', Parnes wrote in an email dated 2 June 2008, 'So it would make sense if the chapters went back to her'.

8 It could have been an oversight; Vawter did acknowledge other sources, thanking Arcade and The Jack Smith Archives in each new programme for his show.

Parnes' meticulous overview of these publications is likely where Vawter obtained the bulk of his details about Smith's performances.

In his dissertation, Parnes identified *Rehearsal for the Destruction of Atlantis* as Smith's 'first theatrical performance in New York' (36). He said it was part of the New Cinema Festival organized by Jonas Mekas, and belonged to the Expanded Cinema genre, 'a hybrid form just emerging that combined live performances with projected imagery' (36). There were also performances by Ken Jacobs, Robert Whitman and John Vacarro, but Smith's piece was 'the most theatrical and included a young Vacarro in the central role of the lobster' (37). Production photographs of Vawter's 1990 Amsterdam tribute feature the performer, bare-chested and wearing a toga skirt, confronting a man-sized lobster.[9] The lobster stands erect with one claw raised high in the air. Vawter faces the creature defiantly. He raises one arm, as if in parody. The script for Smith's *Rehearsal* was published in *Film Culture*. Yet Vawter's 'Synopsis' for his Amsterdam tribute did not draw upon that script. He borrowed only Smith's evocative title and the legendary lobster. Below is an abridged transcript[10] of Vawter's outline for that memorial:

'Synopsis - Rehearsal for the Destruction of Atlantis':
- Ship emerges from pit to Hollywood music
- Slide is already on as sail comes into position
- Chico is sweeping stage and eventually starts the slide show
- 5 to 8 minutes of slides [...]
- Sinbad enters [...]
- Death of a Penguin slide show
- Jack Smith monologue[11]

---

9 See Bob Van Danzig photographs, n.d., box 5, folder 2, Ron Vawter Papers.
10 See "Synopsis - Rehearsal for the Destruction of Atlantis." Box 4, Folder 28. Ron Vawter Papers.
11 'Jack Smith Monologue' may have been Vawter's working title for *What's Underground About Marshmallows*.

- After chopping onions: Maria Montez film list and Ibsen Ghost Tape and Doris Day Tape
- Ship sinks to final good-bye.

Vawter's reference to the 'Death of a Penguin slide show' suggests an even more direct relationship to Parnes's dissertation. There, Parnes discussed how poverty affected Smith's choices of media: By 1971, Smith 'began devoting his endeavours to 35 mm slides', since 'he lacked money for expensive 16 mm film stock' (55). During a funded trip to Italy, Smith took along 'a toy penguin found on 14th Street to which he added breasts and [. . .] many layers of paint and glitter' (55–56). In Rome, Smith shot extensive slides featuring the penguin, dubbed 'Yolanda La Penguina' (56). Someone, perhaps Vawter, underlined Parnes's account of Smith's slide shows. Meanwhile, in Amsterdam, Vawter staged and photographed scenes similar to the ones in Smith's slides with the help of the photographer Bob Van Dantzig.[12] He then projected these slides during his portrait of Smith. In one slide, Vawter's glittery penguin meets a real penguin at the zoo. In another slide, Vawter poses beside a Holocaust memorial to Holland's Jews. There are many slides of Vawter and Yolanda navigating the city together. A final slide depicts Vawter huddled alone in a doorway, the older Smith personified: a man whose tragedy was, according to Vawter, that he 'allowed himself to be marginalized' (Pacheco 1992: 8).

The backdrop for Vawter's Amsterdam tribute was a life-sized rowboat filled with Jack Smith-style treasure: coins, costume jewellery, and other shimmering objects. A rowboat is roughly consistent with the idea of a ship that he first shared with Arcade. His goal was 'to put together a 40-minute condensed evening with Jack Smith where you get an idea of his whole work: the kinds of projections he would use, the kinds of settings he would make. I wanted to give people who never saw Jack a sense of who he was as a performer' (Schechner 1993: 25). To this end, Vawter borrowed heavily from Parnes' account of Smith's *I Was a Male*. In his dissertation reconstruction of that piece, Parnes included a list of 'Maria Montez's feature films' (1988: 123),

12 See Bob Van Danzig slides, n.d., box 5, folder 2, Ron Vawter Papers.

180

recited at the end of Smith's performance to honour the dead actress. Smith's list is nearly identical to the one read aloud by a performer named 'Chica' (sometimes 'Chico') at the end of Vawter's portrait. 'Chica' functioned as Vawter's technical assistant. This character sat inside an Arabian tent at stage left, played some music used in the monologue and read the list of Maria Montez films. Smith had relied on similar assistants during his own performances.

The most striking resemblance of all, however, is the one between Parnes's dissertation photos of Smith's 'Dance with his Headdress' (111–112) and Vawter's closing dance with a veil. Parnes photographed Smith wearing a turban-like headdress with a long and billowy train. As Smith danced with the headdress, his assistant (Ela Troyano) sat in the background and 'kept track of the script' (111). Parnes wrote that Smith's headdress dance took place during the March 1982 perform-ance of *I Was a Male*. It is unlikely that Vawter saw Smith's dance in person, partly because he was on tour in Amsterdam from 16–28 March 1982, and partly because *I Was a Male* had a run of just three performances.[13] However, Parnes stated via email that he helped to organize a 1989 memorial for Smith at Performance Space 122 (gen-erally known as P.S. 122), where he presented rare visual documents of Smith's work: 'As I personally selected the images shown [...] I know mine were the only images of either *I Was a Male* or *What's Under-ground* that Jack possessed' (2008). Perhaps Vawter attended the P.S. 122 memorial, or saw photos of Smith's headdress dance in the mate-rials that Arcade copied for him.

At some point in the evolution of his tribute to Smith, Vawter dropped his original idea to end with a sinking ship, and instead con-cluded with a haunting veil dance. In the video of *RC/JS* filmed in February 1992 at the Wexner Center, Vawter began his dance by draping a diaphanous veil to cover the length of his body, then slowly

---

13 Parnes wrote in his dissertation that *I Was a Male Yvonne De Carlo* was 'scheduled to run throughout 1982' (91), but was cancelled in March 1982 after only three performances due to a disagreement between Smith and the owner of the club in which he performed.

revealing his torso. He proceeded to dance while whirling the veil high above his head. He fell to the floor, covering himself with its shimmering surface. At last, Vawter rose aggressively, displaying the veil a final time before moving to a corner of the stage while 'Chico' read the Maria Montez film list.

Parnes' attention to detail was the basis upon which Vawter could reconstruct otherwise undocumented elements of Smith's work, such as his headdress dance. Parnes' dissertation is a textual and photographic remnant of Smith's short-lived, embodied acts. Vawter studied and slowly immersed himself in the archival remains at his disposal, using them to visualize, revitalize and inevitably alter Smith's unique persona. Despite its shortcomings, Vawter's effort to memorialize Smith was arguably far more historically invested than any surrogate act he had previously undertaken with The Wooster Group—such as donning the grotesque mask of an old person while 'standing in' for Gray's grandmother, or wearing blackface during the company's take on a Pigmeat Markham comedy routine originally performed by black actors in 1965.

For Penny Arcade, the publicity generated by Vawter's portrait of Smith ultimately outweighed her concerns about his allegedly distorting and unauthorized use of materials she gave him: 'Because of Ron, we got attention that [. . .] the *New York Times* etc. would never have given us on Jack Smith alone. So it was a weird tradeoff.' Marianne Weems, who began working as a producer and assistant director on *RC/JS* in 1992,[14] noted during our interview that Vawter's portrait rekindled a widespread interest in Smith, who proved so significant to New York's diverse communities of experimental artists:

> Jack Smith was the root of so much of that whole Wooster Group, Robert Wilson, and Richard Foreman aesthetic. [. . .] All these people came out of the woodwork [. . .] and their deep, strong identification with Ron impersonating Jack

---

14 Weems left The Wooster Group in 1992 to found her own theatre company, The Builders' Association. During that transition, she also helped to research and produce Roy Cohn/Jack Smith.

Smith was really great to see. [. . .] Ken Jacobs and a lot of early filmmakers came to see the show several times. Many theatre people from that era really enjoyed seeing Jack's work revived (2003b).

Much of Vawter's piece was rooted in reconstructing the external details of 'this world, this universe' (Schechner 1993: 25) that Smith created. Nevertheless, there are also traces of Vawter's efforts to fathom Smith's troubled relationships, and his overt displays of queer sexuality in a culture (New York of the 1980s and early 1990s) that became extremely hostile to gays due to the AIDS crisis. In an interview with Stephen Holden, Vawter said he first met Smith in the early 1970s: 'It was around the time that I was coming out homosexually' (1992: 5). In 'Strange', an interview published in *New York Quarterly*, Vawter contrasted Smith's flagrant homosexuality with his own more cautious approach to being gay: 'He was the queerest thing I ever saw. I couldn't imagine being that out' (1992). And in an interview with Jessica Hagedorn, Vawter spoke of his reluctance to befriend Smith: 'I didn't seek to get close to him. He scared the shit out of me as a person' (1992: 48). Given Vawter's professed fear of the older artist, it is not surprising that his examples of Smith's 'menace' (48) all came from other people's anecdotes. When Hagedorn asked if Vawter stuck his tongue out at viewers to recreate a gesture done by Smith, he responded by quoting the late Ruth Maleczech: 'She said that whenever she saw Jack perform, he would just *look* at her { . . .] as if *she* had ruined the evening simply by showing up' (48). Later in the interview, Vawter quoted another performer who told him about a show in which Smith 'stuck his finger down his throat, and vomited right on [the audience]' (48). He added that Maleczech assessed his 1992 portrait as lacking Smith's usual contempt for the audience: 'You're being too respectful' (48), she told him.

By and large, Vawter avoided referencing or judging these disturbing aspects of Smith's public persona in his various tributes. In 1991, however, he began working on a second portrait, 'Roy Cohn', directed by Gregory Mehrten, his longtime lover and life partner. This

183

time, Vawter found it impossible to sidestep the personal and political challenges of reviving another gay man who had died of AIDS. No longer willing to remain neutral on the issue of Cohn's public behavior, and guided by more ambiguous archives, he and Mehrten diverged from The Wooster Group's foundational practice of using the performer as 'stand in', instead adopting a more traditionally mimetic and arguably more psychological approach to Cohn's persona.

Roy Cohn: From Reconstruction to Self-Disclosure

In his interview with Schechner, Vawter explained that his early tributes eventually led him to create 'another portrait that in some way balanced Smith' (1993: 20). Roy Cohn, a powerful New York lawyer, was 'such a different personality' compared to Smith, and Vawter felt that placing them together 'would make for an interesting spectrum of male homosexuality' (1992: 48). On the surface, they seemed to have little but AIDS in common; even in their homosexuality, they were worlds apart. Smith was defiantly gay, whereas Cohn stayed deep in the closet until his death. Smith despised commercialism and profit-driven art, which is partly why he lived in poverty, refusing to pay rent or electricity, and becoming increasingly marginalized. By contrast, Cohn grew up the son of a prominent Jewish judge and devoted his career to climbing through America's legal and socioeconomic ranks. Cohn was raised on Park Avenue in the Jewish Bronx, but liked to imply that he hailed from ritzy Park Avenue on Manhattan's Upper East Side. While Smith often made enemies of influential artists, Cohn often made deals with prominent people on both the left and right side of the political spectrum.

The TV image of a young Roy Cohn whispering into Senator Joseph McCarthy's ear had lingered in Vawter's memory since childhood. He recalled his uncanny attraction to Cohn in an article titled 'Strange': 'I didn't know I was queer. I didn't know he was queer. But I recognized something in Cohn that was like me [. . .] it initiated a haunt in me, and consequently I just followed his career my whole life' (1992).

Mindful of Vawter's tendency to compartmentalize parts of his life, it makes sense that Cohn's alleged duplicity intrigued him. Vawter often lied to loved ones in effort to shield them, or tell them what they wanted to hear. Prior to his 1986 hospitalization for a seizure, he went to great lengths to conceal his homosexuality from his biological family. Where Smith's explicit brand of gayness frightened Vawter, Cohn's keen ability to repress his homosexuality was more familiar to the actor, who spent his own youth trying to please his military parents by attending Officer Candidate School, earning his commission as a 2nd Lieutenant, and briefly getting engaged to a woman. Yet, as he performed these heteronormative gestures, Vawter met his first boyfriend at college and hid their sexual relationship from other friends and family.

As preliminary research for his portrait of Roy Cohn, Vawter began reading Nicholas von Hoffman's biography, *Citizen Cohn* (1988). Vawter admitted his fascination with a specific scenario described in that text:

> Cohn's chauffeur talked about driving Cohn—all dressed up in his tux—and his boyfriend to a dinner given by the American Society for the Protection of the Family. Cohn [. . .] gave this speech attacking homosexuality. That idea really might be fun, I thought, and so I just wanted to recreate that speech. (1993: 20)

Vawter's quest to recreate Cohn's anti-gay speech led him and Mehrten to collaborate with writer Gary Indiana and dramaturge Marianne Weems. Weems left The Wooster Group in 1992 and founded her own theatre company, The Builders Association, in 1994. During that transitional period, she also helped to research, create and produce *RC/JS*. During a 7 March 2003 interview, Weems recalled looking for a transcript of Cohn's 1978 speech. She spent months exploring various archives, but never found proof of the reputed event. In the process, however, Weems located an important article by Ken Auletta, and transcripts of two *60 Minutes* interviews featuring Cohn. Copies of these documents are included in the Ron Vawter Papers.

Auletta's 'Don't Mess with Roy Cohn' appeared in a 1978 issue of *Esquire*. At the time, Cohn was one of the most notorious yet powerful lawyers in New York, and widely perceived as immune to prosecution after beating three separate felony indictments. Cohn was indicted in 1964 for bribery, in 1968 for conspiracy, and in 1969 for extortion and blackmail. The third indictment was tried first, and Auletta described a brilliant courtroom performance that contributed to the legend of Cohn's invincibility:

> [Cohn's] attorney, Joseph E. Brill, was felled by a heart attack. It tells you something about Roy's Machiavellian reputation that there are those who believe the heart attack was feigned so Roy could offer his own summation. For two days, without a note, Roy delivered an eloquent, seven-hour summation, ending with a protestation of his love for America. Tears streamed from Roy's eyes and the jurors' cheeks. Then the jury was sequestered to deliberate. (1978: 44)

In addition to his formal acquittals, Cohn sidestepped accusations of tax evasion and even murder. According to Cohn's enemies, some of whom Auletta quoted in his article, Cohn the lawyer had no respect for legal protocol: 'He actually thinks it normal to be reprimanded by a judge' (44). According to many of his clients, however, Cohn lived to protect the underdog. Auletta ultimately presented a man full of contradictions: 'Roy's liberal, jet-setting lifestyle doesn't square with his conservative politics' (57).

Composing the speech that Vawter and his collaborators imagined Cohn giving unfolded in several phases. First, Indiana worked with the details in Auletta's article and the *60 Minutes* transcripts gathered by Weems. He often drew upon Cohn's actual remarks, incorporating aspects of Cohn's language choices and diction into his script. Mike Wallace interviewed Cohn for *60 Minutes*. In that interview transcript, Wallace urged Cohn to admit he was dying of AIDS. Four months shy of death (Cohn died on 2 Aug. 1986), the visibly ill lawyer (who was disbarred in Jun. 1986) denied it fervently: 'I . . . I ain't dying from nothing, to start with, number one. Number two, I'll tell you categorically, I do not have AIDS!' (Wallace 1986: 11).

Indiana never mentioned Cohn's struggle with AIDS in his script (Vawter's portrait of Smith also avoided any references to HIV or AIDS). However, Indiana did cite Cohn's explanation for persistent rumours about his homosexuality: 'Take this set of facts: bachelor, unmarried, middle-aged—well, *young* middle-aged. And then, all the stories go back to the McCarthy–Schine days' (Wallace 1986: 11). Indiana also quoted verbatim from an interview with Morley Safer, aired on *60 Minutes*. In the transcript of this interview, Cohn reflected on how he 'totally broke' with his background in the early 1950s: 'Here I was, a young Jewish Democrat from New York, supposedly one of the most liberal cities in the United States, going down to become Chief Counsel for a fellow like Joseph McCarthy' (Safer 1979: 19). Overall, Indiana depicted Cohn as vaguely ashamed of his 'true' self, and willing to sacrifice the more marginal co-cultures to which he belonged (gays and Jews) in order to please America's power brokers.

During an interview, Weems explained that Indiana's solitary writing process was informed by 'a series of dinners and endless drinks' (2003a). On those occasions Mehrten, Vawter and Weems talked with Indiana about the ideas in the script. When asked to compare 'Roy Cohn' to her prior work with The Wooster Group, Weems stressed a basic difference: 'We started with a script, and we stuck to it' (2003a). Mehrten, a professional editor, cut a third of Indiana's Cohn speech along with revising or adding to it. Weems concluded that working on Cohn's portrait was 'antithetical to the Wooster Group's process because it wasn't about layering; it was about stripping away and solidifying' (2003a).

The methodological difference identified by Weems is important to consider on other levels. One is temporal. Whereas The Wooster Group, to date, is famous for taking years to develop a show, Weems stressed that Vawter's HIV-positive diagnosis gave him a new sense of urgency:

It wasn't so much that he felt politically that he wanted to split off [from The Wooster Group] and do something more oriented around the issues that were really pressing for him; he felt that he had a very limited amount of time left. He felt like he didn't have a choice, in a way. As much as he loved working with Liz LeCompte and The Wooster Group, he wanted to do something that felt extremely pressing to him. And those were the terms in which he expressed it. (2003a)

The relative absence of audiovisual media in 'Roy Cohn' also relates to the difference that Weems identifies between layering and stripping away. Vawter's minimal use of media allowed him to complete his second portrait far more quickly than 'Jack Smith', since he did not need to find, assemble and manage multiple layers of slides, music and audiotape. Only two pieces of music played during the 'Roy Cohn' segment: One, a feisty, patriotic selection used to rouse viewers when Vawter-as-Cohn approached the podium to begin his speech; the other, played at the very end of the portrait when Vawter-as-Cohn invited his audience to join him in singing what he described as his favourite song, 'God Bless America', by Irving Berlin.

Although LeCompte and Vawter were moving in different directions by 1991–92, LeCompte and The Wooster Group enthusiastically supported *RC/JS*. Garage Productions was formed to help with the administrative support of the show. Vawter and Mehrten used the Performing Garage to rehearse *RC/JS*. They also launched *RC/JS* there while The Wooster Group toured *Brace Up!* with actor Paul Lazar now performing Vawter's score as Vershinin. Mehrten's 'Director's Notebook' indicates that rehearsals for *RC/JS* began in December 1991, and continued almost daily until it premiered at the Performing Garage as a work-in-progress on 24 January 1992. After each run through, Mehrten gave Vawter notes on what he could do to improve the show. In reading these notes, it becomes apparent that Vawter's greatest challenge was related to traditional acting, or pretending to be someone *other* than himself. For example, he resisted adopting Cohn's Jewish accent, or acting overtly gay. 'Don't be embarrassed at [being] Jewish', Mehrten wrote on 4 December 1991. 'More Jewish, swishier', he appealed on 2 January 1992. On 4 January, Mehrten noted that Vawter's Cohn portrait was still 'too negative at the beginning'. On 9 January, he advised that Vawter's delivery of Smith's line, 'I don't like to be fucked', not be 'confrontational'.

'What Ron went through to get Cohn's character right' (2002b), Mehrten acknowledged in an interview. A crucial turning point came when Mehrten asked Vawter to imitate Cohn's Bronx accent. 'I'm sorry', the director implored, 'but you have to listen to tapes and try to sound like him' (2002b). Initially, Vawter refused: 'His big fear was that the piece would be like *Mark Twain Tonight*. You know, an actor puts on a wig, and he's Abraham Lincoln' (2002b). Over time, Vawter learnt Cohn's distinct dialect. Nevertheless, the performer's abiding discomfort with impersonation led him to add a third component to the pairing of *RC/JS*: 'That's why he insisted on having an introduction before the play: to explain that the point was not how well he could be like Cohn or Smith' (Mehrten 2002b).

On a basic level, Vawter's 'Introductory Remarks for the Performance of *Roy Cohn/Jack Smith*', were a tactical response to Mehrten's call for him to act 'as if' he were Roy Cohn or Jack Smith. Yet what began as Vawter's reluctance to forfeit the non-psychological aesthetic he had crafted over two decades with The Wooster Group slowly evolved into a new mode of performing where Vawter did not 'stand in' for Cohn or Smith as he had done for much of his career with The Wooster Group. By contrast, Vawter did not simply stand in place for the deceased subjects of his portraits in *RC/JS*, but rather, stood *beside* them: relating to their extreme lives and some of their tragic choices. For example, although Vawter described his portrait of Cohn as akin to 'spitting on Cohn's grave', he nonetheless recognized aspects of his own experiences in Cohn's difficult story:

> I mean, I can say I hated the man, but when I went into rehearsal and permitted these things to come out of me, I connected to all sorts of things from the time when I was first coming out [...] in the early 1970s, when I was leaving

the military. Before then, everything I did, even though I felt homosexual, felt like a veil and a dodge: ways of passing. So when I began working on Cohn, I realized the tragedy of his life in trying to pass all the time. I connected with that, and it gave me a kind of sympathy or empathy. (Schechner 1993: 22)

Little by little, Vawter discarded the audiovisual tools he had previously used to stand in for (and distance himself from) absent others. Each night at the start of his 'Introductory Remarks', Vawter used only a microphone to share aspects of his own story with audiences: 'Good evening and welcome to the Performing Garage. My name is Ron Vawter, and you are about to see a performance of *RC/JS*' (Hughes and Román 1998: 456). He then introduced Cohn and Smith, briefly explaining their cultural significance. Finally, Vawter alluded to his private reasons for juxtaposing scenes from their lives:

I am a person living with AIDS, and for my own purposes, I've taken only particular aspects of their personalities and balanced one against each other [...] This is not documentary, but rather a subjective reaction, a response, to the lives of two very different white male homosexuals who had two powerful things in common: a virus, and a society which sought to repress their homosexuality. (457)

During a 19 March 2003 interview, Marianne Weems proposed that Vawter's 'Introductory Remarks' marked the first time he shared his theatrical motives directly with an audience:

Ron very carefully crafted that himself. And I thought it was ultimately the most interesting part of the show, because [...] it was really Ron enacting Ron Vawter as a public figure. It was the only time he ever did that publicly, in a performance. And the way he explained the show was also a radical departure for Ron because, coming from The Wooster Group, explaining *anything* is anathema to the idea of performance. (2003b)

Mehrten helped Vawter adapt and revise his 'Introductory Remarks', so the crafting that went into this section was not solely Vawter's own. Nevertheless, Weems is right to point out Vawter's stark departure from The Wooster Group's usual working methods. Indeed, *Poor Theater: A Series of Simulacra* (2004) constituted The Wooster Group's first-ever use of a subtitle to give audiences a hint about their intentions. Prior to that show, they had gone 30 years with no explanations. For Weems, Vawter's earlier disclosure worked on at least two levels: 'He came out as a person with AIDS, so there was a political coming out. But there was also an aesthetic coming out: risking to explain what the piece was about, and to unpack it for people before they saw it' (2003b).

At the heart of The Wooster Group's aesthetic is a paradox. On the one hand, the company is known for creating self-based performance personae, as opposed to staging fictional characters. On the other hand, these self-based personae are typically stripped of an individual performer's emotions—instead developed and perfected around a task-based, physical score. In LeCompte's theatre, the performer is ideally a 'stand-in' for many things and thus accrues many layers of meaning, yet rarely gets to share their multifaceted self. While productions often draw upon life events affecting specific company members, they also tend to distract viewers from a single, biographical interpretation, instead opening up the reference so that it can signify multiple things. In reflecting on Vawter's role as Vershinin, and his repeatedly thwarted efforts to say goodbye to Masha in *Brace Up!* (1991) and *Fish Story* (1994), I recognize the extent to which The Wooster Group's signature style may have constrained Vawter at that point in his life. At once originated by Vawter and part of a larger score, Vershinin hinted at the possibility that Vawter would use this role to express his feelings in performance, yet ultimately resisted any direct and unmediated farewell to the colleagues and audiences he loved.

Weems explained that as a lifelong Wooster Group member, Vawter was 'deeply, firmly embedded in a tradition of obfuscation. For him to get up there and be almost polemical—I think that, to him, was the most beautiful act' (2003b). Meanwhile, Schechner vividly recalled a moment during the introduction when Vawter lifted his shirt and showed his AIDS-induced lesions. According to Schechner, 'it was brave and horrific'.(2008b).

Vawter's HIV-positive diagnosis had been fraught with fear and shame. By contrast, his aesthetic coming out as a performer with AIDS was a brave and liberating act. AIDS, rather than having the effect of erasure that usually comes with illness, allowed the performer a remarkable script of vitality as he took centre stage and *became* Ron Vawter—finally himself, finally out of the closet about his HIV status, finally free to be direct, intimate and unmediated.

CHAPTER 8

On Endings (and Beginnings)

According to Norman Frisch, a former Wooster Group dramaturge, Ron Vawter's explicit wish was to die in the theatre:

> He said this to people, and he said it to me. Ron really wanted to die on stage. If you look at the rehearsal videos from the last few days of *Philoktetes-Variations*, you will see that he was trying to do that. [. . .] I'm speaking very literally now: Ron was staging his own funeral' (2002a).

Under normal circumstances, staging one's funeral seems like the height of high drama: a sumptuous way to find out who attends, and how survivors respond to one's death. Yet mindful of the forms of erasure that often accompanied the funerals and obituaries of those who died in the AIDS crisis, Vawter's desire for others to witness his death was a powerful act of resistance. At a time when artists with AIDS were routinely pushed to the margins, Vawter's reported effort to die on stage, his illness out in the open, was remarkable. Equally amazing was the flurry of new projects that he launched from 1992–94. This concluding chapter charts the performances, films and other initiatives that Vawter undertook during the last two years of his life.[15] In doing so, it is important to focus on why his aesthetics, politics and lived realities increasingly merged.

---

15 To make this project feasible in terms of scope and length, I will not discuss the many films and videos in which Vawter appeared late in his career (including several videos made by The Wooster Group) and have instead focused on Vawter's performances in the contexts of theatre and everyday life.

In the previous chapter, we examined *Roy Cohn/Jack Smith* (1992), an evolving piece in which Vawter the consummate performer finally addressed the audience as himself. Vawter ended his 'Introductory Remarks' by disclosing that he, like the subjects of his theatrical portraits, was a gay man with AIDS, an extremely courageous move at a time when people with AIDS faced countless forms of discrimination. Intertwined with his bravery, Vawter's last two years were remarkable in their irony. The man who was not a solo artist, who was so private about his gayness and his illness, became a subtle yet influential AIDS activist. Vawter's signature method of acting also changed during this period. For decades, he had relished the meticulous, task-based work of creating characters based on physical scores—even in college, with the Little Theatre, he had resisted trying to access a character's inner state. However, his work with Elizabeth LeCompte positioned the performer as a non-representational surrogate for absent others. This non-psychological approach proved integral to The Wooster Group's aesthetic, and changed experimental theatre as we know it today.

Towards the end of Vawter's life, however, the performance style he had helped to perfect became increasingly difficult to sustain. As his illness progressed, Vawter could not afford to 'stand in' for deceased gay men like Cohn and Smith. Instead, he gradually chose to stand beside them, to identify with some of their tragic choices, because their struggles and losses were also his own. In his 'Introductory Remarks', Vawter candidly proposed that HIV was symptomatic of an older sociopolitical problem: the pressure put on gay men to deny or suppress their same-sex desires. Vawter outlined the divergent lives and careers of Cohn and Smith, concluding that both men shared not only a virus, but a society that sought repress their homosexuality. He, too, had experienced their shame, their need to hide behind extreme behaviours that sometimes pushed away friends and allies.

Vawter originally performed *RC/JS* as a work-in-progress at the Performing Garage in January/February 1992. His full-fledged production premiered in that venue from 1 May to 15 June 1992. Greg Merhten, Coco McPherson (one of many performers who played

'Chica' in the Smith portrait[1]), and Vawter toured the show in Europe in 1993. They maintained a robust schedule: Brussels from 15-24 April; Berlin, 12–15 May; Frankfurt, 26–30 May; Vienna, 8–9 June; Amsterdam, 17–27 June; and London, 8–11 July.

Back in the U.S., a filmmaker and University of Notre Dame professor named Jill Godmilow worked with Vawter's producer, Marianne Weems, and an independent film company, Good Machine[2], to raise money for a film version of *RC/JS*. As soon as *RC/JS* opened in 1992, Vawter wanted to make a film of it. He asked Johnathan Demme, but after over a year of negotiations, Demme dropped out as director. (Demme had wanted to make a video of *RC/JS* interspersed with personal remarks by Vawter about AIDS. Vawter insisted on shooting the show on film as is). That is when Jill Godmilow stepped forward. Many factors impeded her desire to make a film of *RC/JS*, including funding, scheduling and Vawter's unstable health. Nevertheless, on 31 October and 1 November 1993, Vawter revived *RC/JS* one last time at The Kitchen in Manhattan. Godmilow filmed his backstage preparations, introductory remarks to the audience, the portraits themselves and audience reactions to the piece.[3] Godmilow's riveting and controversial film, *Roy Cohn/Jack Smith*, came out in 1995. Vawter approved the rough cut, though he died before the film's official release.

RC/JS was the by far the most famous and polished capstone of Vawter's work apart from The Wooster Group. However, he also became involved in other projects that explored canonical texts from gay and lesbian perspectives. Indeed, Vawter's commitment to gay and lesbian political theatre became much more visible after he came out

---

1 Pedro Rosado was the first 'Chico', followed by Clay Shirky.

2 Good Machine was founded in 1990 by Ted Hope and James Schamus, two independent film producers based in New York City. In 2001, the partners sold Good Machine to Universal.

3 Godmilow was sharply criticized by some of Vawter's fans for her decision to cross-cut and intercut sections of 'Jack Smith' with sections of 'Roy Cohn', so that the portraits spoke to one another. Some critics also disagreed with Godmilow's inclusion of audience reactions to Vawter's portraits, arguing that this interrupted the viewer's experience of watching Vawter perform.

as a person with AIDS. In 1992, he met the performance artist Karen Finley in Los Angeles, where she was presenting her *Memento Mori* installation at the Museum of Contemporary Art. Finley began working on this installation in 1991, as part of a festival titled *Burning the Flag*, focused on American live art and censorship, having experienced censorship first-hand as one of the 'NEA Four': four solo performers whose grants from the National Endowment for the Arts were revoked after Congress passed the 'Decency Clause' in 1990.[4] Art about sex and AIDS was often deemed indecent during that era, but several prominent artists, including Finley, refused to look away.

Later, Finley would explain during a lecture at NYU that *Memento Mori* was 'a grieving ritual for people who had died of AIDS or were dying of AIDS' (2002). Vawter had seen her installation at about the same time as she saw *RC/JS*. Inspired by each other's pieces, they decided to collaborate on their own queer rendition of Edward Albee's *Who's Afraid of Virginia Woolf?*

As noted in Chapter 1, Albee greatly influenced Vawter early in his theatre career. Albee's brash characters and their gradual yet striking violations of social norms captured the young man's imagination on some level. Finley said in her NYU lecture that she identified deeply with Vawter's need to break the rules: 'When I met Ron Vawter, I fell in love. […] I felt this transgression in his performance that I really related to, and for a moment I wasn't lonely' (2002). While they would go on to work together on commercial projects like the Hollywood film *Philadelphia* (1993), she felt it was equally important to work with Vawter on Albee's play—a piece staged only once—as a reading at The Public Theatre.

Finley also stressed how much Vawter loved having a new theatre piece on which to work. Both of them were aroused and revitalized

---

4 'The NEA Four' were Karen Finley, Tim Miller, John Fleck, and Holly Hughes. The 'Decency Clause' stated that the NEA must consider not just artistic merit, but 'general standards of decency and respect for the diverse beliefs of the American public'. For articles referencing this controversy and its outcomes, see 'Finley v. NEA' (1990); Joan Biskupic (1998: A01).

by the risks of altering Albee's well-known work, and were far enough along that they invited another pair of actors, Lola Pashalinski and Wallace Shawn, to join them as Honey and Nick (the younger couple) and Peter Sellars as the director. However, Finley became pregnant during their work-in-progress, and that put her on a different path than Vawter's own: 'It was a very moving experience. Here it was that I was going to be giving birth, whereas he was going to die' (2002).

Though he was experiencing AIDS-related complications by 1992, Vawter did not let that discourage him; if anything, he became more determined to secure new roles. Already known as nonconformists in the theatre, Vawter (as well as Finley) was cast in Jonathan Demme's *Philadelphia*, only the second Hollywood project to tackle the subject of AIDS (a TV movie, *And The Band Played On*, was the first one) and was inspired in part by the true story of Geoffrey Bowers, an attorney who in 1987 sued the law firm Baker & McKenzie for unfair dismissal in one of America's first AIDS discrimination cases. Despite undergoing treatment for a blood clot in his lung, Vawter spent the fall of 1992 working on the movie where he played Bob Seidman, a lawyer working for the same law firm as Andrew Beckett, the HIV-positive lead played by Tom Hanks. In 'The Non-Conformist', C. Carr wrote that Vawter was 'particularly pleased to be cast as a heterosexual. And uninfected' (1993: 35). Carr added that Vawter was 'the first actor cast in the first big-budget Hollywood movie about AIDS' (1993: 35) as Demme had known of Vawter's long career in experimental theatre, and had championed him as a lead in *Philadelphia*. Ironically, even as *Philadelphia* featured a character who successfully challenged a legal system that refused to employ him based on AIDS, most Hollywood underwriters would not insure the Vawter, the real-life HIV-positive actor on the grounds of his unpredictable health. Had it not been for Demme's determined support, Vawter would have been forced to forfeit this important role.

Philadelphia provoked a sea-change in public attitudes about people with AIDS. Tom Hanks won an Academy Award for Best Actor in a Leading Role, while Bruce Springsteen's 'Streets of Philadelphia' won Best Music, Original Song. One major effect of the film was that mainstream audiences finally saw people with AIDS as worthy of activism and empathy. *Philadelphia* also began a subtle shift in Hollywood towards more multifaceted depictions of gay men. Gay men began to be portrayed as committed partners, educated professionals and caring family members. For years, Vawter had aspired to break into Hollywood like his colleague, Willem Dafoe. Now, he finally played a supporting role in one of the most socially transforming films of its time.

As Vawter completed work on *Philadelphia* in late 1992, he became a founding member of the Pomodori Foundation. A tribute to Vawter's Italian heritage, *pomodori* means tomato: a robust, fertile fruit. Gregory Mehrten and Rosemary Quinn were the Pomodori Foundation's other founders. Their agenda was to develop vibrant, socially engaged gay and lesbian theatre. The newly minted company decided to stage *Queer and Alone*, based on a novel by Jim Strahs. Mehrten created a script by editing the novel. He also played the main character, Desmond Farquhar, who went on a sea voyage and met various people. Mehrten said part of the reason for staging this play was to have Vawter direct him, since he had just finished directing Vawter in *RC/JS* (2002b). Weems also came in as a co-director because Vawter was quite ill by then, and could not always attend rehearsals as the production neared its opening. In October and November 1993, Vawter and Weems co-directed *Queer and Alone* as part of the artist-in-residence programme at The Kitchen. Mehrten recalled staging the complexities of Strahs's plot, and noted how vastly his own approach to character differed from Vawter's:

> A lot of Jim [Strahs's] writing is about things that aren't true. People say things, and then you realize fifty pages later that this was all a big lie. But you're never sure, at first. It might be true. That's the whole thing about the main character Desmond: he's the one telling the story, and he's very unreliable. I tried to create a narrative that showed that process of making things up. [. . .] Eventually, I was in a hospital bed,

198

all wrapped up. There was wrapping around my face and then it was unwrapped, like the story unraveling, revealing itself. [...] Ron wanted it to be very unreal and non-naturalistic. But I really loved playing this person. It wasn't like *Roy Cohn/Jack Smith*, where the whole point was that he's not Roy Cohn or Jack Smith. I really did play Desmond. I wasn't supposed to be me; I really was supposed to be him. (2002b)

Whereas Mehrten fondly internalized characters, Vawter resisted psychological approaches. Instead, he built his career around precise physical scores and self-referential yet multilayered performance personae that undercut any direct relationship between the actor and his roles. There was always a distance between Vawter and the characters he performed onstage, no matter how much they seemed to resemble him. As he grew ill, however, the Wooster Group's hallmark separations between performer, persona and role became harder to sustain.

On 30 November 1993, during a run of *St. Antony* that lasted from 11 November to 5 December 1993, Vawter revived his role as Frank Dell for a video recorded by and in the collection of The Theatre on Film and Tape Archive at Lincoln Center. Although the actor appeared exhausted at the end of this video, people who saw the piece live remarked on his amazing strength. Weems said performing was at the heart of Vawter's self-concept; just being in front of an audience gave him the will to go on:

Ron was a performer; he wanted to be able to do his job, so it was almost like a pragmatic thing. Doing the show meant being a performer who performed, [and that] is what kept him alive. [...] [T]he last run of *St. Anthony* [...] was incredible! That show is so physical, and Ron could barely walk before the show some nights; and then you'd see him hopping around with his pants down in the third part. It was just incredible; *that* was really transcendent! (2003b)

Still in search of new projects to sustain him, Vawter began talks in 1993 with Susan Sontag, an essayist, cultural analyst, novelist, and filmmaker who had survived stage IV breast cancer in 1975. Joined by Mehrten and Weems, they began planning a piece they tentatively called *Dark Victory*, borrowed from a 1939 movie starring Bette Davis. In the original *Dark Victory*, Davis played Judith Traherne, a young socialite diagnosed with an inoperable brain tumour. At first, the character responded with despair to the news that she had only months to live, drinking heavily and exhibiting reckless behaviour. Over time, however, she realized that she would rather spend her remaining days with her true love: the surgeon who had tried to save her life. Weems described Sontag's and Vawter's approach to their own *Dark Victory* as 'a meditation on representations of death and dying in cinema, and some literature' (2003b). Mehrten added that *Dark Victory* was a project for 'me and Ron to act in together (after having directed each other), alternating the roles of a person dying and the person caring for that person' (2017). The piece included scenes from *Dark Victory*, *Uncle Tom's Cabin*, *The Brothers Karamazov* and other famous texts.

In spring 1994, Vawter and Mehrten travelled to Bellagio, Italy, where Sontag and Weems were busy assembling a script for *Dark Victory* at the Rockefeller Foundation's Bellagio Center. *Dark Victory* was one of two projects that brought Vawter and Mehrten to Europe in early 1994. They also travelled to Belgium that spring for the world premiere of a play titled *Philoktetes/Variations*, in which Vawter played Philoktetes. They planned to finish a run of *Philoktetes/Variations* in Brussels, then join Sontag and Weems in Bellagio, and work as a group on *Dark Victory*. However, that plan unfolded in shocking ways as Vawter's illness intensified, with his mental and physical state abruptly approximating that of the expiring Philoktetes character whom he portrayed. This junction between the actor's lived reality and his final performance warrants our careful attention.

Last Acts

While still performing *RC/JS*, Vawter asked John Jesurun, a New York writer and multimedia artist, to compose a section of a project he wanted to do based on Sophocles' ancient tragedy, *Philoktetes*. Jesurun and Vawter met in the early 1980s and knew each other's work very well. According to Jesurun, Vawter had studied Sophocles's *Philoktetes* in high school, and its details came back to him as he grew ill. Vawter provided Jesurun with the drama's basic plot, but also gave him great freedom to do his own thing: 'He really said, "Just write whatever you want. Whatever you write, I'll say it"' (2002).

In addition to the drama by Sophocles, Vawter planned to explore other versions of the Philoktetes legend. Mehrten said the resulting production, *Philoktetes/Variations* (1994), was 'always conceived as a triptych (Sophocles, André Gide, and Jesurun)' (2017). To clarify, Jesurun did not write the whole play—only his section. Mehrten added that Vawter initially envisioned a large, multimedia production with visuals by Leslie Thornton and music by Henry Threadgill. Perhaps based on his years as an administrator whose duties included arranging international tours, or perhaps due to the climate of arts censorship in America, Vawter sensed that European theatres were more likely to fund his ambitious project than American ones. Working with Jan Ritsema, an acclaimed Dutch director, was another way to generate European interest and support. Jesurun's section, more focused on language play than on literary traditions, entered into that mix. On his personal webpage, 'Philoktetes-1993–2007', Jesurun suggested other factors that drew Vawter to this collaboration:

> He felt connected to the character at this tenuous point in his life, but not only because of the obvious 'disease'. He said he came to me because he didn't want a gay play, an AIDS play, or a play about him. [. . .] He loved my writing and I loved his acting so the race was on—a thrill and a challenge.[5]

Jesurun's statement implies that Vawter began *Philoktetes* with the same detached approach to character that typified most of his prior work. He did not want to compare his AIDS-related illnesses to the wound of Philoktetes. His foremost concern was having another role to play. Yet Vawter clearly trusted Jesurun to explore themes and concerns that were meaningful to him.

---

5 See John Jesurun, 'Philoktetes-1993-2007'. Available at https://bit.ly/-2URNTbr (last accessed 4 February 2017).

At the heart of *Philoktetes* is a war hero who suffers a horrific infection and subsequent exile. In Sophocles' drama, Philoktetes was an archer to whom the great Heracles had gifted a magic bow and arrows. As a youth, Philoktetes alone had fulfilled Heracles' plea to set him on fire in order to end the dying hero's suffering, thus embracing the controversial ethics of assisted suicide that others in their community shunned. Years later, while marching on Troy with the Greek army, a snake bit Philoktetes and left a wound so putrid that his fellow warriors abandoned him on the island of Lemnos as they could not stand the stench of his injury.

Like Cohn and Smith, Philoktetes was cast out of the community that mattered most to him. New York's legal establishment disbarred Cohn. Smith died a recluse, alienated from the prominent filmmakers who had once championed his work. In each case, a stigmatized illness became a terminal turning point. It distanced men from friends and supporters, and stripped them of dignity and power. Though Vawter had resisted a play overtly about AIDS, there were palpable links between the humiliating exile of Philoktetes and the sense of abandonment that many HIV-positive people, including himself, experienced in relation to their government and society at large. Vawter clearly learned from the isolation suffered by Cohn and Smith and instead sought to retain the community that gave him a public identity: his beloved audiences.

Even in the last months of his life, Vawter still had crucial things to say to his audiences, but he grew too weak to perform using his usual techniques. Vawter's physical limits led to a final shift in his aesthetic: from theatre to activism, from scripted performance to sharing the realities of his life. The Ron Vawter Papers include an undated interview transcript titled 'Ron Vawter (The Wooster Group) and Frank Vercruyssen (STAN): A Dialogue on Acting'.[6] Near the end of the transcript, while discussing an unnamed performance, Vawter

---

6 See 'Ron Vawter (The Wooster Group) and Frank Vercruyssen (Stan): A Dialogue on Acting', Box 1, Folder 3, Vawter Papers.

confided to Vercruyssen that his mode of engaging with audiences was changing as a direct result of his AIDS:

> I had this extraordinary experience this week [...] for the first time in my life—because of my health—I had to cancel two shows. I had respiratory complications. So we decided in the next performances to turn the whole thing into a kind of documentary. I had to talk to the audience [...] and try to join the performance a couple of times. [...] I'm not sure that what I do now is even theatre. It's more social; it's trying to wake people up a bit.

As he had done throughout his career, Vawter adapted to change. This time, however, the transitions to which he responded were not those of an ensemble or its leaders; the changes were in his body. Long known for his readiness to take risks, Vawter now faced a profoundly poignant gamble: sharing his daily efforts to live and work with viewers who paid to see theatre.

At the NYU symposium, Jesurun said he tentatively asked Vawter if making *Philoktetes* would be too much for him:

> Ron was walking around very gingerly; he was turning into a wisp. I got very nervous and worried. I said to him, 'Are you going to be able to finish this thing'? He said, 'You know, we may not be able to finish this thing. This may be you walking me to the gate here'. (2002)

Despite what Jesurun described as the real possibility that Vawter 'would die during this project' (2002), he and Vawter continued developing the script. They met regularly to share ideas, and Jesurun wrote dialogue based on their conversations: 'We talked a lot about ideas, and drank, and drank, and adored each other in lots of ways when we talked about this stuff' (2002). Jesurun described their collaboration as 'a new way of working or being with an actor. You kind of walk along the path together, even though you do it separately' (2002).

After reading several variations of the Philoktetes legend, Jesurun realized he was in effect, writing an ending for Vawter: 'I said to Ron,

"You know, in some of these versions, Philoktetes dies". Ron said, "Just write whatever you want to write. Whatever way it goes, that's the way it's going to go". That was his attitude, and it really was a spiritual attitude' (2002).

By the time Vawter started rehearsing *Philoktetes*, he was too weak to stand for the duration of the play so he practiced his role, lying down in an open coffin. Vawter's delivery of his lines to Odysseus and Neoptelemus from this liminal space dramatized the anger and isolation of his protagonist, at once commenting subtly yet forcefully on the social stigmas faced by people with AIDS.

Changes in blocking made to accommodate Vawter's health also changed his relationship to the work itself. His longstanding role as a 'stand-in' for others evolved into a need to address his own circumstances: Vawter could no longer comfortably stand or stand in as he was now a performer suffering the tremendous physical deterioration caused by AIDS. As a gay man, he had watched in anger and sorrow as the Reagan and Bush administrations showed various forms of indifference to the AIDS crisis, focusing instead on defeating foreign armies. From 1981 well into the 1990s, AIDS meant social death along with physical death. Not only was there no cure, but people with AIDS often lost jobs, housing and relationships because others feared contagion. Vawter was fortunate to have supporters who loved him unconditionally. Nevertheless, he knew the challenges of finding safe and effective medical treatment. Marianne Weems, who was very involved in ACT UP (AIDS Coalition to Unleash Power) at the time, helped Vawter to evaluate his options:

> I went to many doctor's appointments with Ron: everything from a Chinese acupuncturist to radical ACT UP doctors. [. . .] We spent a lot of time on the phone and in person, talking about different treatment programs. That led to a larger discussion about communities and sub-communities, and what is available to different people in our culture. There was a whole political aspect of Ron's illness that he really started to unpack (2003a).

Most notably, Vawter faced the pressure and uncertainty of experimental treatments like AZT. In March 1987, when AZT first became
available by prescription, thousands of people wanted to take it. yet
many patients soon experienced debilitating side effects. Mehrten
recalled that Vawter wrestled with a decision about AZT, and ultimately opted to try it because there were no other viable options left:

> By the time we did *Roy Cohn/Jack Smith*, I think he had start-
> ing taking AZT, the only drug they gave to people back then.
> AZT was a horrible drug. It gave him all these bad side
> effects like neuropathy, which makes the nerves on your feet
> hurt. That affected his work with The Wooster Group, too.
> Not enough not to do it, but he wouldn't work as many hours
> per day (2002b).

Vawter's decision to start AZT reaffirmed his need to take a break
from group dynamics. The painful effects of treatment soon required
him to work on his own terms and schedule.

Philoktetes/Variations premiered at the Kaaitheatre in Brussels on
3 March 1994, roughly four months after Vawter's filmed revival of
RC/JS in October 1993. By the time Vawter flew to Brussels, he
seemed ready to acknowledge that his life was ending. This was a new
development in Vawter's approach to death, and in his approach to
acting. Frisch echoed Weems's sense that having new roles and projects kept Vawter alive, describing him as 'someone who did not like
to think about or dwell on death' (2002a). Yet the rehearsal tapes
recorded in Brussels signalled the actor's acceptance that *Philoktetes*
would be his last show: '

> Ron [...] lay in a casket at center stage, and I think he really
> wanted to die on stage during the run of that show. [...] I
> think that would have been his wish: not to die in a hospital,
> not to die in an airplane, but to die on stage. (Frisch 2002a)

Putting aside what some might view as its incredible morbidity,
Vawter's wish to die on stage was also a gesture whereby he ceased to
stand in for others, and became himself and only himself. In Jesurun's

play, Philoktetes' fate is ambiguous: even at the end, we are not sure if he dies or lives. By contrast, Vawter's performance inside the open coffin candidly avowed the future. Through that grim yet purposeful act, Vawter enacted his transformation from playing a role in a drama, to participating in a ritual on the cusp of life and death: his own last rite of sorts.

Vawter's trusted European collaborators, Kaaitheatre and director Jan Ritsema, honoured the way in which the actor chose to present himself on stage. By contrast, the image of a person with late-stage AIDS speaking from the inside of a coffin provoked anxiety among some of Vawter's American peers. Jesurun recalled his discomfort with the circumstances under which the show went on:

> Ron got very sick on the second evening. He literally was in a kind of delirium, and if anybody sees tapes of those performances, they're horrifying. This is where I found there was, as far as AIDS was concerned, a split between Europe and America. I thought personally that this director and the theatre were putting on a freak show. (2002)

Conversely, one might argue that Ritsema and Kaaitheatre were incredibly brave to present the realities of late-stage AIDS usually hidden in private rooms and hospices. The 3 March 1994 premiere was Vawter's only full performance of *Philoktetes*. Due to his failing health, Kaaitheatre cancelled the rest of the run. Prior to that time, Vawter had never missed a performance with The Wooster Group or of *RC/JS*. Jesurun noted that Vawter sometimes did readings of *Philoktetes* in the United States: 'The readings I heard Ron do were amazing and very quiet. For Ron, it was a quiet time. [I]f he couldn't act it, then at least he could say it. That was really important for him' (2002).

Jesurun's remark about the value of communicating with an audience, even if by means of speaking rather than acting, recalls Vawter's undated interview with Frank Vercruyssen, a Flemish actor. Vawter may have referenced *Philoktetes* when he told Vercruyssen about the changes made to an unnamed show due to his respiratory problems: 'I'm not sure that what I do now is even theatre. It's more social; it's trying to wake people up a bit. So many artists are dying of AIDS. This performance has a more decidedly political bent'.[7]

Dying on stage in Belgium during *Philoktetes* would have sent a stark political message back to the United States: that American artists with AIDS were forced to leave home for their deaths to be recognized as the casualties of a callous political regime. This was also the plight of Philoktetes: a venerable warrior until his infection, Philoktetes' torment over his exile could only be witnessed by others on Lemnos, far from his home in Greece. Apart from its likely political impact, Vawter's reported desire to die on stage makes sense on a personal level, since theatre had been the centre of most of his life. Theatre was Vawter's place of work and community, but also his site of self-transformation. Weems described *RC/JS* as a kind of rehearsal for the greater transition underlying *Philoktetes*: 'You know his whole thing—he used to mix Jack Smith's ashes with his make-up—as corny and superstitious as that is, I think it really was his intention: he was practicing crossing [over]' (2003a).

Sadly, timing foiled the actor who sought to cross to another state with his beloved audience around him. The rapid deterioration caused by AIDS forced Vawter to stop performing in *Philoktetes*, but did not end his will to collaborate. After Brussels, Vawter and Mehrten travelled to Italy, where they were scheduled to work on *Dark Victory* with Sontag and Weems. Weems explained the horrible irony of Vawter's arrival in Bellagio: 'He was in the final stages of dying, basically. It was really one of the most beautiful places in the world. But Ron was too sick to even know where he was' (2003a).

Although Vawter had been very positive throughout his illness, Weems admitted that his optimism finally gave way:

> He was afraid of dying. In the end, when he was very sick, it was terrible because he was really suffering. There was a huge amount of anxiety and fear there. But in the whole time that

7 Born in 1965, Vercruyssen identifies himself in the text as a 28-year-old actor belonging to a Flemish theatre company, tg STAN, so his conversation with Vawter likely took place in 1993.

we were making *Roy Cohn/Jack Smith*, he was very loving about the whole thing, very embracing and accepting. That enactment was a kind of rehearsal for him (2003a).

Mehrten and Vawter spent about ten days in Bellagio with Sontag and Weems. They all hoped Vawter would recover, but he only grew more ill. Weems recalled taking him to a hospital in Milan, where The Rockefeller Foundation paid for him to go home on a hospital plane. Mehrten's personal friends, Cherie Fortis and Gregory Turner, arranged to meet Vawter's plane at the airport. Weems also notified The Wooster Group of Vawter's emergency flight: 'Kate [Valk] was supposed to call me and tell me that everything was fine' (Weems 2003b).

Sadly, Weems never received Valk's phone call, and Vawter never made it home to New York. Richard Schechner explained the heart-breaking details of Vawter's death in his TDR eulogy for the actor: 'On 16 April 1994, [Ron] died on a Swiss Air flight from Milan to New York. He was being transported under strict medical supervision. Next to him when he died was his longtime partner and artistic collaborator, Greg Mehrten' (1995: 11). Schechner added, 'Ron [. . .] worked intensely until almost the moment of his passing' (11).

The Wooster Group's archive includes condolences sent to the company after Vawter's death. Among the cards and letters there, one message stood out. It was a fax from Marianne Weems, still in Bellagio, writing to express her grief at Vawter's passing, and to recount his final days. In her fax, Weems recalled how urgently Vawter had wanted to go home. Slipping between clarity and dementia, he said calmly, 'I think it might be time . . . to retire'. At the hospital in Milan, as medical staff prepared him to board the plane bound for New York, Weems whispered 'Ronnie' and stroked his forehead. Vawter briefly opened his eyes. At last, on the tarmac, he finally seemed relieved.

Knowing all along how Vawter's story ends, there is little comfort in closure. In reflecting on what I have learned about Vawter in the years since I first began this research project, I would say, ironically, that some of my own key claims about Vawter are ones he might reject.

Though I provide strong evidence throughout this book for Vawter's role as an unsung hero of both The Performance Group and The Wooster Group, he would surely resist taking credit away from his collaborators, particularly Schechner and LeCompte. Vawter would not call himself a shadow governor, even though he played an influential administrative role in both companies. Instead of seeking to stand out, I suspect Vawter would take the greatest pride in being known as a team player: someone who did his part, and who wore his multiple hats very well.

Perhaps most of all, Vawter would want to be remembered as an artist who took a stance on the some of the burning sociopolitical issues of his time. From the Vietnam War protests that Vawter led while in college to leaving the Army and coming out as a gay man; from his enthusiasm for joining Schechner's environmental theatre revolution to the impassioned critiques and debates that The Wooster Group ignited when they donned blackface together as part of their first, fumbling efforts to explore their complicity in American racism; from his unwavering support of women in the theatre to his final projects addressing American homophobia and dehumanizing treatment of people with AIDS, Vawter did not stay silent. He championed underdogs, valued listening to others, and seemed to view theatre-making as a combination of technical, intellectual, and embodied research. Much like LeCompte, Vawter did not chase commercial success, privileging enduring exploration over critical acclaim—and would likely have remained with The Wooster Group until today had AIDS not redirected his life and altered his sense of urgency.

Today, more than 20 years after Vawter's death, his willingness to take risks and to use art for advancing dialogue about controversial issues still is of vital importance. Just as his work in theatre and film continues to be relevant to many communities, his offstage life matters, too. Known for developing an enduring performance aesthetic as a 'stand-in' or surrogate for absent others, it is painfully poignant to realize that Vawter can never be replaced. We can, however, honour, remember and further analyse the import of Vawter's remarkable life in performance.

References

ADCOCK, Joe. 1978. '*Rumstick Road* Is Superb'. *Philadelphia Evening Bulletin* (28 January).

ALBEE, Edward. 1980. *Who's Afraid of Virginia Woolf?* New York: Antheneum.

———. 2004. *The Collected Plays of Edward Albee*, Volume 1. New York: Overlook.

ARRATIA, Euridice. 1992. 'Island Hopping; Rehearsing The Wooster Group's *Brace Up!*' *The Drama Review* 36(4): 121-42.

ASCHEIM, Skip. 1984. 'Acid Reign'. *The Tab* (2 May), p. 24.

AUGERI ROWE, Jo Ann. 1984. 'L.S.D. is Worth the Trip'. *Daily Evening Item*, (20 April).

AULETTA, Ken. 1978. 'Don't Mess With Roy Cohn'. *Esquire Magazine*, (5 December), p. 39–60.

AUSLANDER, Philip. 1992. 'L.S.D. from the Crucible: The Wooster Group'. *Presence and Resistance: Postmodernism and Cultural Politics in Contemporary American Performance*. Ann Arbor: University of Michigan Press, pp. 83–104.

———. 1997. 'Task and Vision: Willem Dafoe in *LSD*'. *From Acting to Performance: Essays in Modernism and Postmodernism*. New York and London: Routledge, pp. 39-45.

———. 2005. 'Performance as Therapy: Spalding Gray's Autopathographic Monologues', in Carrie Sandahl and Philip Auslander (eds), *Bodies in Commotion: Disability and Performance*. Ann Arbor: University of Michigan Press, pp. 163-74.

BANES, Sally. 1985. 'Junk Alchemy'. *Village Voice*, 19 March, p. 89.

BARLOW, Helen. 1995. 'Curtain Call'. *HQ Magazine* (July–August), p. 34–6.

BEER, John. 2009. 'Five Minutes with Kate Valk'. *Time Out Chicago*, 8-14 January. Formerly available at http://bit.ly/2Y5Zh6l (last accessed on 5 February 2009; page no longer exists).

BELL, Phaedra. 2005. 'Fixing the TV: Televisual Geography in the Wooster Group's *Brace Up!*' *Modern Drama* (48)3: 565–84.

BERGMAN, Ingmar (director). 1958. *The Magician (Ansiktet)*. 1958. Film. Criterion Collection Blu-Ray, 2015.

BERRY, William Jan and Dean Ormsby Torrence. 1963. 'Dead Man's Curve'. From *Surf City/Dead Man's Curve*. Available at http://bit.ly/2YSWryJ (last accessed 7 September 2015).

BESONEN, Julie. 'The Accidental Actor: Late Bloomer Ron Vawter'. Box 1, Folder 9. Ron Vawter Papers. Billy Rose Theatre Collection. New York Public Library for the Performing Arts.

BIERMAN, James. 1979. 'Three Places in Rhode Island'. *The Drama Review* 23(1): 13-30.

BISKUPIC, Joan. 1998. ' "Decency" Can Be Weighed in Arts Agency's Funding'. *Washington Post* (26 June), pp A01.

BRECHT, Bertolt. 1977 [1964]. 'A Short Organum for the Theatre', in John Willett (ed. and trans.), *Brecht on Theatre: The Development of an Aesthetic*. New York: Hill and Wang, pp.179-205.

BREUER, Lee. 1977. 'Guest View: The Actor Evolves'. *Soho Weekly News*, 7 July.

BURIAN, Jarka M. 1956–1991. 'Marat Sade, Peter Weiss, November 1972', Series 1: Play Files, 1956-1991, Box 1, Jarka M. Burian Papers, State University of New York, Albany.

BURKE, Roberta. 1974. 'NFA Graduate Returns with Theatre Group'. *Norwich Bulletin* 4 July, p. 6.

CALI, Joseph. 1969. 'VM Days Stress Local Action'. *The Indian,* 12 November, p. 1, 5.

CAMPBELL, Dan. 1969. 'Masterful and Powerful Acting Characterizes *Luther*'. *The Indian,* 4 November, p. 3.

CARLOMUSTO, Jean. 2000. Panel discussion at 'Fever in the Archive': An Exhibition of AIDS Activist Videotapes from the Royal S. Marks Collection of the New York Public Library. New York, NY, 6 December.

CARR, C. 1993. 'The Non-Conformist'. *Village Voice* (27 April), pp. 35–8.

———. 2004. 'Flaming Intrigue'. *Village Voice* (2 March). Available at http://bit.ly/2Y5ByDu (last accessed 15 August 2015).

CASEY, Neil. 2011. 'Spalding Gray's Tortured Soul'. *New York Times* (6 October). Available at https://nyti.ms/2JCYtg0 (last accessed 4 January 2016).

CLAY, Carolyn. 1984. 'Everybody Must Get Stoned'. *Boston Phoenix* (1 May), Sec. 3, p. 6.

COE, Robert. 1978. 'Making Two Lives and a Trilogy'. *Village Voice,* 11 December, p. 119–21.

EDER, Richard. 1978. 'Spalding Gray's Youth'. *New York Times* 19 December, p. C7.

FALK, Florence. 1978. 'Autobiographical Theatre'. *Soho Weekly News* (1 June), p. 21.

FEINER, Marjorie. 1972. 'Sade Play at SUNYA a Horror Story of Insane'. *Knickerbocker News,* 21 October, p. 7A.

FEINGOLD, Michael. 1978. 'Plainclothes Naturalism'. *Village Voice* 3 April, p. 73.

'FINLEY V. NEA'. 1990. Center for Constitutional Rights. Available at http://bit.ly/2ShYSbF (last accessed on 24 January 2017).

FOX, Terry Curtis. 1978. *Cops: A Full Length Drama.* New York: Samuel French Inc.

GAARD, David. '*The Marilyn Project* 1974–1975, 2004'. Box 9, Folder 4. Gaard (David) Theatrical Works and Short Stories Collection. Online Archive of California. California Digital Library.

GENET, Jean. 1962. *The Balcony*. (Bernard Frechtman, trans). New York: Grove Press.

GIESEKAM, Greg. 2008. Review of The Wooster Group Workbook, by Andrew Quick. *Times Higher Education*. Available at http://bit.ly/30C5lB8 (last accessed on 5 August 2015).

GOFFMAN, Erving. 1959. *The Presentation of the Self in Everyday Life*. New York: Doubleday.

GORDON, John B. 1980. Review of *The Balcony*, by Jean Genet, as performed by The Performance Group, New York. *Theatre Journal* 32(2): 264–5.

'GRAY Areas: More Angry Words on *Route 1 & 9*'. 1987. *Village Voice* 27 January, p. 87.

GRAY, Spalding. 1978. 'Playwright's Notes'. *Performing Arts Journal* 3(2): 87–91.

———. 1979. 'About Three Places in Rhode Island'. *The Drama Review:* 23(1): 31-42.

GRAY, Spalding and Elizabeth LeCompte. 1978. 'Play: *Rumstick Road*'. *Performing Arts Journal* 3(2): 92-115.

GUSSOW, Mel. 1984. 'Theatre: *Pretty Boy* and a Beckett'. *New York Times* 15 June, p. C3.

HARRIS, William. 1977. 'Looking At One's Self'. *Soho Weekly News*, (14 April).

HAYES, Edward. 1972. 'Marat: Interesting and Well-Done'. *Albany Student Press*, 27 October, p. 1A.

HERBERT, John. 1967. *Fortune and Men's Eyes*. New York: Grove Press.

HOBERMAN, J. 1979. 'The Theatre of Jack Smith'. *The Drama Review* 23(1): 3-12.

HOFFMAN, Ted. 1978. 'The Ineluctable Word-of-Mouth'. *Villager,* 6 April, p. 13.

HOLDEN, Stephen. 1992. 'Two Strangers Meet through an Actor'. *New York Times,* 3 May 1992, Sec. 2, p. 5+.

Indian, The. 1967. 'Little Theatre Schedules One-Act Plays This Week'. *The Indian,* 5 December, pp. 6, 9.

Indian, The. 1969. 'Little Theatre Presents Melodrama: *The Drunkard*. *The Indian,* 18 February, p. 3.

INSTITUTE FOR ADVANCED TECHNOLOGY IN THE HUMANITIES (IATH). 1998–-2012. '*The Drunkard*. U of Virginia. Available at https://at.virginia.edu/2JC3bMo (last accessed on 20 February 2013).

JESURUN, John. 'Philoktetes-1993-2007'. Available at http://bit.ly/2Sg6pYE (last accessed on 4 February 2017).

Jesurun, John. 1993. *Philoktetes*. Collection of Theresa Smalec, New Jersey.

JONES, John Bush. 1984. 'L.S.D.: The Theatre as a High Time'. *Patriot Ledger* (21 April), p. 13.

JUNG, Daryl. 1989. 'The Wooster Group: New York's Icon-Smashing Performance Artists Launch Quay Works'. *NOW: Toronto's Weekly News and Entertainment Voice* January–February, p. 20.

KAYE, Nick. 2007. 'Multiplication: The Wooster Group'. *Multi-Media: Video—Installation—Performance.* New York: Routledge, pp. 164-180.

KELLY, Martin P. 1969a. 'Area Productions and Tryouts'. *Albany Times-Union,* 21 February, p. 26.

——. 1969b. 'Siena Little Theatre Offers Osborne's *Luther*'. *Albany Times-Union,* 1 November, p. 3.

——. 1971. 'Siena Play Lacks Cohesive Fire'. *Albany Times-Union,* 20 March, p. 6.

——. 1985. 'Colonie Native Recognized with Obie'. *Albany Times-Union* (27 May), p. A5.

KIRBY, Michael, (ed.). 1965. *Happenings: An Illustrated Anthology*. New York: E.P. Dutton & Co.

KOLIN, Philip C. 2005. 'Albee's Early One-Act Plays: "A New American Playwright from Whom Much Is to Be Expected"' in Stephen Bottoms (ed.), *The Cambridge Companion to Edward Albee*. New York: Cambridge University Press, pp. 16–37.

LAUTMAN, Joan. 1984. 'High Times at the Theatre'. *Boston Ledger* 23–30 April.

LECOMPTE, Elizabeth. 1978. 'An Introduction'. *Performing Arts Journal* 3(2): 81–6.

——(director). 1979. 'The Fifth Examination of the Text: "The Cocktail Party"', from *Nayatt School*. Filmed by Ken Kobland; New York.. DVD.

——. 1981a. 'Always Starting New: Elizabeth LeCompte'. Interview by Lenora Champagne. *The Drama Review* 25(3): 19–28.

——(director). 1979. 'By the Sea', from *Point Judith*. Film. Filmed by Ken Kobland; New London, Connecticut.

——. 1981b. 'Point Judith'. *Zone* Spring-Summer: 14–27.

——(director). 1992. *Brace Up!* Performing Garage, New York. Video recording of a live performance .Theatre on Film and Tape Archive, 23 April.

——(director). 1993. *Frank Dell's The Temptation of St. Antony*. Video recording of a live performance. Performing Garage, New York. Theatre on Film and Tape Archive, 30 November.

——(director). *Fish Story*. 1994. Video recording of a live performance. Performing Garage, New York.

LEVERETT, James. 1978. 'Mapping Rhode Island'. *Soho Weekly News* (21 December), p. 71.

LOH, Jennifer. 2011. ' "Borrowing" Religious Identifications: A Study of Religious Practices among the Hijras of India. *The SOAS Journal of Graduate Research* 3 (March). Available at http://bit.ly/2SfgQLW (last accessed on 16 July 2019).

LUFT, Friedrich. 1986. 'Review of *The Zoo Story*, 1959' in C. Kolin and J. Madison Davis (eds), *Critical Essays on Edward Albee*. Boston: G.K. Hall & Co., p. 41.

MANCINI, John. 1990. 'The Elite Indiana Rangers Were the Only National Guard Infantry Unit to Fight in the Vietnam War'. *Vietnam* (June): 68.

MARRANCA, Bonnie. 1975. 'Mirroring the Marilyn Mystique'. *(Weekly News* 25 December).

———. 2003. 'The Wooster Group: A Dictionary of Ideas'. *PAJ* 25(2): 1-18.

MEHRTEN, Gregory. 1984. 'Pretty Boy script: Final Version'. Box 3, Folder 8. Ron Vawter Papers. Billy Rose Theatre Division. New York Public Library for the Performing Arts.

———. 1991. 'Director's Notebook'. Box 4, Folder 12. Ron Vawter Papers. Billy Rose Theatre Division. New York Public Library for the Performing Arts.

MILVY, Erika. 1992. 'Cohn Do'. *Variety Fair* (June), p. 88.

MYDELL, Joseph. 1977. 'Performing Garage Digs Environmental Dirt as Seneca's *Oedipus* Buries Sophocles". *Villager* 8 December, p. 19.

NASON, Richard. 1978. 'Mega-Realism in the Precinct: Smashing Shootout Caps *Cops*'. *Villager* (30 March), p. 15.

OSBORNE, John. 1961. *Luther.* London: Faber and Faber.

PACHECO, Patrick. 1992. 'Self-Hate Crimes'. *Los Angeles Times* 2 August 1992, p. 8+.

PARNES, Uzi. 1988. 'Pop Performance: Four Seminal Influences, The Work of Jack Smith, Tom Murrin-The Alien Comic, Ethyl

Eichelberger, and the Split Britches Company'. Doctoral Dissertation, New York University.

PERFORMANCE GROUP. 1970. *Commune*, in Arthur Sainer (ed.), *The New Radical Theatre Notebook*. New York: Applause Books, 1997. pp. 128-61.

Programme Notes. 1978. *Nayatt School*. Performing Garage, NY. 6 May-11 June.

Programme Notes. 1987. *Frank Dell's The Temptation of St. Antony*. Performing Garage, NY. 8 October–9 November.

Programme Notes. 1988. *Frank Dell's The Temptation of St. Antony*. Performing Garage, NY. 16 September-15 October.

Programme Notes. 2004. 'Selections from the Archive in Honor of Spalding Gray'. Performing Garage, NY. 16 September.

QUICK, Andrew. 2007. *The Wooster Group Work Book*. New York and London: Routledge.

REGELSON, Rosalyn. 1975. 'Love and Death and Sick Psychiatry'. *Soho Weekly News* (23 October.

Richard Schechner Papers and The Drama Review Collection; 1943-2007 (mostly 1960-2007), Manuscripts Division, Department of Rare Books and Special Collections, Princeton University Library.

ROACH, Joseph. 1996. *Cities of the Dead: Circum-Atlantic Performance*. New York: Columbia UP.

SAFER, Morley. 1979. Interview with Roy Cohn. *60 Minutes*. CBS. New York. 30 December.

SAINER, Arthur. 1975a. *Radical Theatre Notebook*. New York: Avon Books.

——. 1975b. 'Walking Souls, Travelling Whites'. *Village Voice* (23 June), p. 86.

——. 1975c. 'The Brilliant Kids Show Us How'. *Village Voice* (15 December), p. 137.

——. 1976. 'Marilyn's Back and Wooster Street's Got Her'. *Village Voice* 5 January, p. 73.

——. 1977. 'The Courage Not to Know'. *Village Voice* (25 April), p. 79–80.

SALLE, David and Sarah French. 2008. 'Kate Valk'. *BOMB Magazine* 100. Available at http://bit.ly/2LnDwsU (last accessed on 7 September 2015).

SAVRAN, David. 1988. *Breaking the Rules: The Wooster Group*. New York: Theatre Communications Group.

——. 2005. 'Death of the Avantgarde'. *TDR* 49(3): 10–42.

SCHECHNER, Richard. 1977. 'A Place to Pick Up New Ideas'. Interview by Thomas Lask. *New York Times* 25 March, p. C2.

——. 1994[1973]. *Environmental Theatre*. New York: Applause Books.

——. 1982. 'The Decline and Fall of the (American) Avant-Garde'. *The End of Humanism: Writings on Performance*. New York: PAJ Publications, pp. 11–76.

——. 1983. *Performative Circumstances: From the Avant Garde to Ramlila*. Calcutta: Seagull Books.

——. 1985[1982]. 'Playing with Genet's *The Balcony*: Looking Back on a 1979/1980 Production'. *Between Theatre and Anthropology*. Philadelphia: U of Penn P, pp. 261–93.

——. 2002. 'Reflections on Ron Vawter'. Lecture, New York University, New York, 29 October.

SHEWEY, Don. 1981. 'Elizabeth LeCompte's Last Stand?' *Village Voice* (11 November).

'*Sly Mourning* by Shaman Company'. 1975. Advertisement. *Village Voice* 13 October, p. 12.

STERRITT, David. 1978a. 'Experimental Theatre Festival in New York'. *Christian Science Monitor* 5 January, n. p. .

——. 1978b. 'Nyatt School Makes a Diverse Evening'. *Christian Science Monitor* 24 May, p. 22.

STRAHS, James. 1981. *Rig* script in Elizabeth LeCompte, 'Point Judith'. *Zone* Spring-Summer: 14-27.

———. 1987. *Queer and Alone*. New York: PAJ Publications.

TAUBIN, Amy. 1990. 'Cameos: Actor Ron Vawter'. *Premiere* (February), p. 40.

VAWTER, Ron. 1970. 'Little Theatre Production Nears Final Stages'. *The Indian,* 13 October, p. 6.

———. 1979. 'Piero della Francesca: An Analysis of his Paintings Performance Documentation'. Master's thesis, New York University.

———. 1992a. 'Ron Vawter'. Interview by Jessica Hagedorn. *BOMB* Magazine (Fall): 46-49.

———. 1992b. 'Strange'. 1992. *New York Quarterly* 16 February, n. p. .

———. 1993. 'Ron Vawter: For the Record'. Interview by Richard Schechner. *TDR* 37(3): 17-41.

———. 1994. 'Ron Vawter'. Interview by Ross Wetzsteon. *Village Voice* (3 May), p. 96.

———. 1998. 'Introductory Remarks for the Performance of *Roy Cohn/Jack Smith*' in Holly Hughes and David Romàn (eds), *O Solo Homo: The New Queer Performance*. New York: Grove Press, pp. 456–7.

———(n.d.). 'Ron Vawter (The Wooster Group) and Frank Vercruyssen (Stan): A Dialogue on Acting'. Undated interview transcript. Box 1, Folder 3. Ron Vawter Papers. Billy Rose Theatre Division. New York Public Library for the Performing Arts.

WALLACE, Mike. 1986. Interview with Roy Cohn. *60 Minutes*. CBS. New York. 30 March.

WALLACE, Robert. 2003. 'John Herbert (1926–2001)'. *The Literary Encyclopedia*. Available at http://bit.ly/2Y31Kyt (last accessed on 18 January 2013).

WEDEKIND, Frank. 1972. *German Expressionism: The Lulu Plays and Other Sex Tragedies*. London: Calder and Boyars.

WETZSTEON, Ross. 1989. 'Saint Ron: New York's Best Unknown Actor'. *Village Voice* (17 October), pp. 37–41.

What Happened on the Way Here. 1981. Advertisement. *Village Voice* (28 January–3 February), p. 90.

WHITMAN, Robert. 2005. 'Biography'. *Local Report.* Available at http://bit.ly/2JB19wc (last accessed on 13 November 2015).

WHITTEMORE, Tom. 1969. 'Melodramatic Drunkard Entertains SRO Audiences'. *The Indian*, 25 February, p. 3.

WILLIAMS, Mike. 1971. 'Fortune: Gut Experience.' *The Indian*, 18 March, p. 19.

WITKEWICZ, Stanisław Ignacy. 1968. 'On a New Type of Play' in Jan Kott (ed.), Daniel C. Gerould and C. S. Durer (trans.), *Four Decades of Polish Plays.* Evanston: Northwestern Press, 1990, pp. 99–100.

WOOSTER GROUP. 2015. 'Production History'. Available at http://bit.ly/2GcqFW8 (last accessed on 3 September 2015).

——. 1981. *Route 1 & 9: The Last Act. Benzene* 5/6: 4-16.

Interviews and Email Correspondence

ARCADE, Penny. 2003. Interview with the author, 25 May.

BURIAN, Grayce. 2006. Interview with the author, 4 March.

CALI, Joseph. 2004. Interview with the author, 7 October.

CHAPMAN, Linda and Lola Pasholinski. 2003. Interview with the author, 8 July.

CLAYBURGH, Jim. 2004. Interview with the author, 24 May.

COLEMAN, Meghan. 2008. Interview with author, 9 November.

DAFOE, Willem. 2008. Interview with the author, 24 April.

DALY, Kevin. 2005. Interview with the author, 13 February.

DEVLIN, Vianney, 2004. Interview with the author, 10 September.

FRISCH, Norman. 2002a. Interview with author, 20 November.

——. 2002b. Interview with author, 22 November.

GRAY, Spalding. 2004. Interview with author, 9 January.

GONZÁLEZ Nieves, Roberto. 2008. Email to the author, 6 November.

GRIFFITHS, James. 2004. Interview with author, 17 February.

GOCKLEY, Emily. 2006. Interview with author, 18 September.

LECOMPTE, Elizabeth. 2005. Interview with the author, 12 May.

MACINTOSH, Joan. 2004. Interview with the author, 7 April.

MEHRTEN, Gregory. 2002a. Interview with the author, 14 June.

——. 2002b. Interview with the author, 27 June.

——. 2017. Email message to the author, 6 September.

NELSON, Daniel. 2004. Interview with the author, 24 November.

PARNES, Uzi. 2008. Email message to the author, 2 June.

PORTER, Bruce. 2004. Interview with the author, 15 April.

PRIBRAM, Bruce. 2011. Email to the author, 7 September.

RAYVID, Bruce. 2004. Interview with the author, 21 May.

REILLY, Nancy. 2008. Interview with author, 20 December.

SACK, Leeny. 2004. Interview with the author, 22 March.

SCHECHNER, Richard. 2003. Interview with the author, 23 June.

——. 2006. Interview with the author, 7 November.

——. 2008a. Email to the author, 11 April.

——. 2008b. Email to the author, 22 October.

——. 2009a. Email to the author, 9 March.

——. 2009b. Email to the author, 10 March.

——. 2013. Email to the author, 20 June.

SCHLATTER, David. 2004. Interview with the author, 14 August.

VAN PATTEN, Michael. 2005. Phone interview with the author, 25 February.

VAWTER, Matilda Buttoni. 2004. Interview with the author, 22 November.

WEEMS, Marianne. 2003a. Interview with the author, 7 March.

——. 2003b. Interview with the author, 19 March.